How to Read
THE LANDSCAPE

How to Read
THE LANDSCAPE

Patrick Whitefield

Permanent Publications

Published by
Permanent Publications
Hyden House Ltd
The Sustainability Centre
East Meon
Hampshire GU32 1HR
United Kingdom
Tel: 0844 846 846 4824 (local rate UK only)
         or +44 (0)1730 823 311
Fax: 01730 823 322
Email: enquiries@permaculture.co.uk
Web: www.permanentpublications.co.uk

Distributed in the USA by
Chelsea Green Publishing Company, PO Box 428, White River Junction, VT 05001
www.chelseagreen.com

© 2014 Patrick Whitefield
The right of Patrick Whitefield to be identified as the author of this work has been asserted
by him in accordance with the Copyrights, Designs and Patents Act 1998

Photographs © Patrick Whitefield, unless stated otherwise

Patrick Whitefield's website: www.patrickwhitefield.co.uk

Designed by Two Plus George Limited, www.TwoPlusGeorge.co.uk

Cover illustration by Jane Bottomley

Printed in the UK by Cambrian Printers, Aberystwyth

All paper from FSC certified mixed sources

The Forest Stewardship Council (FSC) is a non-profit international
organisation established to promote the responsible management
of the world's forests. Products carrying the FSC label are
independently certified to assure consumers that they come from
forests that are managed to meet the social, economic and ecological
needs of present and future generations.

British Library Cataloguing-in-Publication Data
A catalogue record for this book is available from the British Library

ISBN 978 1 85623 185 5

Contents

Introduction

I'VE ALWAYS been fascinated by the landscape. When I was a student at agricultural college I remember a friend saying, "It's not safe to take a lift with Patrick. He 'farms' as he drives." I don't know if people use the word 'to farm' in that sense any more. It meant to observe and assess the land and decide what should be done in each field. It goes back to the days when most farms employed a lot of workers and the job of the farmer was to think and make decisions rather than to put those decisions into practice. Farming in that sense is one aspect of landscape reading.

As it turned out I never became a farmer, although I did work on farms for a number of years. When I acquired some land of my own it was a nature reserve rather than a farm and so I learnt to read the landscape from a somewhat different perspective, that of the wild plants and animals rather than the cultivated ones. Eventually I became a teacher of permaculture, and both of these perspectives are relevant in my present work, in fact they have merged into one, more holistic view of the landscape. Permaculture is all about creating productive landscapes that work in harmony with nature and are thus truly sustainable. It's a way of designing such landscapes, whether gardens, farms, villages or towns. Observation is the absolute bedrock of permaculture design. We can only design a truly harmonious landscape if we have a good knowledge and understanding of what's already there before we start.

I originally intended this book to be a permaculture workbook, covering the all-important observation stage of the design process. But my enthusiasm for the subject couldn't be bound by such a utilitarian plan. My notebook started to fill with all sorts of observations that might not be directly relevant to permaculture design but were just too interesting to pass by. I began to visualise my reader not so much as a designer but more as someone who spends time outdoors, whether for enjoyment or in the course of their job, snuggling down with the book in an armchair on a winter's evening. But in the end I realised there may not be that much difference between the useful and the simply fascinating. Who can say which piece of information may be of use and which will not? In fact the kind of thinking which divides things up into, on the one hand, the useful but boring and ugly and on the other, the useless but interesting and beautiful, belongs to an age which is rapidly passing. It was an idea born in the industrial revolution and its time is over. So I hope that all of you who read this book will both enjoy it and find it useful.

Its focus is on the rural landscape. This is not to say that I think the urban landscape is less worthy of attention, but as I've lived almost all my life in the country I don't know much about urban landscapes and I'm not the right person to write about them. In fact that job has already been brilliantly done by the late Oliver Gilbert in his book *The Ecology of Urban Habitats*. (See Further Reading on page 217.)

Nor is this book mainly about the history of the landscape. Many people assume that landscape reading and landscape history are one and the same. Perhaps this is because so many excellent books have been written about the history of the landscape while the broader field of landscape reading has been largely ignored. I have included a chapter on landscape history, as it's clearly impossible to understand something without knowing about its past. But the history of the landscape is just one aspect of it, the human influence. The other influences – rock, soil, climate, plants and animals – also play their parts, and the landscape we see is the result of an ever-changing interplay of all these.

The result is a complex picture that can only be broadly sketched in a single book. There just isn't space to go into all the complexity. In fact if I were to try to do so the clarity of the picture would be lost, so I've often simplified. For example, I've sometimes had to ignore regional variations and make broad statements that are true for the country as a whole. I hope I've never simplified things to the point of distorting the truth but everything you read in the pages that follow must be taken with the added comment that actually it's more complicated than that. In any case my intention is not to tell you exactly what's going on in the landscape around you. It's to open a door on a new way of looking at that landscape and understanding it. The descriptions I give of individual landscapes are no more than examples and you may find something quite different in your own locality.

I've tried as much as possible to write from personal experience but inevitably quite a lot of research has been necessary to fill in the gaps. Since landscape reading is such a wide field this has meant casting my net wide and getting snippets of information from many different books and papers on a variety of subjects. But I must mention a special debt of gratitude to Oliver Rackham, the great authority on the history of the landscape. His books and face-to-face teaching have been a source of both inspiration and information. Special thanks also go to my sister, Cristina Crossingham, who has carefully read each chapter and made many useful suggestions.

Introduction to this New Edition

SOMETIMES you don't really know what you've written until you have the printed book in your hand. *The Living Landscape* was a big, thick book. Some time after its publication I realised that, in my enthusiasm for the subject, I'd included a lot of things which interest me but wouldn't necessarily interest the reader. These were side tracks and sub-plots that obscured the central theme rather than clarifying it.

So this new edition, with a new name, is much shorter than the old one but with all the best bits left in. The publishers also took the opportunity to produce it in full colour throughout and I've added many new photographs. I think it's much better and I hope you will too.

Ash Dieback

One specific point needs mentioning and that's the fate of the ash tree. As I write, in the spring of 2014, we don't yet know how the ash trees of Britain will react to ash dieback disease. I wrote the first version of this book before we'd even heard of the disease and when I came to revise it, although I was aware that it had killed 95% of the ash trees in Denmark, I had yet to see an example of it. Will it do the same here, or will it behave differently and take a lesser toll on British ash trees? We don't know.

The ash is one of the most important trees in the British landscape. If it does become virtually extinct, the landscape you read about in this book will be significantly different from the one you can see around you. No doubt other trees will fill the niche now filled by ash; and the few individual trees with genetic resistance to the disease will breed and slowly repopulate the countryside, both naturally and through human plant breeding programmes. But it will be a slow process and even the end result, some hundreds of years from now, will undoubtedly look very different from the landscape of today.

There's no way I can predict the nature of these changes beyond the general remarks I've made here, so I've made no changes to the text of the book in response to ash dieback.

Please note there is a glossary of words that may be unfamiliar on pages 221-222.

This view shows how landform affects land use:
woodland on the steepest slopes, mixed farming on the
gentle slopes and meadow on the flood-prone riverside.
Lancaut, lower Wye valley.

1

Introducing the Landscape

THE LANDSCAPE we see around us is formed from the interaction of four factors: the rock, the soil, the climate and living things.

Rocks

The kinds of rocks that lie under the landscape determine its shape. To put it simply, hard rocks are slow to erode and make hills while soft, erodible rocks make valleys. Altitude has an influence both on natural vegetation and on land use, while the degree of slope often has a very close influence on land use. The nature of the rock also has a big effect on the nature of the soil, which in its turn has its effect on the vegetation.

Soil

The influence of soil on vegetation can most often be seen in places where human influence is lightest, such as on moorland. Amongst all the moorland plants the most competitive is bracken. It grows tall, with horizontal fronds which cast shade on other plants, and also gives out chemicals that inhibit their growth. Not many other plants can hold their own against it. But there are some things which bracken can't tolerate. One of them is shallow soil and you can often see bracken give way to heather as the soil becomes thinner around the edges of exposed rock. Another is wet soil and you can see bracken grow happily on a hillside but give way to

1

grasses and sedges in flatter areas where water drains away more slowly. Thus the patterns of vegetation reflect the soil conditions below.

Climate

The climate affects the landscape of the country as a whole. Compare the green landscape of rainy Britain with the arid starkness of the Mediterranean countries. But it also affects it on a much smaller scale. To continue with the example of bracken, another thing it doesn't tolerate is too much cold. On the highest hills and mountains there's a certain height, above which it won't grow and this adds another element to the pattern of its distribution. Such small-scale changes in climate are known as microclimate.

Living Things

The fourth influence is living things, plants and animals. Overwhelmingly the biggest influence they have on the landscape of Britain is in the grazing of farm animals. The natural vegetation of this island is woodland and the humble sheep and the stolid cow between them have transformed millions of hectares of land from woodland to grassland and moor. They will eat whatever they can get, but some plants are more able to survive constant nibbling than others. Supreme among the plants that can tolerate, even thrive on, constant nibbling are the grasses. All their buds are below ground, so they can easily regrow after being eaten. Plants with their buds above ground, such as little trees, will eventually die if they are repeatedly bitten back. Old trees can survive intensive grazing, but they can't reproduce because their young ones get eaten. So grazing on its own is enough to turn woodland into pasture, as long as it goes on constantly for the lifetime of the longest-lived trees.

The Natural and the Human

Human beings are strictly speaking included in the fourth landscape-forming factor, the living things. But in a densely-settled country like ours the human influence is enormous, as great as all the other factors put together. So it can sometimes be useful to think in terms not of four factors – rock, soil, climate and living things – but two, the natural and the human.

Every landscape is the result of interplay between natural and human forces. Everywhere people have endeavoured to meet their material needs from the land but the way they've done it in each place has been moulded by natural conditions. Places with the most favourable soils and climate are dominated by the intensive cultivation of cereals and other crops. Where the land is hillier and the climate is wetter, the emphasis is on grass.

Both these broad landscape types usually contain some woodland and it's usually sited on land that's unsuitable for farming in one way or another, often because it's too steep. In hilly areas you can see a close relationship between woodland and slope, with the steeper slopes wooded and the flatter land farmed. While the general division between woodland farmland is determined by the landform, which in turn is determined by the rocks, the exact point at which it was considered that a particular slope was too steep for farming would have been determined by various human factors. When there's a strong demand for farm produce marginal slopes are often cleared of trees, and then allowed to revert to woodland in times of economic downturn. The frame of mind or even the whim of individual farmers and landowners can also play a part. Not every decision taken by people is a strictly rational one.

Seeing the natural and the human as two complementary forces is a useful way of understanding what's happening in the landscape. But at the same time it's important to remember that we're part of the ecological community, with no more right to be here and thrive than any other species. Certainly we're much more powerful than any other and our effect on the world ecosystem is correspondingly great. But that's all the more reason to remind ourselves that we're part of the web of life, not superior to it or outside it. When we forget this we destroy the very living systems on which we depend for survival.

Semi-Natural Ecosystems

All landscapes are a result of the interplay of human and natural forces. Even in the most urban scene you can find weeds poking up between the paving stones and the odd buddleia in the brickwork. As for wilderness, in the sense of places where humans have no influence at all, it's doubtful that such a thing has existed for thousands of years. Even hunter-gatherers have more influence on the ecosystems they inhabit than used to be believed, especially where fire is used to improve the hunting.

Most of the land here in Britain lies between these two extremes. Over two-thirds of it is farmland and most of the rest is moorland and other rough grazing. Cities, towns and villages take up less than a tenth of the area. Virtually all of the land would be woodland if it weren't for humankind. The small area of woodland that does remain has been used as a resource by people down the ages and bears little resemblance to the wildwood of prehistoric times. Every bit of the island has been modified by us or our grazing animals, except for the peaks of the highest mountains that were always above the tree line.

So we have no wilderness in Britain. Even the Highlands of Scotland are the result of a blend of human and natural forces. We might like to think of the Highlands as the next thing to a wilderness. But what could be less natural than an open, treeless moor where naturally there would be woodland?

These Highland moors are an example of what's known as a semi-natural ecosystem. Semi-natural means that the ecosystem has been modified by human action but the vegetation has not actually been planted. In the case of moorland, that human action is grazing. The plants that are there now have either survived from the time it was woodland or have moved in of their own accord since then.

There are also semi-natural grasslands, composed of wild, self-selected grasses and wildflowers, but they are a tiny percentage of the total grassland area. Most of the grassland in Britain is cultivated, just like any other agricultural crop.

There are also semi-natural woods. Many of these are coppiced woods, which have been felled and allowed to regenerate many times over hundreds or thousands of years. The structure of a coppice wood is quite unlike that of a wild wood. The trees are smaller and there's very little accumulation of dead wood. No-one has ever planted a tree there, but it's not a natural wood, it's semi-natural.

Semi-natural ecosystems are jewels of biodiversity, the last refuge of wild plants and animals in an intensively humanised landscape. They're rare in the more fertile parts of the country, where almost all the land has been converted to productive farming. The ones that survive are now mostly nature reserves. In the uplands, where the productive potential of the land is lower, there's still a lot of moorland and rough grassland. It's the closest thing we have to wilderness, but it's not wild. It's the fruit of the long, long dance between people and nature.

Regional Landscapes

The different ways the dance has been played out from place to place have given us distinctive regional landscapes. A fine example is the West Country, that curiously-shaped peninsula which snakes out from the south-west corner of England. I live near the West Country but outside it, in central Somerset. The county is like a shallow bowl, with a ring of hills round the edge and broad, shallow valleys in the middle. The rocks of Somerset are mostly young, soft and alkaline.

Lime-loving plants, like the climber, old man's beard, are frequent. On the whole the villages are large, though there are some hamlets too.

The western rim of this bowl is the Quantock Hills. You cross them and suddenly you're in the West Country, still in Somerset but in that western tip which has more in common with Devon and Cornwall than with the rest of the county. Everywhere there are hills, separated by narrow valleys. The rocks are old, hard and mostly acid. Plants of acid soils, such as foxgloves, are common and the hedges are raised up on great solid banks a metre or more high. There are few big villages, most parishes consisting of scattered hamlets and isolated farms.

There is variety within the West Country of course, but it's a variation on a theme. One of these variations is to be found in the South Hams, that part of Devon which juts out into the sea to the south of Dartmoor. The land is a plateau of broad, flat-topped hills, all of much the same height, dissected by steep V-shaped valleys. The hilltops are intensively farmed. They're exposed to strong, salty winds, so trees are few and usually sculpted by the wind. By contrast, the narrow valleys are too steep for farming and are mostly wooded. I call this the combe and plateau pattern of landscape. It's not confined to the South Hams of Devon and can be found in other areas where a dissected plateau lies near the sea.

While the West Country landscape can be seen as variations on a theme, moving east to Wiltshire we find a county divided into two distinct landscape types, the chalk downs and the clay vales. The downs are wide, open hills, formerly unfenced sheepwalk, now wire-fenced into big fields and mainly growing corn. Trees are mostly in isolated clumps or occasional large woods. It's a dry landscape with no surface water. By contrast, the clay vales have smaller, thickly hedged fields with hedgerow trees, frequent small woods, streams and rivers. There are fewer long views. The heavy soil holds water well and grows lush grass that is ideal for dairy farming. The old expression 'as different as chalk and cheese' refers to these two landscape types.

Natural succession: clumps of hawthorn and bramble moving into an old pasture (see next page). Yarley Fields, Somerset.

Processes and Relationships

You can see the landscape as a series of objects, here a wood, there a field and so on, but it becomes more interesting and meaningful if you see it as a series of processes and relationships.

Take a field of grass. It looks fairly static but of course the grass is growing and this is a process, one that goes on through most of the year and means that the field is forever changing. But the process of growth doesn't go on uninterrupted. People mow the grass or pasture animals on it and the state of the field at any one time is a result of that relationship between growth and human management.

Natural succession is another process. Suppose that field was left alone and neither grazed nor mown, it wouldn't stay as a field of grass forever. Shrubs such as bramble and hawthorn would establish and bit by bit it would turn into scrub. How fast this would happen and the kind of shrubs that would move in, both depend on a whole host of relationships, involving the soil, the microclimate, the kind of grasses which grow in the field, which shrubs grow nearby to provide seed and so on.

Cycles of Change

Process means change through time and the landscape is indeed constantly changing. The shortest time cycle is that of annual growth.

The annual cycle of deciduous trees is familiar to us all but herbaceous plants have one too. They start in spring with lush green leaves, which turn the sun's energy into food. Everything looks fresh and young. In high summer comes the mature, reproductive phase when they flower and set seed, using the energy they have accumulated for reproduction. The plant is usually taller at this stage, to give the seeds more chance of moving away from the mother plant and colonising new ground. In many cases the leaves, now no longer active, go brown and tatty – hence the expressions 'gone to seed' or 'seedy-looking' for people who look uncared-for and past their best. The countryside loses the fresh, clean look it had in May and June. Not all herbaceous plants follow exactly this annual cycle, but it's common enough to dominate the feel of the landscape as the warmer months pass by.

If annual cycles are about the maturing of seeds and fruits, succession is about the maturity of whole ecosystems. We've just seen how shrubs can take over from grassland if the human influence is removed. If the process is allowed to continue the shrubs in turn will be taken over by pioneer trees to form new woodland. But young woodland is very different from a mature one. Even the species of trees are different, so at least one generation of tree must come to the end of its life before the woodland even approaches maturity. You can't see the whole cycle of succession in a single human lifetime.

There are other changes that happen on a moderate timescale that falls between the two extremes of annual and successional changes, with a rhythm of a few years or decades. They are often caused by human action and can be called rotational.

A classic example is the coppicing of ancient woodland. This is a mature ecosystem, but over the centuries it's been repeatedly cut down and allowed to grow again, mainly through the trees resprouting from the stump. When a part of the wood has been felled it may look as though the ecosystem has suffered a major change, one that plunges it back to an earlier stage of succession. But no, this is just part of the medium-term cycle which the wood has experienced many times. The key difference between rotational change and successional change is that the mix of plants and animals that make up the ecosystem is not drastically altered by a rotational change. Some animals and plants will migrate from one part of the wood to another to find the conditions of light or shade that they prefer, but the ancient woodland remains an ancient woodland.

Great hairy willowherb favours damp places.

Multiple Causes

Everything we see in the landscape is the result of a complex of different causes. We don't like complexity. We would always much rather put something down to a single cause. It's never true but it's easier on our brains.

For example, I might say, "Rosebay willowherb is growing here but great hairy willowherb is growing over there because the soil is that bit wetter." What I really mean is that there are masses of different reasons for the presence of these two plants, related to soil, microclimate and biotic factors, but the difference which most likely accounts for their split distribution is soil moisture. All the other factors are near enough the same to leave them as understood. It's a useful shorthand. But the danger is that we tend to focus on one factor and ignore the others. Then we can miss something significant.

So if I sometimes attribute something to a single reason, please remember that I'm simplifying.

METHODS AND TOOLS

Identifying Plants

You can start out reading the landscape without knowing how to identify plants. For example, if you see young trees growing in a field of grass it's reasonable to deduce that you're looking at a process of grassland turning into woodland. The young trees will grow and as they get bigger they'll become the dominant life form and shade out the grass. You don't need to know what kind of trees they are.

A wood consisting of a few big old trees with wide-spreading branches surrounded by lots of young trees growing close together suggests a later stage in the same process of wood formation. A tree with spreading branches can't have grown up in woodland surrounded by other trees. In that situation it would have grown tall and narrow, shaded by its neighbours on all sides and reaching for the light above. So this is a new wood growing up around trees that formerly stood far apart on grassland or heath.

But you can discover more about the landscape if you can identify plants. Some indicate specific things about the soil, others tell about the history of the ecosystem. For example, certain plants are characteristic of ancient woodland rather than more recently formed woods.

The first thing to do is to get yourself one or more guides, as identification books are known. The most important groups are trees and wildflowers and a guide to each of these is worthwhile. For advice on choosing guides, see Further Reading, on pages 217-222.

When you start out learning to identify trees, look closely at individual structures like leaves, twigs and bark. Later you'll get to know trees by their overall character but to begin with be specific. Trees are usually identified by leaf shape, but do be sure that the leaf you're looking at really is attached to the tree you're trying to identify. The branches often intermix and it's a common mistake to spend time examining a leaf that turns out to belong to a neighbouring tree! In winter you can sometimes identify a tree by the dead leaves at its foot. But this can be misleading. Leaves get blown around by the wind and there's no guarantee that the leaves on the ground come from the tree above them.

Maps

Maps are most useful for the historical aspect of landscape reading. The patterns made by the fields tell us a great deal about the history of the land and they usually show up better on a map than on the ground. Maps can also show you things that you might not have noticed. Springs, for example, are important features but sometimes not very conspicuous.

The Explorer series of Ordnance Survey maps are the best for reading the landscape. They are at a scale of 1:25,000 and show all the field boundaries. The Landranger, at 1:50,000, doesn't show enough detail to be of any use. Geological maps can also be useful. They're quite easy to understand once you know the names of the various rocks that occur in your area. Soil maps, on the other hand, are full of jargon and not much use to a lay person.

Local People

Local people can sometimes tell you things that you couldn't have worked out for yourself, as this extract from my notebook illustrates.

Harbournmeford, Devon

Phillip told me the story of the patch of docks in the little field across the stream by the quarry. A neighbouring farm across the valley had their slurry pit overflow during a flash flood. The slurry came down the lane, in the gate and all along the bottom of the valley. The cows that produced the slurry had been eating silage full of docks, so it was full of dock seeds. They germinated in a swathe where the flood had been, right along the valley. But they only survived in the little field because it's not grazed by sheep, because the fencing's too bad to hold sheep.

Sheep will eat docks and cattle won't, at least not if they can avoid it. Sheep also need much better fencing to keep them in than cattle do. The little field by the quarry was the only one in the valley with fencing too bad to take sheep and that's why the docks survived there. I could never have reconstructed that story simply by looking at what was there.

It's not just information you get from talking to people but a different perspective. A farmer or forester may see things that pass a nature conservationist by and vice versa.

Once I was designing a garden for a young farmer and his wife. He's generally a person of radical views with an open mind. At the time he was converting his farm to organic and looking at installing a wind farm on part of his land. But his reaction to my design revealed how dyed-in-the-wool a farmer he is.

I'd placed the things they'd asked for – vegetable garden, fruit trees, chicken run, flower beds and lawn – on the design but there was still plenty of land left over. Rather than give him a large area of lawn that would shackle him to the lawnmower for the rest of his life, I proposed a shrubbery for the surplus space, mainly of native shrubs. It would look attractive throughout the year, provide wildlife habitat and need virtually no maintenance.

He looked very serious and said, "Well, I like most of the design, but not the shrubbery. I don't want to lose that much land." It was almost as though he believed that once you plant trees or shrubs on a piece of land it ceases to exist as land. On the farm there is a grain of truth in this. Once you plant a field up with trees you can't farm it, in the sense of growing arable crops or grass. But in a garden?

He is by no means the only farmer I've come across with this attitude to trees. But it was really brought into contrast for me one day when I heard a forester refer to 'bare ground'. What he meant was not soil without plants on it at all, but land without trees. It's a normal forestry term and this wasn't the first time I'd heard it, but it reminded me of the farmer and the shrubbery. The forester's perspective is exactly the opposite: if a piece of land doesn't have trees on it there's nothing going on there at all.

I don't mean to put people in compartments. After all, sometimes the farmer and the nature conservationist are one and the same person. But we do all have our own approach to the land and the challenge for all of us is to see it in the round, from every point of view. On the other hand we can never know everything about a landscape. Living processes are just too complex for that. A sense of mystery and wonder will always remain.

2

The History of the Landscape

THE INFLUENCE of people on the land is clear to see: where once there was wildwood from coast to coast now there's a cultivated landscape of fields and hedges, woods and plantations. What's less clear is how long this has been going on. Is agriculture a new invention that has come in at the eleventh hour to disturb a wildwood that had slumbered untouched by human hand for countless eons? Far from it. Our ancestors started turning wildwood into fields and hedges some six thousand years ago, which was not long after the wildwood recovered its full extent in Britain after the desolation of the last Ice Age.

THE PREHISTORIC LANDSCAPE

Timescale of landscape history. (BP = Before Present.)

Approximately fourteen thousand years ago the last Ice Age ended, leaving behind it a landscape of tundra. About twelve thousand years ago the temperature had risen enough for the first trees to appear in the south of the island. First came the cold-tolerant kinds like birch and pine, then the more temperate like oak and lime.

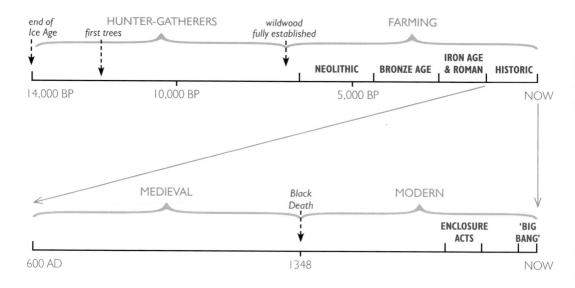

end of Ice Age | first trees | HUNTER-GATHERERS | wildwood fully established | FARMING

NEOLITHIC | BRONZE AGE | IRON AGE & ROMAN | HISTORIC

14,000 BP | 10,000 BP | 5,000 BP | NOW

MEDIEVAL | Black Death | MODERN

ENCLOSURE ACTS | 'BIG BANG'

600 AD | 1348 | NOW

10

Ash and beech arrived later and thousands of years passed before the trees spread out and occupied the range they do now. Bit by bit the wildwood was formed. Around seven thousand years ago it had spread over the whole island except for a band of bog along the northern coast of Scotland, the outer isles and the tops of the highest mountains.

Just how dense and continuous the wildwood was is not known for certain. The traditional view is that there were virtually no gaps in the wildwood at all. But then where have all the plants of open country come from? Could the grasses and grassland wildflowers all have immigrated with the first people who brought grazing animals and started opening up the wildwood? It is just possible. In North America almost all the pasture grasses are European immigrants. There are native grasslands there of course but the indigenous species aren't adapted to intensive grazing. The spear-like leaf of plantain, a common grassland herb, was called the white man's footprint by the Native Americans. (See page 43.) As for the weeds, no agriculture means no weeds. A glance down a list of weeds in an American book reveals at least half of them to be familiar ones from this side of the water. Here in Britain many of the weeds may be immigrants too, though from a much earlier time.

However that may be, most landscape historians now think in terms of the wildwood having more in the way of gaps and clearings than was previously thought. There is even a theory that the primeval landscape was one that periodically alternated between grassland and woodland, with large herds of wild herbivores playing a key role. This theory doesn't really stand up to close scrutiny and it's most likely that the pre-agricultural landscape of Britain was predominantly wooded. (See page 79.)

There were people living in Britain at the time but they can't have had much effect on the landscape. There were very few of them and they lived by hunting and gathering. There is some archaeological evidence that they occasionally set fire to the wildwood. Fire can turn dense woodland into something more like parkland, making it easier for hunters to see their prey and increasing the amount of grass to feed the prey animals. This burning of the woodland seems puzzling because, except for the Highland pinewoods, British native woodland just doesn't burn. But the woods we know today are not the wildwood. They have been managed for centuries and trees have been harvested regularly. In virgin woodland the trees die naturally and remain in situ, decomposing slowly. A large proportion of the total biomass at any one time can be dead wood. At the end of a long dry summer it might have been possible to get a fire going hot enough to kill some of the live trees.

The Neolithic Age

The first farmers were the people of the Neolithic, or New Stone Age. Farming started ten thousand years ago in what we now call the Middle East and spread slowly from there. Although it was also invented in other parts of the world, it came to this island direct from its first homeland and arrived here some six thousand years ago. The crops that form the backbone of our agriculture to this day come from the Middle East.

The Middle East is a dry region with extensive deserts, with steppes in those areas having a little more moisture. Out of the steppe came wheat, barley and oats, grasses with seeds big enough to make them worth growing as food crops. The Neolithic farmers of Britain ate these along with the meat and milk from their herds. The hunter-gatherers of earlier times had eaten hazelnuts and the starchy tubers of bulrushes with their wild meat. But by the time agriculture arrived in north-west Europe the cereals had been improved by thousands of years of plant breeding and the methods of cereal farming were well developed. It was an efficient and well-known package. No-one went to the trouble to invent a northern form of agriculture using the indigenous edible plants. If they had the landscape might look very different now, perhaps more like the native wildwood and less like an imitation of the south-west Asian steppe.

Animal farming was part of the same package and here too exotics reigned. It wasn't the native roe and red deer but the imported cattle, sheep and goats that made up the herds. Domesticated herds have much more impact on the landscape than wild herbivores because they can be kept in much larger numbers. The key to this is haymaking. The population of wild animals is controlled mainly by starvation during winter. When summer comes there just aren't enough of them to keep up with the abundance of plant growth and any effect they have on the vegetation can only be marginal. But making hay during summer and feeding it to domestic animals in winter means they can be kept at an artificially high population. As we've already seen, trees can't survive intensive grazing but grasses can. (See page 2.) So the inevitable result was the gradual replacement of woodland with grassland. Over the thousands of years since the dawn of the Neolithic age grazing animals have destroyed many more square miles of British woodland than the axe and the plough.

The Neolithic people started managing the wildwood and turning it into the kinds of woodland we would recognise today. Right at the beginning of the Neolithic age they were already working some woods on a regular coppice cycle. This means felling the trees every few years and allowing them to regrow from

Cattle, sculptors of the landscape.

the stump. They regrow in a multi-stemmed form and the same trees can be cut again time after time. We know they did this because large quantities of unmistakable coppice poles have been found preserved in the peat of the Somerset Levels. They form part of the structure of wooden trackways that they built to cross the marshes. The earliest of them dates back to some six thousand years ago, the early Neolithic.

But why should the Neolithic people have bothered with coppicing when they had unlimited access to wildwood around the modest clearings where they grew their crops and pastured their animals? Because coppice wood is much more accessible and easier to use. If you want firewood it's much easier to cut a crop of young poles at ground level than to fell giant virgin trees and chop up their huge trunks and thick branches with stone axes and wooden wedges. The coppice poles will also be fairly straight and much the same size, perfect raw material for building a house, a fence or a trackway. They also coppiced to make leaf hay for their animals. Before the invention of metal it was much easier to cut wood than to mow grass. You can't make a scythe with stones. Leaf hay, which has been a minor animal feed into historical times, consists of small branches, or the tops of larger poles, cut in the summer when they are in full leaf and dried for winter use.

This tree has been coppiced just once. When the current crop of poles is harvested new ones will grow and this can be repeated indefinitely.

Farming communities spread all over these islands, including less favourable areas like the Scottish Highlands. In fact the Highlands had a higher population during much of the prehistoric period than they do now. Nevertheless the impact of the new way of life on the landscape may have been slight to begin with. The population was still very low and at first farming would only have supplemented hunting and gathering. There's very little you can see in the modern landscape that was made by the hands of the Neolithic people. Nevertheless their legacy is important because they gave birth to the semi-natural ecosystems that are with us to this day. This isn't to say that individual coppice woodlands and semi-natural grasslands have necessarily survived on the same sites from that day to this, although in some places this may have happened. It's more that these types of ecosystem have been in continuous existence since then. Whether they have stayed put or migrated around the landscape there's been continuity of habitat for the wild plants and animals that inhabit them.

Moorland and heath are two other semi-natural ecosystems. Both of them are basically places where heather grows: moors in the uplands and heath in the lowlands. Most moorland was formed from woodland in much the same way as grassland, by grazing, though some of it does have a more natural origin. (See page 169.) Heath may also have been formed by grazing but it's equally possible that it started out as abandoned arable land. The light sandy soils of what is now heath would have been attractive at first to people with the most primitive of farming tools. But such extreme sandy soils would soon have become too acid and impoverished to continue cropping.

Prehistoric Remains

The age of prehistoric agriculture lasted something over five thousand years, from the beginning of the Neolithic to the end of the Roman period. We must include the Roman in the prehistoric because there are no written records from Roman times that shed any light on the landscape. This is almost four times as long as the historical period, which started in the seventh century AD when the Anglo-Saxons learned to read and write. Throughout the prehistoric period people made fields, planted hedges, built walls and houses. Bit by bit the humanised area extended and the wildwood shrank. It wasn't a continuous process. Land came into cultivation, was abandoned and then re-occupied, sometimes after a gap of centuries. But by the time the historical period dawned there was very little wildwood left.

In some parts of the country there are almost certainly fields still in use today that were first laid out in prehistoric times. But more often prehistoric fields are overlain and obliterated by later reorganisations. The best places to see the remains of prehistoric fields are hill areas that were cultivated then, perhaps when the climate was warmer, but have remained uncultivated ever since.

The most characteristic prehistoric fields are small and square. They can be seen on some unploughed areas of the chalk downland of southern England. They make a chequered pattern with low banks enclosing little fields of an acre or less. The square shape reflects the kind of plough used in those times. This was a scratch plough, or ard, which cuts into the soil like a chisel but doesn't turn it upside down like the later mouldboard plough. To use it effectively it was necessary to plough each field at least twice, in different directions. Hence the square-shaped fields. A long narrow field would have been easy to plough from end to end but tedious from side to side. You would have spent more time turning the plough than ploughing. These little fields are often accompanied by the remains of lanes and farmsteads, which suggest a landscape of small farms and hamlets.

A completely different landscape is suggested by the remains of a much more impressive kind of prehistoric field, the reaves. These are stony banks that march across the country in regular parallel lines, not quite straight, about a hundred

Traces of prehistoric fields on chalk downland. Sydling St Nicholas, Dorset.

metres apart, with occasional cross-reaves forming rectangular fields. The most extensive remains of a reave landscape are to be seen on the southern part of Dartmoor, covering tens of square miles in a pattern that can only have been planned by a strong central authority. They appear to have been used mainly for animal farming with a little cropping. Excavation of the associated buildings dates them to the late Bronze Age. There's a small set of reaves in Perthshire which are also Bronze Age while a set in County Mayo date to the Neolithic.

We can do no more than wonder about the social and political setup that created the reaves. Archaeology tells us nothing of such things. But we can say for sure that the country as a whole must have been quite densely populated if such effort was put into organised agriculture in such a marginal area as Dartmoor. Even given the milder climate of the Bronze Age, this infertile granite upland must have been a less favoured area. If people put that amount of effort into developing such marginal land there can't have been much unused space left in the country as a whole.

In some places reave fields may still be in use today. Part of the parish of Toller Porcorum in Dorset is laid out in a very reave-like pattern, which contrasts strongly with the irregular field pattern of the surrounding vale country. (See map below.) The straight field boundaries are certainly very old. Some of them consist of huge banks with ancient coppice stools on them. No-one built such big banks in modern times, and though they could be medieval the resemblance to the Dartmoor reaves is too close to dismiss lightly.

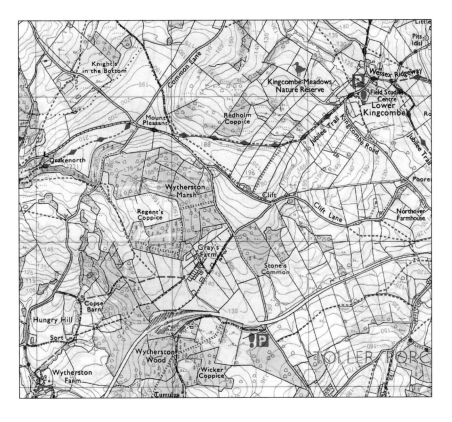

The Romans left their mark on the landscape with their straight main roads and the first towns to be built in Britain. Many of them are still in use, both roads and towns. But the roads were like a modern motorway system, connecting the towns but hardly relating to the rest of the road network. This was made up of the winding lanes that had been there before. The towns were islands of urban life in a hardly-changing landscape of hamlets and little fields. Villas were built in the countryside, but they fitted into the existing pattern rather than replacing it. Villages did not yet exist. Nevertheless it was a densely settled landscape. Roman remains show up well in the archaeological record and they tell us that farmsteads and hamlets were spaced about half a mile apart over most of lowland Britain and more densely in some areas.

Here and there the Romans did impose order on the countryside. An example is the Gwent Levels, on the Welsh coast of the Bristol Channel, either side of Newport. The Romans drained land in various parts of the country, including the Fens of eastern England. In most places their work has been overlaid by that of later generations, but the present layout of the Gwent Levels has been shown by excavation to be Roman. It's a highly organised landscape, with long, narrow, rectangular fields bounded by straight, parallel ditches, evenly spaced and pointing to the sea.

The fall of Rome marks the start of the Middle Ages. The economic collapse that took place when the Roman armies left Britain was total. The towns crumbled and export markets ceased to exist. People no longer had to grow a surplus of food to support the army and the civil service. Britain slipped back into a subsistence economy. People stopped using coins, and in the west of the country they even stopped making pottery. Trees spread back over abandoned farmland, at least in some places.

Nevertheless it was still a farmed landscape and in most parts a fully occupied one. When the Anglo-Saxons moved in to fill the power vacuum left by Rome they took over a landscape already organised into estates, not a wilderness from which they had to hack out new farms and settlements from scratch. There's evidence for this in some modern parish boundaries, which are based on those of medieval manors, which in turn sometimes date back to early Anglo-Saxon estate boundaries. Anyone carving out a brand new estate would surely use an obvious landmark, like a ditch and rampart that ran more or less where the boundary was to be. On the Marlborough Downs in Wiltshire there is just such a rampart, called Wansdyke, which was built right at the start of the Anglo-Saxon period. Several parishes meet approximately along this line, on what was then open downland, but the boundaries completely ignore the dyke. They are clearly older than it. The new Anglo-Saxon lords were taking over established estates with recognised boundaries. In other places parish boundaries ignore Roman roads in much the same way. We can only wonder how old they are.

There's more continuity in the landscape than we often think. Although there have been major reorganisations, most things are much older than they seem. Boundaries are often the oldest things of all. After all, boundaries are all about land ownership and this is a very touchy subject, one on which people have been reluctant to give an inch.

WOODLAND AND CHAMPION

In the Middle Ages we begin to see the different regions of Britain emerging, each with its own distinctive character. This is particularly so in England where historical records are more plentiful and landscape historians have been more active. The main division is into two landscape types, which used to be known as woodland and champion. In champion country there were big open fields, with each farmer's land holding split into a number of strips that were intermingled with those of his neighbours throughout the fields. All the farmers lived together in one village. Woodland country had small, hedged fields, each one privately owned. There were few villages and farmsteads stood alone or were grouped into hamlets of half a dozen houses or so.

The word champion may come from the French Champagne region, which is an extreme example of the type. Woodland comes from the abundance of

Typical ancient countryside. Ragmans Farm, Forest of Dean.

trees in the hedgerows, compared to the wide hedgeless spaces of the open fields. Oliver Rackham has renamed them planned and ancient countryside. Indeed, the woodland countryside is ancient. This is how the landscape was in prehistoric times and any changes to it have mostly been piecemeal. The champion country was indeed planned. The open fields of each village were laid out in a highly ordered manner and the people who made them had to

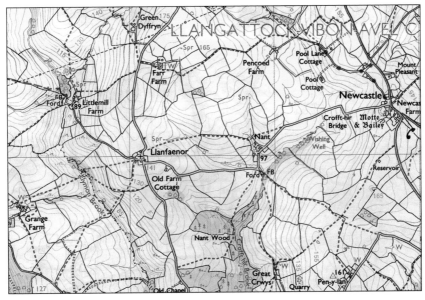

Map, ancient countryside, Monmouthshire.

sweep away the previous layout. In their turn the open fields were swept away by the Enclosure Acts of the eighteenth and nineteenth centuries and replaced by large, rectangular fields.

No-one knows why the open fields were made, still less why they were made in some parts of the country and not in others. The planned countryside lies across England in a swathe from Yorkshire to Dorset, with ancient countryside on both sides. (See map.) All of the planned countryside is in the fertile lowlands, but the distinction is not all down to geology and climate. Why, for example, does the boundary make that dog-leg corner across the flat plain of East Anglia? Historians may have their theories, but the people who actually made the open fields are no longer around and they left no written record of their reasons.

The planned countryside of England.

The open fields were very much an arable landscape, formed by the nature of the mouldboard plough. This is the plough that turns the soil upside down in a slice. Cross-ploughing is not necessary, so a long, narrow strip of land is an efficient shape to work as it keeps unproductive turning time to a minimum. The plough always moves the soil to the right, so as you plough up one side of your piece and down the other, the soil is turned towards the centre from both sides. Thus the soil gets progressively piled up along the centre and removed from the edges, and over the years this resulted in a series of permanent rounded ridges. These ridges were the basic unit from which the open fields were made up.

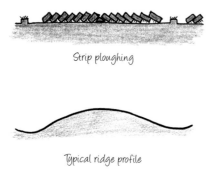

Strip ploughing

Typical ridge profile

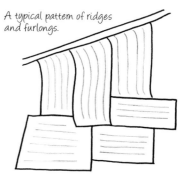

A typical pattern of ridges and furlongs.

A strip was a parcel of one or more ridges belonging to a single person. A number of strips lying parallel together made a furlong and the furlongs were grouped together to make two, three or sometimes more fields. In the Midlands the field was the unit of rotation. A two-field village would have one field under crops and the other under fallow. A three-field village would have one under autumn-sown crops, one under spring crops and the third fallow. In East Anglia the furlong was the unit of rotation, so the number of fields in the parish was less significant.

The open fields would be available for common grazing both after harvest and in the fallow year and in addition there was common land for pasture. Meadow for haymaking was often the most valuable land of all. It was usually situated on the rich alluvial soils along rivers and streams. These soils might be too wet for arable farming but would have both the moisture and the plant nutrients needed for a good hay crop year after year.

There are four villages in England that still have working open fields: Laxton in Northamptonshire, Soham in Cambridgeshire, Portland in Dorset and Braunton in Devon. If you visit one of these you'll see that the strips are not always straight. Just as often they are curved, either like a C or like a reversed S. These shapes arose due to the practicalities of ploughing with a team of six or eight oxen. Once they'd stopped ploughing at the end of a furrow they could be turned, yoke by yoke, but until then they had to keep in line, pulling. This meant there was an unploughed, and thus unproductive, headland left at either end of each furlong. The width of the headland could be kept to a minimum if the team approached it at an angle, which is just what would happen if the ridge was curved. The ridges may have been deliberately laid out in a curved shape or they may have gradually grown curved through use. No-one knows for sure.

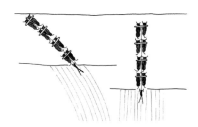

You may have noticed that one of the surviving open field systems is in Devon, well outside the planned countryside as shown on the map on the facing page. There were indeed open fields in some parts of the ancient countryside, though usually they only covered part of a parish, with hedged fields on the rest of the land. Mostly they were introduced relatively late and done away with relatively early compared to the open fields of the champion country.

In Scotland and some upland areas of northern England there was a different kind of open field system, the infield-outfield. The fields had the same kind of ridges and their remains may not look that different from the southern ridge and furrow I've already described. But the common arable of the village was divided up in a different way. The infield was cropped every year and fertility was maintained with manure from animals that were overwintered indoors. The outfield was occasionally cropped and grazed at other times. Both were enclosed by a large bank or wall, the head dyke, beyond which was common grazing land. In Scotland the term run-rig is often used for the system, though strictly this applies to the legal arrangements rather than the physical layout.

Medieval grain yields were tiny by modern standards and very erratic from year to year. It was normal for the farmers to harvest only two or three bags of grain for every bag of seed sown. In a bumper year it could be ten bags but in a bad year they harvested less than they had sown – or nothing at all. For comparison, present-day organic farmers get between twelve and forty to one. Production could be increased by changing from a two-field to a three-field system. This reduced the proportion of fallow land from half the arable area to a third. But it was the fallow that restored fertility to the soil so the change could be self-defeating in the long run. Grain was also grown in the ancient countryside but in many western and upland areas, where it's easier to grow grass than cereals, milk was a staple food.

The Black Death

The Middle Ages are generally held to run from about AD 500 to 1500. But from a landscape point of view, 1348, the year of the Black Death, has more sense as the end point. These eight centuries were a time of steady population increase. They also saw a steady increase in the proportion of land under open field. Perhaps in part this was a response to an increasing shortage of arable land. What later ages saw as inefficient the medieval mind must have seen as efficient. It was very much a communal system. A plough and a team of oxen were beyond the means of an individual farmer. So they clubbed together, those who could afford it providing an ox, those who couldn't only their labour. Matters such as the crop rotation and the date at which cattle could be let in to graze the fields after harvest had to be decided communally, and there was a manor court or village assembly to decide and enforce such things. In a dangerous world where death by starvation was a reality people saw safety in numbers and security in conformism.

Towards the end of the period land hunger became acute. Open field farming spread onto increasingly steep slopes. This led to the formation of large earthen terraces, which we call strip lynchetts. They usually occur in groups, like a huge staircase, and they are often marked on the Ordnance Survey map in Gothic script. The amount of labour required to make them must have been punishing. They are a sign of desperation: there was no land left that was flat enough to plough, so it had to be created. The country was full.

Around the year 1300 the population stopped growing. It even fell a bit, with runs of bad weather that the malnourished people were ill-fitted to cope with. Then in 1348 came the Black Death, the bubonic plague, which killed somewhere between a third and half the population. Suddenly the population pressure was gone. There was land to spare, not enough people to till it and little market for surplus food. But an alternative land use was waiting in the wings, one that

Strip lynchetts. (The transverse lines on the steep faces of the lynchetts are terracettes. See page 154.)

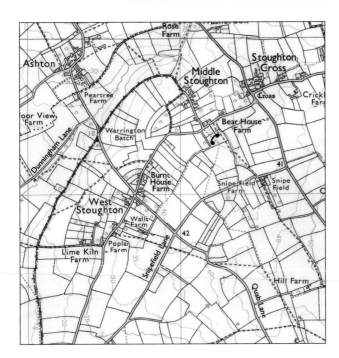

Strips and furlongs fossilised in the present landscape. Wedmore, Somerset.

required little labour and had a ready market just across the English Channel in the growing cities of Flanders. It was wool production. Much of the land in both woodland and champion country went down to grass to feed the sheep.

During this period most of the open fields in the ancient countryside were enclosed by agreement between the occupiers. Often this was a matter of neighbours exchanging strips till each had enough in one place to be worth enclosing them with a hedge. So the shapes of the old strips and furlongs are often preserved in the shapes of the fields we see today. These patterns can be easier to recognise on a map than on the ground. In some places there are narrow parallel fields that are obviously based on former strips. They may be reversed-S-shaped, C-shaped or straight. In others just the occasional hedge or field wall with a reversed-S shape gives the clue.

A hedge with that tell-tale reversed-S shape.

Another clue is field boundaries with seemingly irrational right-angled turns in them. These preserve the boundaries of the old furlongs, which were small and interlocked with each other in an irregular way. As the furlongs were amalgamated to make larger fields these irregular shapes

Dog-legs in field walls and parish boundaries. Chewton Plain, Somerset

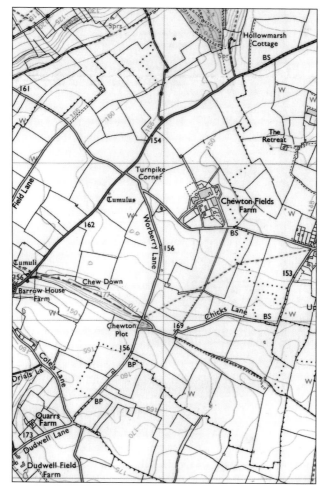

became dog-legs in the new field boundaries. Lanes often follow the outline of the old furlongs, giving them an irrational zigzag course. So can parish boundaries, which are shown on the Ordnance Survey Explorer maps as dotted lines. These are relatively late boundaries that were only finalised when the open fields of adjacent villages spread out to meet each other. Just the occasional dog-leg in a field boundary is not diagnostic because it could result from the amalgamation of ancient fields. As with almost every aspect of landscape reading, we're looking for a pattern.

Where the enclosed land was put down to grass and never ploughed again from then till now the ridges themselves were preserved. This gives a corrugated surface to the land, composed of ridges usually about ten metres wide and either curved or straight. It's known as ridge and furrow. The later parliamentary enclosures could also preserve ridge and furrow in this way, but in that case the new field hedges would ignore the old furlong boundaries and cut across them, while enclosure by agreement followed the old boundaries of strips and furlongs.

Woodland, Parks, Commons and Forests

In England at least, woodland became valuable as the population rose through the Middle Ages. Wood was virtually the only fuel and coppice woodland was the main source. In fact almost everything in medieval life, from houses to tools, was made of wood, though the great majority of it was used for fuel. Coppices were enclosed to keep out farm animals that would eat the new shoots that spring up after coppicing and thus prevent the trees regrowing. The barrier was usually a bank with a ditch on the outside and a hedge on the top. In the east of England these woodbanks can be massive earthworks. In the west they may be little bigger than a typical hedgebank but they are usually distinctive enough to mark out the wood as ancient. Another sign of an ancient coppice wood is often a zigzag boundary, the result of successive generations of farmers carving roughly rectangular fields out of the woodland edge.

A completely different approach to woodland was to combine grazing animals and trees. This gave a savanna-type woodland with grass between the

An enclosure-by-agreement landscape. In the foreground there are faint traces of ridge and furrow and beyond the farmstead the fields are bounded by curved and dog-leg hedges. The large, rectangular fields in the distance suggest later, parliamentary enclosure. Glastonbury, Somerset.

trees, now known as wood pasture. Coppice was clearly impossible in these woods but trees could be pollarded for a regular crop of poles. Pollarding is just the same as coppicing except the tree is cut two or three metres from the ground, out of reach of the animals. (See pages 112-114.) A new generation of trees might only get going at very rare intervals, perhaps when there was an epidemic of animal disease. Many wood pastures were commons or deer parks.

In Scotland the situation was different. Peat and coal were much more widely available as alternative fuels so woodland wasn't as highly valued and it declined more rapidly. Scotland may have had as little as five percent woodland in the Middle Ages, compared to perhaps fifteen percent in England. This lack of woodland can be seen in the way the Scots started to build in stone earlier than the English and Welsh, who used timber right into modern times. Some Scottish woods were managed intensively by coppicing and pollarding but most ancient woods north of the border that survived did so not because they were conserved but because they were remote from human settlement.

Parks were specialised wood pastures where private landowners kept deer. They had banks round them but with the ditch on the inside to keep the animals in. The bank was topped with a wooden fence, known as a pale. This was expensive to maintain, so parks usually have the economic shape of a rectangle with rounded corners, which encloses the greatest area for the least perimeter. Sometimes the banks were never finished, or didn't keep to the oval shape because the emparker didn't own all the land he would have liked to. Occasionally a 'park pale' is marked in Gothic script on an Ordnance Survey map, or a Park Farm or Park Wood will give a clue to the presence of a former park.

One of the best examples of a medieval deer park is Moccas Park in Herefordshire. It still has its herd of fallow deer and ancient trees of fantastic shapes, known as the Old Men of Moccas. In one corner of the park the trees are growing on ridge and furrow, which indicates that that part had been cultivated before it became a park.

Moccas Park, Hereforshire

The Old Men of Moccas give me a tangible feeling of how old the countryside is. We gaily toss about words like Medieval and Neolithic, and hundreds of years run off our tongues like grams in a cake recipe. But these old, old trees, fuller of dead wood than live, sitting there, growing by tiny rings each year or perhaps dying a little bit more than growing, give a real visual experience to the word 'age'. And when I saw the ridge and furrow under their feet I had some tangible idea of just how long ago it was that those men and oxen made those ridges and furrows.

Common land was the land left over when that needed for more intensive purposes had been fenced off. Commons could be grassland, moorland, heath, wood pasture or wetland. Their primary function was summer grazing, but they provided much else besides: wood, gorse or peat for fuel; bracken for animal bedding; wild fruits, herbs and fungi; wildfowl and fish. They belonged to specific communities and only members of the community had the right to use them.

If overgrazing threatened to become a problem individual commoners were awarded stints, a stint being the right to graze a certain number of animals on the common.

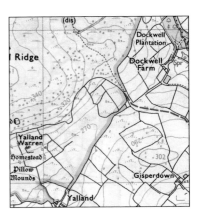

Roadside verges were common land and where a road met a common it usually widened out gradually into a funnel or horn shape. This shape was formed partly as a result of new fields being enclosed from the common. The most economical way to enclose land is with a curved hedge or wall, and if new fields of this shape were taken out of the common on either side of a road it left a road that gradually widened as it entered the common. Another reason for funnels is that they are a useful shape for rounding up animals that have been grazing on the common. These horns can often be seen on surviving commons.

A 'horn' on the edge of Dartmoor. (Note, the boundary between moorland and fields follows the black lines, which represent field walls, not the brown tint.)

In the Middle Ages over a third of the land of England was common. The commons were a great medieval institution with a complex set of customs and traditions regulating the various uses that different people could make of them. The forests were another great medieval institution and they were often located at least in part on common land. A forest was not necessarily woodland. It was a tract of land where the king or some other great lord kept his deer. There were moorland forests, such as Bowland and Dartmoor, heathland ones, such as the famous Sherwood and even one or two in fenland. People sometimes look at moorland forests and say, "This was forest in Medieval times, and just look at it now. It shows how much woodland has been lost in modern times." But the truth is they lost their trees thousands of years before they were declared forests.

Those forests that were based on woodland usually had a core of wood pasture and a much larger surrounding area of farmland that was also legally part of the forest. Here a special set of laws applied, ostensibly to protect the deer and their habitat but more realistically to give the king some extra income from fines. At the peak of forests in the high Middle Ages forest law held sway over vast swathes of the country but very little of that land was wooded. A forest was a place of deer rather than a place of trees.

Most forests were disafforested in early modern times. Plantations of oaks were made in some of those that remained in royal hands and the new meaning of 'forest' was born. However the real foundations of commercial plantation forestry were laid not by the state but by Scottish aristocrats of the seventeenth and eighteenth centuries. They were the first to experiment with exotic conifers. They have left us with notable forested landscapes, such as that between Blair Athol and Dunkeld on Tayside. But plantations didn't cover a significant area of Britain till the birth of the Forestry Commission in 1919.

Woodland, as opposed to plantation, remained an important economic resource through much of modern times. Charcoal was used more and more as the iron industry grew, till it was replaced by coke during the eighteenth century. Even into the nineteenth, when coal was taking over as the mass heating fuel, there was an increasing demand from industry for wooden goods such as bobbins, barrel staves and wheel spokes. Oak bark for tanning leather was a product that boomed in the early nineteenth century and the oak coppices of Argyll switched from charcoal to tan-bark production. Both of these markets led to reduced diversity in the woods as species other than oak were weeded out.

It's surprising how many people still come up with the old canard that woods were destroyed by industry. Far from destroying the woods, industrial demand saved them. Cutting trees down does not destroy a wood. Coppice woods have survived thousands of years of regular cutting, and pine can regenerate from seed. Woods are destroyed by grubbing them up for another purpose, usually agriculture, or by grazing them constantly at an intensity that prevents regeneration. The coppices of the charcoal age had an economic value so their owners had every incentive to keep them as woodland. The proof of this lies in the modern landscape: those areas that had the biggest charcoal-fired industries are now the areas with the most surviving woodland. Argyll, the Lake District, the Forest of Dean and the Weald are all examples. Iron masters didn't change to coke because there was a shortage of wood but because coke was cheaper. In a day's work a coal miner could produce more than twice the thermal equivalent that a woodcutter could.

Some woods were lost. In upland areas there must have been losses due to intensive grazing by sheep, though woods that disappear in this way often leave few traces. In lowland areas they were grubbed out to make new fields. In ancient countryside the site of a lost wood often stands out on the map as an island of

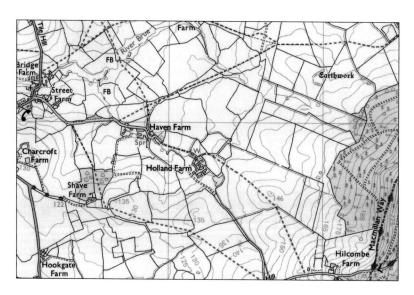

Ancient and modern intakes from the wood (which is now coniferised). Selwood Forest, Somerset.

regular, straight-sided hedges against a background of irregularly shaped fields. Sometimes there's a tell-tale name such as Southwood Farm in a place that is now far from any woodland. But when the demand for wood products finally tailed off in the later nineteenth century woodland was not grubbed out wholesale because by then farming was in decline.

ENCLOSURE

After the end of the Middle Ages the ancient countryside underwent modest changes. It lost its few remaining open fields through enclosure by agreement and bit by bit most of its common land was enclosed. By contrast the planned countryside was utterly transformed, from one kind of planned layout to another.

At the heart of the change were new crop rotations. Unproductive fallow could now be replaced with fodder crops, which gave fertility to the soil and produced animal feed. Clover, which can enrich the soil with the nitrogen 'fixed' by the bacteria that live in its roots, was an important one. Turnips and swedes, which produce large quantities of sheep fodder and thus equally large quantities of manure, were another. In the Norfolk four-course rotation, crops of clover and roots were alternated with crops of wheat and barley. Other rotations alternated cereals and temporary grassland, sown with high-yielding grasses and clovers. Yields of both corn and animal produce could be much higher with the new rotations.

The snag was you couldn't introduce a new rotation on open fields. The very essence of the system was that everyone followed the same rotation and the same annual cycle, both of which had gone on from time immemorial. An integral part of this annual cycle was throwing open the fields to the whole community's

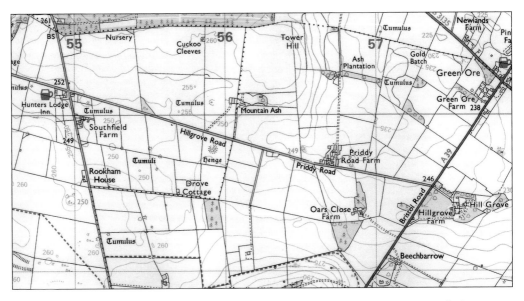

Enclosure act country, Mendip Hills, Somerset. Here the field boundaries are stone walls rather than hawthorn hedges.

cattle after harvest and during the fallow year. There was no point in growing a crop of swedes for the winter if they would be polished off by the cattle of the whole village on the first day of communal grazing.

If the medieval psyche had seen safety in numbers, the modern mind saw profit in individualism. The open field system had to go, at least in the minds of

This landscape, though outside the main area of planned countryside, shows every sign of parliamentary enclosure. Stringston, Somerset.

the landowners and larger farmers, who had the financial resources to capitalise on the new methods. Enclosure would mean exchanging their scattered strips for a private farm within a ring fence where they could do exactly what they pleased.

Not so the poorer land-holders who had just a few strips, the right to pasture one or two beasts on the common and the right to collect sticks for fuel. With these and the odd spell of work for their richer neighbours they could live a life of independence and dignity. Enclosure meant they lost all this in return for a small field that wouldn't make a viable holding. Faced with the expense of hedging the new field and a pressing neighbour who wanted to buy it, it might not stay in their hands very long. They became landless day-labourers, a class that was mercilessly exploited.

The enclosers resorted to Parliament to enforce their will. In the Scottish Lowlands a series of general acts of Parliament in the seventeenth century allowed the run-rig to be enclosed. In the English champion counties a succession of individual enclosure acts picked off the open field parishes one by one over the eighteenth and nineteenth centuries.

The new layout of enclosed fields completely ignored the old pattern of fields and furlongs. The enclosure act landscape is one of big straight-sided fields bounded by hedges of pure hawthorn. The winding lanes were replaced by straight roads with wide verges, that are sometimes mistaken for Roman roads. It's a mechanical landscape produced by an industrial age. Occasionally you will see a crooked hedge of mixed shrub species among the straight lines of enclosure act country. Often it's a parish boundary. These had always been hedged and, as we've already seen, boundaries can be very persistent. Woodland was also left unaffected and sometimes remains as irregular islands in the ruthless rationality of the modern chequerboard.

The large villages of the English planned countryside also remained intact after enclosure, though soon farmsteads began to appear on the new compact farms. Names like Trafalgar or Waterloo Farm often give a clue to the date of the new buildings, if not of the actual enclosure. But it was in Scotland that the Enlightenment ideal of an efficient modern landscape reached its most perfect form. On the north-eastern plain, between the firths of Tay and Moray, the former settlement pattern was swept away and replaced by model farms and cottages in a landscape that became among the most productive in Europe.

Along with the open fields went almost all the common land in both planned and ancient countryside. In ancient countryside enclosed commons often stand out on the map as an island of rectangular fields. Commons on very sandy soils were often heathland. With the new farming methods heath could now be converted into productive farmland. Lime could be brought in to correct acidity and the new rotations could boost the humus level to make up for the lack of clay in the soil. Most of the heathland of England disappeared in the nineteenth century.

Moorland commons, of which enormous areas were enclosed in Wales and the north of England, were sometimes more intractable than heath. Unlike lowland heath, high moorland has a severe climate to contend with as well as poor soil. There were attempts to turn moors into improved grassland but they were more successful in some regions than others. A modern version of ridge and furrow was sometimes used in vain attempts to turn moorland into arable. Its remains are quite easy to distinguish from medieval ridge and furrow. Apart from being found on moorland, where medieval ridge and furrow is rare, it's much narrower, typically five metres wide, and always straight.

The loss of the commons is one aspect of a general process of simplification that was going on in the landscape. Commons were often wild places with a mixture of trees, scrub, bracken, furze and marsh as well as heath and rough grassland. All this was replaced by fields of uniform grass and arable land. Simplification was a trend that was to gather pace in the twentieth century.

In the Highlands of Scotland the notorious Clearances were the equivalent of enclosure. With callous cruelty the peasant population was thrown off the land and replaced with a monoculture of sheep, which brought in a greater return to the landowners. But within a generation the fragile fertility of the Highland soils had been exported in the wool clip and the land could no longer support the sheep. They were replaced by deer, which rich people would pay for the privilege of shooting. One gamekeeper can manage an area that would once have been home to hundreds of people and the Highlands have remained largely deserted ever since. The people emigrated to the colonies or to the industrial cities of the Lowlands. Terrible though the Clearances were, for every family evicted some ten families left of their own accord. For the first time in history there were alternatives to the hard way of life that their ancestors had followed for six thousand years.

It was the start of globalisation. On an unprecedented scale people could move out and food could be brought in. There had been trade from Medieval times, when timber was imported from the Baltic and wool was exported to Flanders. Both had their effect on the landscape but Britain remained self-sufficient in food. Then in the 1870s railways opened up the interior of North America and steamships shrank the Atlantic. The virgin soils of the prairies were cashed in for grain which could be sold on Liverpool dockside cheaper than local farmers could grow it.

Imported food became so cheap that farming went into a depression that lasted till the Second World War. There was a brief respite during the First

World War but during the inter-war years almost every crumb on British plates was imported. Many farmers could do no more than keep their farms out of bankruptcy while the family survived on what their wives could get for the eggs, butter and vegetables they took to market each week. Much land reverted to scrub and rabbits roamed where the land lay idle.

THE BIG BANG

The enclosure acts took place over a period of centuries and, in England at least, they only affected about a fifth of the land. But the changes in the British countryside since the Second World War have happened in half a century and affected the whole country. Compared to any previous period of change this one rates as an explosion.

Similar changes have gone on all over the world and in town as much as country. Everyone has been caught up in a race for more material consumption. The twin drivers are a rapidly changing technology and fossil fuels that are, in the long view, vastly under priced. Farmers and foresters have done nothing different from what everyone else has done, yet they have been roundly criticised for it by people who happily eat the cheap food that the new methods have made possible.

The low price of fossil fuel hasn't only powered the new technology of tractors, fertilisers and sprays; it's also unleashed a level of globalisation that couldn't have been imagined a hundred years before. Technology has driven up world food production to the point where, until very recently, there was a constant surplus. Meanwhile the low cost of fuel means that food can be moved around the world at a fraction of the cost of producing it. The price for any commodity has become the lowest price at which anyone anywhere on the planet can produce it.

In the case of farming, a third factor has been subsidies. Paid at first by the national government and later by the European Union, subsidies have attempted to cushion farmers from the effects of globalisation. They have never managed to make farming as profitable as other businesses but for a long time they guaranteed a steady return for anything which farmers produced. Farmers responded by going all out for maximum yield.

From a landscape point of view the most obvious effect of all this has been the loss of hedges. You need big fields to operate big machines and a bulldozer can remove in seconds what a man with hand tools could grub out in a day. Where hedges have gone soil erosion has increased and wildlife has suffered. In the east of England, where the rate of loss has been ten times the national average, the whole character of the landscape has been changed.

Nevertheless it hasn't obliterated the difference between champion and woodland counties. Suffolk, for example, is still quite unmistakably ancient countryside. The hedges that do survive there contain a rich mixture of species and follow a curvy or crooked course, quite unlike the straight hawthorn hedges of parliamentary enclosure. Old farmsteads, many of which date from medieval times, stand alone amongst the fields.

As the fields have got bigger so have the farms themselves. Farmers have needed ever more land just to stay economically level with their urban counterparts. Greed is not always the motive for farm amalgamations, as this entry from my notebook relates.

Sprint Mill, Cumbria.

Hillary, a hill farmer from Tebay, said that most of the high fell farms are now abandoned and their land farmed by neighbours with farms at a lower level. It was electricity and the motor car that killed them off. They could support a family, but not with a car and a full range of electrical equipment. A young man couldn't go courting with any hope of success without these things.

Farms have also become more specialised. In the east, fertilisers and pesticides have done away with the need for rotations and the economies of scale mean that costs are lower on a pure arable than a mixed farm. In the west, the low cost of transport means that it's cheaper to buy straw from the other side of the country than to grow a little corn to provide winter bedding and grain for the animals. There's always been a predominance of grazing in the west and arable in the east but this was a matter of emphasis on what were essentially mixed farms. Now it's rare to find a field of wheat in Wales or a cow in Cambridgeshire.

Simplification of the landscape: hedges are lost to excessive browsing by sheep, while heathland succeeds to wood through lack of grazing. Simmonds Yat, Herefordshire.

31

The landscape is getting simpler all the time. It's not just the loss of hedges, moors and ancient woodland or the increasing specialisation of farms. It's also a general tidying up and a form of triage in which land is either farmed intensively or not at all. You can see this in grassland country, where flat fields tend to be improved with fertilisers or by reseeding, while sloping fields, which are difficult to mechanise, are allowed to succeed to woodland. The great variety of grassland types is lost in this process. Coppice woods also become simpler when they are no longer managed. Where once there was a mix of patches in different stages of regrowth, each with its distinctive community of plants and animals, now there's a dense canopy overall. Little field quarries and redundant ponds have been filled in and small marshy patches have been drained. The rich mosaic of the countryside, so important to a diversity of wildlife, has increasingly become monochrome.

By the 1980s people began to wonder whether this single-minded pursuit of production at all costs was altogether what they wanted. Food surpluses had grown so great that disused aircraft hangers were hired to house the notorious 'grain mountain'. The cost of this surplus food in terms of lost wildlife was shown by a report from the Nature Conservancy Council that detailed the loss of semi-natural ecosystems during the previous forty years. The losses ranged from upland grassland, which had decreased by a third, to lowland flower-rich meadows, which had decreased by 97%. Half of the ancient woodland that had been here in 1945 was gone. This was the same amount of woodland as had been lost in the previous nine hundred years, since the great survey of Domesday Book. One result of this was a great interest in nature conservation. Nature reserves had existed since around the turn of the century but from the mid-80s they expanded by leaps and bounds. But nothing serious was done to stop the continued destruction of biodiversity on the rest of the land.

By around 1990 it became generally accepted that we were paying subsidies for the wrong thing. If the public wanted to pay farmers for anything it was for a beautiful countryside full of wildlife – the very thing that was being destroyed by over-production. It took fifteen years to make the change, and in 2005 subsidies were switched to a flat rate, with supplements for wildlife-friendly practices. A decade later this has made no difference to the decline in wildlife.

OBSERVATION TIPS

Ancient and Planned Countryside

Ancient or Woodland	Planned or Champion
Hamlets or a mix of villages and hamlets, with old farmsteads standing alone.	Villages, with 18th-19th century farmsteads standing alone.
Fields of irregular shape, or showing the outlines of former strips and furlongs.	Regular shaped fields with straight boundaries.
Hedges of mixed species.	Hedges mostly of hawthorn.
Lanes frequent, crooked and narrow.	Roads less frequent and straight, often with wide verges.
Frequent woods, including small ones.	Woods large or absent.

Two rules of thumb:

- Small, irregular-shaped fields are older than large, regular-shaped ones.
- The older a hedge is the more species of trees and shrubs there are in it. (See pages 189-190.)

These are only general tendencies and there are exceptions.

Ridge and furrow

There are two kinds of ridge and furrow, and three other kinds of earthworks that can be mistaken for it:

- Medieval ridge and furrow is usually about 10m wide with a rounded profile to the ridge. It may be straight or curved, shaped either like a C or like a reversed S.

- Post-medieval ridge and furrow is narrower, usually about 5m wide, always straight, and usually on marginal land.

- Watermeadows are always in a valley bottom, usually on land too wet for arable. Carrier ditches may still be visible along top of the ridges. (See page 150.)

- Gutters or grips are straight, shallow furrows, spaced about 10m apart with flat ground between them. They spill into a ditch at the edge of the field and are part of an intensive drainage system, e.g. on the Somerset Levels.

- Where land has been 'ploughed' for a forestry plantation and later reverted to grassland or heath, the resulting ridges have an asymmetrical profile, with a narrow ridge on one side and flat ground on the other, typically 2m wide overall. (See page 126.)

Faint traces

- Ridge and furrow or other earthworks may be worn away to the point where they can only be seen when conditions are just right.

- In grassland the best time of year is winter or spring, when the grass is short and the sun is low. Sometimes there's a brief moment in early morning or late afternoon when the sun strikes a landscape of short grass at just the right angle and a whole medieval landscape jumps out at you in sharp relief.

- Melting snow can also highlight faint earthwork patterns, as can heavy rainfall, which can flood even the slightest of furrows while leaving the ridges dry.

- In ploughed land former earthworks can reveal themselves as soil marks. Darker soil indicates former furrows or ditches and lighter soil indicates ridges or banks.

- In growing crops, former ditches and banks can show up as crop marks, especially during dry weather. In the deeper topsoil of a former ditch the crops grow greener and taller than in the rest of the field, while in the shallow topsoil over a former bank they grow paler and shorter.

- Former hedges or field walls in grassland often show up as a step or terrace if they lie across the slope. (See page 198.) If they run up and down the slope or if the land is flat they may be revealed as low banks or not show at all.

3

The Rocks and the Soil

THE BRITISH landscape is remarkably varied. Looking out of the front window of my house I can see no less than four distinctive landscapes. On the right are the Mendips, a plateau of stone-walled fields and ash woods. Straight in front of me, stretching away to the sea, are the Somerset Levels, former marshes with drainage ditches instead of hedges. Beyond them lie the Quantocks, a range of old hills topped with heather, bracken and oak woods. To the left is the much lower ridge of the Polden Hills, a belt of hedged fields and stone villages.

If you travel from here to the south coast, some thirty miles away, you pass through yet more kinds of country: chalk downs, sandy heaths, deep clay vales and hills of the golden yellow Ham stone which gives a special glow to the houses in those parts. To the north, just over the Mendips, there's a jumble of hills and valleys that harbour a former coalfield and patches of land with a soil so red that till recently it was quarried for pigment. In most countries of the world you would have to travel hundreds of miles to see the varieties of landscape you can see here in dozens, and most of this diversity is down to the diversity of the rocks. To find out why this should be we need to go back about 60 million years.

Before then the various layers of rock that make up Britain lay more or less in layers one on top of the other. But around that time, deep below the Earth's solid crust, a convection current in the hot, molten magma lifted the north-western part gently upwards. Whenever rocks are lifted like this the rate of erosion speeds up and in the north-west the younger, softer rocks that lay on top were eroded away to reveal the hard old rocks below. The south-east, which had not been lifted up, kept its covering of young, relatively soft rocks. From that day to this the north and west of the island has been higher than the south and east.

This isn't so much because of the initial uplift but because the old rocks which are exposed over most of Scotland, northern England and Wales are hard and less erodible than the softer rocks that lie to the east and south. It's this difference in the hardness of the rocks, rather than the initial uplift, which has given us the contrast between the highland and lowland zones of the country.

In the south-east, the layers of younger rocks were tilted by the uplift. As the raised, north-western part of each layer was lifted it eroded away, leaving some of the layer below it exposed. There they lie, like the edge of an open carpet sample book, each sample different from the next and each leaving a little bit of the one below it showing. This is of course a greatly simplified scheme of the rocks of Britain and there are parts of the island where the structure doesn't

Highland and lowland Britain

conform to it. But in general it explains why there is so much variety in the rocks that appear at the surface and thus so much variety in the landscape.

KINDS OF ROCK

Although the rocks are mostly hidden from the eye they have a huge effect on the landscape and this is expressed in three main ways:

- Hard rocks make hills and soft rocks make valleys.
- Some rocks hold water and others don't and you can see the difference because there's no surface water on those that don't.
- Some rocks make a soil that is poor in plant nutrients and acid, while others make a soil that is rich and alkaline. You can see the difference in the vegetation.

The first step to understanding your own landscape is knowing what kind of rocks underlie it. The following sketch of the commoner rock types may get you started.

Sand and Clay

If you've read the Winnie the Pooh books in the original editions you may have memories of the enchanted landscape hinted at by E. H. Shepard's line drawings. This wasn't an imaginary place but a real one, Ashdown Forest. It lies at the centre of the High Weald, a sandstone upland that runs between the clay vales of Kent and Sussex in the south-east of England. Sandstone is harder than clay and this is why the High Weald rises above the two clay vales, known collectively as the Low Weald. The vegetation is different too: the Forest is mostly heathland and contrasts with the green-hedged fields of the broad vales on either side.

Sand grains contain very little of the minerals which plants need for growth and the soil they form is acid. If you add in the fact that a very sandy soil dries out quickly after rain, leaving plants short of water, overall it makes a difficult soil for plant growth. It's hard to grow crops in it and only a few tough plants, like heathers and birch trees, are really at home there. This is why Ashdown Forest has been used as rough grazing land and has developed into a heath. It's a beautiful landscape but not a very productive one from a human point of view.

Clay, by contrast, contains an abundance of plant nutrients and tends to be alkaline. It forms a rich soil. Water moves through it slowly and, though poor drainage can be a problem, drought is less of one. Soils that contain a high proportion of clay grow better crops than sandy soils, as long as the drainage is good. This was especially true in the days before chemical fertilisers, when farmers were far more dependent on the natural fertility of the soil than they are now.

So the difference between sandstone and clay is reflected in the historic land use of these neighbouring landscapes, the one poor common land, the other prosperous farms. This pattern can be carried over to an urban landscape. Hampstead Heath in London is an island of open land in a sea of bricks and mortar. It's also an island of sandy soil surrounded by clay, so it was left as common grazing while the surrounding clay was divided up into privately owned farms. As the town expanded, individuals could sell their land for building but the heath remained common property which no one person could sell. Hampstead Heath owes its survival to the difficulty of getting a group of commoners to agree on disposing of their common property.

Limestones

From the top of Ashdown Forest, looking beyond the Low Weald on either side, you can see the North and South Downs. These hills are made of chalk, the youngest and softest of the various limestones that are found in Britain. Limestones are formed at the bottom of clear seas where the only durable material is the limy skeletons of minute sea creatures, which over aeons of time rain down and form thick layers of pure lime.

Limestones almost always make hills. Some are hard, like the grey carboniferous limestone of the Pennines and Mendips, while others, like chalk, are soft. But even the chalk is resistant to erosion because, like all limestones, it's permeable to water. This means water sinks in and no streams or rivers flow on the surface, and surface water is the main agent of erosion.

The carboniferous limestone makes a mildly rugged landscape. The rock is often exposed on the surface and it can make spectacular cliffs. In the past people have gathered loose stones from the surface and made them into the characteristic field walls. By contrast, the softness of chalk has given its hills a rounded, pillowy profile, and it's mostly too soft to make walls. The Cotswold

The grey limestone of the Mendip Hills. Burrington Combe, Somerset. (The bracken-covered hill in the distance is Blackdown. See page 164.)

limestone is intermediate, less rugged than the Pennines and less rounded than the chalk. The Cotswold country has field walls and is famous for its picture-book villages made of the honey-coloured stone.

Limestones are very alkaline. Although clay soils are usually more alkaline than sandy ones, soils formed from limestone are more alkaline again. On the other hand, limestone soils aren't necessarily rich in the other minerals that plants need for their nutrition, so they are not necessarily fertile. They also tend to be thin. Sandstone and clay can both contribute plenty of mineral matter to the soil which forms over them but most of the bulk of limestone is soluble lime and when this is carried away in the drainage water all that remains are any impurities it contained. Chalk, being the purest limestone, characteristically has very thin soil, which restricts the amount of plant growth it can support.

One of the best places in the country to see the contrast between alkaline limestone and acid sandstone is in the Pennines. Here the sandstone, known as millstone grit, is naturally cemented into a hard, impermeable form so, unlike the sandstone of Ashdown Forest, it holds water. While the limestone drains freely and grows sweet pastures on its alkaline soils, the millstone grit is acid and wet. It tends towards heather and moorgrass, with acid peat bogs in the wettest areas.

Hard, Old Rocks

Over much of Wales, the English Lake District and most of Scotland, the rocks are uniformly hard. Valleys are more often carved out of them by the forces of erosion seeking out some line of weakness in the rock than by the contrast between soft and hard kinds.

Some of these hard rocks are ones that have come straight up from the molten magma below. Granite is an example. Like sandstone, it's acid and poor in plant nutrients. The highest mountains in Britain, Ben Nevis and Cairn Gorm, are made wholly or partly from granite. Heather and peat bogs are characteristic on it. Basalt is another rock that comes straight from the magma, but it's rich in plant nutrients and is not acid. If you buy rock dust to revitalise the mineral content of your garden, it will be basalt or one of its close cousins. Mountains of these richer rocks are likely to have a covering of the more demanding plants, such as bracken, gorse and sweet grasses.

Drift Deposits

From the landscape reader's point of view, shallow deposits on the surface can be more important than the solid rocks below. These deposits are known as drift. Wind-blown sand in coastal dunes is an example. Fine material deposited by rivers is called alluvium, and almost every river that is moving slowly enough to shed some of its load is bordered by a band of it. Peat is formed under waterlogged conditions, both in hill areas where the rainfall is high and in low-lying basins where drainage is poor.

A geological map that shows only the solid rocks and not the drift can be misleading. Much of East Anglia, for example, is shown as chalk but if you look

The watery landscape of the Somerset Levels lies on peat and alluvium. The higher land in the background is on a mix of limestones and clay.

for chalk downland there you will be disappointed. Most of the chalk is covered with a drift deposit called boulder clay, a mix of glacial clay and chalk. It makes very fertile soils, with some of the advantages of both clay and chalk, a rich store of nutrients on the one hand and good drainage on the other.

READING THE SOIL

The Finger Test

One of the first things I do when I come upon a piece of land for the first time is to feel the soil with my fingers. This tells me whether it's predominantly sandy or clay. All soils are a mixture of both but almost always one or the other will predominate. Which one is dominant in any particular soil is important because it suggests what crops can be grown on that land and how it needs to be worked with to get the best results.

Most soils are a fairly even mixture and are called loams. You can have a sandy loam or a clay loam, that's to say a soil that is a fair mixture but definitely dominated by one or the other. Extreme soils are known simply as sand or clay. In fact both of them are mixtures but so predominantly one or the other that we use this shorthand to describe them.

A sandy loam is often preferred for market gardening. Certainly they are rather dry soils and rather poor in mineral nutrients but they have the great advantage that you can work on the land almost any day of the year. This is in contrast with a clay soil, where you have to wait much longer after rain for it to dry out enough so you can work it without fear of causing soil compaction. The deficiencies of a sandy loam, dryness and lack of minerals, can always be cured by the application of compost and manure.

Clay loams sometimes used to be called 'wheat and beans land' or 'four horse land'. They were rich enough in nutrients to grow the more demanding crops before the days of chemical fertilisers, but the heavy, plastic soil was hard to work and needed twice the number of horses for ploughing than lighter soils. The terms, 'heavy' and 'light', are often used to describe clay and sandy soils respectively.

What follows is a simplified form of the finger test but it's enough to give you the most important distinctions between one soil and another:

Take about a teaspoonful of soil, knead it till it's completely homogenous and roll it into a ball. It needs to be at just the right moisture content to form the strongest possible ball. Too wet and it squidges, too dry and it crumbles. You may need to moisten it and if it's a bit too wet you can dry it by kneading it for longer. In fact if you knead a sample for too long it may get too dry and you may need to re-moisten it.

When you have the strongest ball you can make with that soil ask yourself this series of questions:

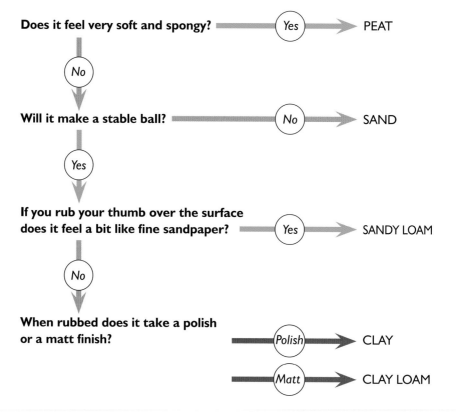

Note: if you can detect a little sand in your sample but not enough to make it feel like fine sandpaper, what you have is a sandy clay loam. This is usually a really fertile soil, with most of the advantages of both sandy and clay soils and little of their disadvantages.

Soil Indicator Plants

We can learn about the soil, and indeed the rocks below, by noting what plants are growing in it. Most plants grow in a wide range of soils and tell us nothing but there are some that have a distinct preference and we call these soil indicator plants.

Rushes.

There are strong indicators and weak indicators. Rushes are an example of a strong indicator. They are usually found in pasture and only grow where the soil is wet. Just this one plant is enough to tell you for certain that the soil is normally wet, whether or not it's wet on the day you see it. Very few plants are strong indicators. Most indicator plants have only a mild preference for one kind of soil but can also be found on others. These are weak indicators and you can't tell anything about the soil by seeing just one species of weak indicator, you have to look out for communities of plants. Three or four indicator plants growing together will tell you something that you couldn't assume from seeing just one.

There are two more rules of thumb about reading indicator plants. One is only to take account of plants that are growing spontaneously, not planted by human hand. Even indicator plants will grow in a wide range of soils if we look after them and weed out competitors. This is what farmers, gardeners and foresters do for the plants they grow. A page in my notebook illustrates how plantations can ignore changes in soil type while spontaneous trees and shrubs closely reflect them.

Teffont, Wiltshire

We went for a walk through the wood. It seems to be a plantation on an ancient woodland site. The top end is beech and ash with bluebells, replacing an older hazel coppice that remains in one corner. There are a few rhododendrons in this part. The bottom end is mainly ash, sycamore and oak, with a very diverse edge of dogwood, spindle, wayfaring tree, native maple, hazel, hawthorn and even a bit of old man's beard. None of these appear to be growing inside the wood, which, as I said, has the appearance of an old plantation.

I took a soil sample on this edge (half a dozen sub-samples). As we walked back up I noticed that the edge gradually changed from the diverse mix to pure spindle, before the path entered the wood and I lost sight of the edge. I took another soil sample at the top end, near where the rhododendrons were growing. The two samples were both a sandy loam but the one from the bottom of the wood was pH 7.25* and the one from the top was 5.5.*

* Alkaline and acid respectively.

41

Rhododendron is a strong indicator of an acid soil. It often self-seeds in woods where the soil is sufficiently acid, if there are seed parents nearby. The rich mix of shrubs on the edge of the lower part of the wood was probably the remains of the semi-natural wood that was there before the plantation. It includes some alkaline indicators and the diversity of plants itself indicates an alkaline soil. You could never have deduced the difference in soil acidity between the two parts of the wood on the basis of the planted trees.

Here we have examples of two different kinds of spontaneous vegetation. The rhododendron is an unwanted plant growing in a cultivated crop, in other words a weed. The shrubs on the woodland edge are the remains of the semi-natural vegetation, left over from the woodland that was there before it was converted to plantation. In general all the plants in semi-natural ecosystems, such as ancient woodland, moorland and unimproved grassland, can be regarded as spontaneous. On cultivated land, which includes arable land, gardens and plantations, only the weeds are spontaneous.

The other rule of thumb is to ignore isolated individuals and plants that are growing poorly. Look for thriving populations of healthy plants. I was once cycling through an oak plantation on an acid soil in the Forest of Dean when I came upon a single plant of old man's beard beside the track. It looked as though it was struggling. Old man's beard, or wild clematis, is a strong indicator of an alkaline soil, so what was it doing there? I dismounted and had a good look: the track I was on had been surfaced with limestone chippings and water draining through the chippings had made the soil beside the track just alkaline enough for an old man's beard plant to survive.

That plant was growing in an untypical place, right beside the track. It's always important to check that the place where indicators are growing is not in any way special. For example, rushes can grow in the compacted soil of tractor ruts while all around is well drained. Gateways, paths, old compost and manure heaps are all untypical places.

Oak trees grow in all soils but where almost all the trees are oak, as here, it suggests a poor, acid soil. Foxgloves are an acid soil indicator, so these two plants between them build up a picture. St Braivels Common, Forest of Dean.

The absence of indicator plants doesn't prove a thing. There may be another factor at work. There may be no suitable seed parents, especially in intensively farmed land and in urban areas. The wild plants of towns are often determined more by what happened to be growing nearby when the soil became bare and available for colonisation than by the nature of the soil itself. Or there may be a biotic influence that is stronger than the soil. Nettles, for example, can out-compete almost anything else where there's a rich accumulation of plant nutrients. But they can't stand repeated mowing, and regular grazing is usually enough to stop them getting established. So they may be absent from farmed grassland even though the soil is rich enough for them.

Checklist
- Look for strong indicators or a community of indicator plants
- Don't count cultivated plants
- Don't count isolated or weakly-growing plants
- Avoid untypical places
- Absence of indicators proves nothing

What They Tell Us

The main things which indicator plants can tell us about the soil are: water content, acidity and plant nutrient content.

Of the three, water content is usually the easiest one to tell. For example: the two common species of buttercup grow on soil which is moist but not wet; rushes on soil which is wet for most of the year; and reeds in really wet places where there's standing water for at least part of the year. (For illustration, see page 187.) Since soil compaction interferes with drainage many plants that indicate poor drainage can also indicate compaction. Silverweed is one of these. Others, such as the greater plantain, only indicate compaction and don't grow in soils that are wet but uncompacted.

Acidity is clear enough to read at the extremes: heather for acid, old man's beard for alkaline. But in the middle range there are no strong indicators so you must look for communities of plants.

Greater plantain, indicates soil compaction.

As for plant nutrients, there's a definite group of plants, mostly garden and arable weeds, which are pretty reliable indicators of rich soils. For example, if you take over a new allotment and find that the weeds there include fat hen, chickweed, annual nettle, annual mercury and black nightshade, rejoice! Your soil is not only high in nutrients but probably fertile in other respects too.

As well as noting individual indicator plants, the overall diversity of plants can be a clue. A high diversity of grasses and wildflowers indicates that the level of nutrients in the soil can't be very high. If it was, a small number of competitive plants would have taken over. (See page 43.) There's also a relationship between diversity and acidity. Here in Europe there are more plants that live in alkaline soils than acid. So a hedgerow with half a dozen species of shrub in it is almost certain to be on an alkaline soil, though there are other factors that affect the diversity of a hedge. (See pages 189-191.)

Ribwort plantain, not an indicator.

The climber, old man's beard, in September. In winter the seed-heads turn white and are clearly visible on the trees and hedges it climbs.

One animal deserves mention as a soil indicator and that's the mole. Moles need well-drained ground. Their main prey is earthworms, which avoid both bad drainage and acidity. So molehills indicate good drainage and a neutral to alkaline soil.

Using the List

Any list of indicator plants you read, including the one below, must be regarded with a degree of scepticism. They're often presented as a series of hard facts, like definitions in a dictionary, but the reality is less clear-cut than that. One reason is that there are a few indicator plants that behave differently in different parts of the country. For example, both suckering elms and creeping buttercup are normally plants of heavy, wet soils. Yet they are common on the very sandy soils around the east Devon heathlands. I've also seen suckering elms on a well-drained gravelly soil on the borders of Suffolk and Essex. These seem to be little pockets of country where these plants, for some unknown reason, behave quite differently from their norm. So please regard the list below as a framework, to be amended according to your experience of your own locality.

Not all the plants on the list will live in your area, so you don't need to learn how to recognise them all. If you don't yet know many wild plants the best way to get started is to identify plants in the landscape first, using a guide, and then consult the list to see if any of the plants you've seen are indicators.

SOIL INDICATOR PLANTS

* = strong indicator, but only for the soil condition so marked;
'poor' and 'rich' refer to the level of plant nutrients in the soil

Trees and Shrubs

Alder
*Wet, usually beside a stream or river. Indicates land liable to flood.

Beech
Well-drained, often suffers from die-back on poorly-drained soils.

Bilberry or blaeberry
*Acid, *poor.

Bramble
Well-drained but moist.

Bog myrtle
*Wet, *acid.

Broom
Acid, sandy.

Chestnut, sweet
Acid, sandy, but often planted on other soils.

Elder
Rich, usually alkaline.

Elm, suckering
Very typical of clay, but in some areas also on sandy and gravelly soils. (See above.)

Elm, wych
Alkaline, often on a clay soil over limestone.

Gorse, common
Well-drained, usually sandy, poor; but increasingly found on a wider range of soils.

Gorse, dwarf and western
Acid, not necessarily well-drained.

Guelder rose
Moist to wet.

Heath, cross-leaved
*Acid, poor, wet.

Heather, bell
*Acid, poor, dry.

Heather, common or ling
*Acid, poor, moist.

Old man's beard or wild clematis
*Alkaline.

Rhododendron
*Acid.

Rowan
Typical of light, acid soils, but very occasionally on limestone.

Scots pine
*Acid, but often planted on other soils.

Spindle
Alkaline.

Wayfaring tree
*Alkaline.

Whitebeam
Well-drained, limestone or light sands.

Willows, except goat willow
Wet.

Yew
Especially common on chalk, but also on other well-drained soils.

45

Herbaceous

Agrimony
  Well-drained.

Birdsfoot trefoil
  Low nitrogen.

Bog asphodel
  Wet, acid* and
  poor*.

Bracken
  *Well-drained, usually
  acid, usually sandy
  when abundant.

Buttercup, creeping
  Moist, compacted or
  heavy.

Buttercup, meadow
  Moist.

Chickweed
  Rich.

Cleavers or goosegrass
  Rich.

Coltsfoot
  Heavy.

Cow wheat, common
and small
  Acid.

Corn spurrey
  Poor, acid.

Cuckoo flower or lady's
  smock
  Moist.

Deadnettle, white and
  red
  Rich.

Dock, broad-leaved
  *Rich.

Fat hen
  Rich.

Fleabane
  Damp.

Foxglove
  Acid.

Harebell
  Well-drained.

Heath bedstraw
  Acid.

Hemp agrimony
  Damp to wet.

Horseshoe vetch
  *Alkaline, *dry,
  limestone or chalk.

Horsetail
  Wet subsoil.

Kidney vetch
  Well-drained, usually
  alkaline.

Marjoram
  Well-drained, usually
  alkaline.

Meadowsweet
  Moist to wet.

Nettle, annual or small
  Rich.

Nettle, stinging
  *Rich, especially in
  phosphorous.

Orache
  Rich.

Orchid, pyramidal
  Alkaline.

Pineapple weed
  Compacted.

Plantain, greater
  Compacted.

Poppy, opium
  Rich.

Pyramidal orchid
  Alkaline.

Ragged Robin
  Wet, not very acid.

Reed
  Usually on soil
  flooded for at least
  part of the year.

Rush, hard
  *Wet, alkaline.

Rush, soft
  *Wet, acid.

Salad burnet
  Alkaline, dry.

Silverweed
  *Compacted or
  damp.

Sorrel, common
  Poor.

Sorrel, sheep's
  *Acid, dry.

Sorrel, wood
  Usually acid.

Stinking iris
  Alkaline.

Thistle, creeping
  Often compacted
  subsoil, fairly rich.

Thyme
  Dry, usually alkaline.

Tormentil, common
  Acid, poor.

Willowherb, great hairy
  Damp.

4

Climate and Microclimate

I REMEMBER standing on the Isle of Erraid on a beautiful June day. The sky was that delicate china blue that's unique to the Hebrides. A soft wind blew in from the Atlantic bringing little puffy white clouds that shone in the sunshine as they sailed over the deep blue sea and the pale golden sands. Erraid is off the western tip of the Isle of Mull, just by Iona. From where I stood I looked inland along the low western peninsula towards Ben More, the highest point on Mull and the first big mountain of the Highlands. It was crowned with a thick black cloud and its flanks were hidden behind sheets of rain.

It always rains more on higher ground. As the wind blows towards rising ground the air is pushed upwards and as it rises it cools. Cool air can't hold as much moisture as warm air, so clouds form and it rains. What I saw that day was a microcosm of the way the climate of Britain conspires with the geology to reinforce the difference between the highland and lowland zones. In Chapter 3 we saw how the whole island is tilted up in the north-west and down in the south-east.

By some cosmic coincidence the climate follows much the same shape. The prevailing westerly winds bring us rain and cloud off the Atlantic ocean, making the west wetter than the east. The weather systems that bring the rain are centred on the north of the island, which makes the north wetter than the south. Even if the country was flat there would be more rain in the north-west but the land form intensifies the climatic gradient. Of course water is essential for life, but there's a happy medium in everything and here in Britain there's more often too much than too little. The rain cools down both soil and air and leaches plant nutrients out of the soil, leaving them poor and acid. The water often can't flow away fast enough and soils become waterlogged, depriving both plant roots and soil organisms of oxygen. The clouds cut out the light and the humidity encourages fungal diseases.

Many of the old, hard rocks of the north-west are poor and acid in the first place and impervious to water, which adds to the drainage problem. So the climate serves to intensify the effect of the rocks, resulting in soils that can support little but moorland and the tougher species of trees. These landscapes can't produce much in the way of human food and they are low in biodiversity. But tourists flock there to see the 'wild', uncultivated scenery of the Highlands, the Lakes and Snowdonia. The paradox is that their visit is so often spoiled by one of the two great forces that created the landscape in the first place – the rain.

Not all western landscapes are so rugged and infertile. Where the rocks are softer and richer in minerals the hills are lower, the rainfall more moderate and the soils more fertile. This is grass country. A constant supply of moisture throughout the growing season keeps up the production of lush green leaves without a break. There may be more rain than you need in winter, but that doesn't matter too much because the cattle are snug in the barn eating the silage that was made from the surplus grass of spring. This is why the west of Britain specialises in animal farming.

To the east of the hills and mountains there's less rain. The air is drier because it's left most of its moisture behind on the high land. It also warms as it falls, and warm air can hold more moisture than cold, so even if it is still moist it gives less rain. The relatively dry area on the lee side of high ground is known as a rain shadow.

In southern and eastern Britain the younger, softer rocks give more fertile soils and lower hills with gentler slopes that can be easily cultivated. All of it is in a rain shadow. You may not think so if you live there, but parts of eastern England have a rainfall that would class them as semi-desert in a hotter and sunnier part of the world. The dry climate has advantages for arable crops. Almost any work on the land, from ploughing to harvesting, needs dry weather, and the crops need a dry spell in late summer to ripen. Certainly grain crops need moisture to grow, but not so much nor so constantly as grass.

MICROCLIMATE

I live on top of a small hill surrounded by flat land. Today, as I write this, the hilltop is in bright sunshine but if I look down in any direction all I can see is fog. The hilltop and the valley have different microclimates. Beyond the flat land there are limestone hills where the wild thyme grows. It likes to grow on the anthills, because it appreciates the slightly drier soil it gets on these little grassy mounds, less than knee high. It tends to grow more often on the south or south-west sides of the anthills, the warm sides that get the noonday and afternoon sunshine. On the north sides of the anthills moss is more common. The contrast between the two sides of an anthill is also a difference in microclimate. There are microclimates on both these scales and every one in between.

Wild thyme favours the south side of an anthill.

The patterns of microclimate in the landscape are particularly important if you're reading the landscape with a practical purpose in view. A precise knowledge of which spots are warm, sunny and sheltered and which are cold, shady or windy is essential to the permaculture designer.

Altitude

Altitude has a more dramatic effect on microclimate in our moist, cloudy climate than it does in other parts of the world. Imagine you're in a sheltered valley, looking up at a high, treeless hill. It's a sunny day with a light breeze, and you're comfortable in a t-shirt. But you just know that if you climb to the top of that hill you'll need to take some warm clothes with you. It's not just that the breeze will be stronger up there but also because the temperature is actually lower at higher altitudes. For every hundred metres you go up the temperature falls by one degree Celsius. This doesn't sound like much, but multiplied by the wind chill factor it makes a very noticeable difference.

I'm talking here of a day when it's as sunny at the top of the hill as in the valley. But so often it isn't. As I saw clearly from the Isle of Erraid, it's usually cloudier on the hills and it rains more. On days when all four factors are combined it can be totally miserable on the hill while it's still quite pleasant in the valley. These differences accumulate over time and can have a marked effect on the vegetation, especially in mountainous areas, where the common pattern is moorland at high altitude and grassland lower down.

This hillside in mid Wales shows how land use changes with altitude. The intensive farming of the valley bottom gives way to open sheepwalk on the hilltop in the middle ground, while the distant mountains are a mix of moorland and conifer plantation. Near Ffarmers, Carmarthenshire.

In merely hilly areas the difference may be less obvious, but if you look carefully you can see it. For example, orchards are notable by their absence from the hills. The damsons of the southern Lake District are an exception, but then damsons are exceptionally tough fruit trees. The effect of altitude on grassland is more subtle. In most western parts of Britain there's likely to be grassland on both hills and vales but the grasses grow for fewer days in the year on the hills. This makes a big difference to the farming economy.

You can 'see' the length of the growing season by comparing the annual cycle of a single plant growing at different altitudes. Hawthorn is often the best choice. It grows almost everywhere and it's very conspicuous when it comes into bloom. Hawthorns which blossom earlier will have started growth earlier in the spring and will stop growing later in the autumn. In fact a difference of a couple of weeks in flowering time may represent several weeks' difference in total growing season.

Very often you can see a strong contrast between the hawthorns separated by a couple of hundred metres vertically, then travel a couple of hundred miles north or south and see very little difference between trees at the same altitude. But you must be sure to compare like with like. Firstly, a hawthorn in an exposed position will flower later than one in a sheltered sun-trap at the same altitude. Secondly, be sure that the hawthorns you're comparing are native ones. Most new planting is done with exotic plants. The seed, or even the plants themselves, may well be imported from Eastern Europe, where labour costs are lower, and these exotic strains are usually earlier flowering. Thirdly, don't look at clipped hedges. Hawthorn flowers on twigs in their second year of growth, so a hedge that is clipped every year never flowers.

Aspect

Aspect means the direction in which a slope faces. North-facing slopes are on the whole cooler and moister than south-facing ones. This makes them slightly less suitable for farming and more suitable for trees, which need moisture more than warmth. There's a slight tendency for the northerly sides of hills to be wooded more often than the south-facing slopes.

The degree of slope also has an effect. At the end of a hot dry summer you can sometimes see how steeper south-facing slopes have dried out more than gentler ones and flat ground least of all. The clue is in the colour of the grass; the moister the soil the greener the grass. This difference isn't entirely due to aspect, as the steeper slopes will drain more freely while the flat ground keeps more moist. (See page 155.) You also have to be sure that any difference in the colour of the sward really is due to drying out. It may be that the grass on the flat has been grazed more intensively than that on the slope. This alone will make it greener, as grazing or cutting keeps grass in its green vegetative stage, while gone-to-seed grass has a dry buff colour, regardless of the moisture content of the soil. (See page 146.)

Frost

In general there are more frosts in the colder climate of higher country but at the microclimate scale this gets turned upside down: there are more frosts in the valleys than on the hills. This is because cold air is heavier than warm air and it sinks. On a morning after a light frost you can often see frost in the lower-lying parts of the landscape while the higher parts are frost free. You may also see a contrast between flat land and sloping, where the cold air has rolled away down the slopes but hardly moved from flatter areas. Frost pockets are those places that always catch the frost on such a night of partial frost. They are low-lying places, valley bottoms and hollows where there's nowhere for the cold air to drain away to. They can be big or small. They can occupy valleys several miles across or measure just a few square metres.

They are places to avoid when planting fruit trees, as a late spring frost can kill the blossom and thus wipe out a whole year's crop. But in summer these very same places can often be warm sun-traps and being low lying they often have the best soil, so they can make good places for vegetable growing, despite the late spring.

To see frost pockets you need to get up early in the morning after a night when there's been a light frost. If there's been a hard frost that has frozen everywhere you won't see any frost pockets. If you go out after an hour or two of sunshine you'll see some places that are frosty while nearby places are frost free, but these are not frost pockets. They are just in the shade and take longer to thaw out. But early in the morning after a light frost you'll see the frost pockets picked out clearly in white rime.

Snow

When snow falls on a windy day it can tell you much about the patterns of wind in the landscape. Areas of thin snow or bare ground indicate the windiest places while drifts form in the sheltered places, where the wind slows down and drops its load of snow. The pattern you see on any one day will only tell you about the microclimates produced by a wind from one particular direction. The south-west is the prevailing wind in Britain, so drifts formed by a wind from that direction are especially useful in predicting microclimates at other times of the year. But snow blown by a north-easterly wind can be even more valuable. The wind doesn't blow from that direction so often but when it does it's colder and can do more harm to vulnerable plants. Both will show you where to place plants which need the most protection and where extra shelter is needed.

When snow falls on a still day it covers the ground to an even depth and while it lies it tells you nothing. But as it starts to thaw a kaleidoscope of microclimate effects is revealed in the pattern of thawed and unthawed patches. The places where it thaws first are the warmer spots and as with drifting you see the whole picture simultaneously. It's like having a map of microclimates drawn for you by nature.

You can see the effect of aspect, with more southerly slopes thawing faster than more northerly ones. The effect of hedges and woodland edges is more localised but often more intense. To the north they cast shade and to the south the rate of thawing is speeded up by sunlight reflected off the vertical surface of the trees and shrubs.

The effects of aspect and edge can reinforce each other. A north-facing slope with a wood at the top, which is the south side, where the sun shines from, will be the last place of all to thaw out. During the rest of the year a slope like this will be one of the coolest and dampest places in the landscape.

A day of thawing snow is like gold dust to a landscape reader. Frost, when it covers the whole landscape rather than just the frost pockets, can tell much the same tale as it thaws. But snow has depth, so it can distinguish grades of warmth by the time it takes to disappear, whereas frost thaws pretty well immediately once the sun strikes it. The only drawback to snowmelt as a guide to microclimates is that the thawing pattern may not be quite the same as the pattern of warm and cool places in summer. The sun is at a higher angle in summer, so shadows will be shorter and there will be less difference between north and south aspects, especially where the slopes are slight. But the general picture will be the same and you can make allowances for these differences.

Flowering Times

A good way to compare microclimates is to go and stand for a while in places of contrasting microclimate, sunny and shady, windy and sheltered and so on. Your body is a sensitive instrument to the combined effect of all the climatic factors that go to make up an individual microclimate.

The limitation of your body is that it only tells you what's happening at one particular time, yet the wind varies in speed and direction and the position of the sun changes from hour to hour and from day to day through the growing season. But you can often get an idea of the accumulated heat and light that each spot receives by looking at the flowering time of plants. If they are blooming in one place but not yet in another then you know that one place receives more sunshine than the other. Often the shadier place is quite obvious. It may be on the north side of a hedge, for example. What's not so obvious is how far from the hedge the significantly shady area reaches. If there's a clear boundary between an area where the plants aren't yet flowering and one where they are, it gives you that information.

Three pictures of nasturtiums taken in my garden on the same day:

Of course the same plant must be growing over a fairly wide area in order to make a comparison. Common wildflowers such as dandelions and buttercups often oblige. When they are in full flower over a grass field the areas where they are not flowering stand out clearly. It is possible that there are no blooms

in full sun, *in half sun,* *in deep shade.*

in one area because the plant itself doesn't grow there, and you have to check this. Dandelions are not just conspicuous when they flower but also when they go to seed. What a contrast there is between the glowing gold of the bloom and the ghostly grey of the dandelion clocks! Gone-to-seed ones have clearly received more sunlight than ones that are still flowering. In late summer you can sometimes see the effect of shade on a field of corn as it ripens. There may be a green strip alongside a north-facing woodland edge when the rest of the field has already turned yellow. The width of this strip is typically two-thirds the height of the trees.

Wind flagging is normally more severe near the coast as salty winds inhibit growth more severely than non-salty ones.

If you're observing the microclimates in a garden you can deliberately plant the same flower in different parts of the garden and compare its development during the growing season. Nasturtiums respond to shade not so much by delaying flowering but by flowering less, as the pictures show. They also reveal the frostiest parts of the garden in a similar way since they die off at the first hint of autumn frost.

Trees

Another way in which plants can show the accumulated climatic effects is the wind flagging of trees and shrubs. It can indicate both the direction and the severity of the prevailing wind.

In extreme cases a wind-flagged tree looks as though it's a once-straight tree that has been blown into its asymmetric shape by the wind. In fact it hasn't. It's rather that the wind is so severe that the tree can only put on new growth on the lee side of its crown, so it grows away from the wind. Less severe wind flagging is less obvious but most trees are somewhat affected by the wind. Where the flagging is slight you have to walk right round the tree to see it, because it's only apparent from a position at right angles to the direction of the wind.

You also need to observe it on a still day because even a light breeze will obscure mild wind flagging.

Over Britain as a whole the prevailing wind is the south-west. But in a steep narrow valley the wind will always blow either up the valley or down it, never across, even if that's south-west. Wind flagging can indicate whether this happens or not in a particular valley. It's also possible for a tree or shrub to be flagged in a direction that isn't the prevailing wind but the strongest. This can happen in a place that is sheltered from the south-west by a hill but exposed to the north-west.

On open hilltops and plateaus the direction of flagging is true to the south-west and its main value here is to indicate just how windy the local climate is. You can also use the direction of wind flagging as a compass to guide you on a cloudy day. On Dartmoor, which is exposed to strong winds and also prone to prolonged mist and fog, I'm told the locals find their way in a fog by the lean of the rushes and taller grasses.

It's not just individual trees that get wind flagged. The canopy of a whole clump can be moulded into a single shape by a strong prevailing wind. These three trees I sketched on the Mendip Hills are a sign of what the climate's like up there. You'd never see anything like it down here in the vale. Note how the most windward tree, which takes the full brunt of the wind, has been stunted by it.

Evergreens such as holly and box can indicate the direction of the prevailing wind by dieback of the leaves or even whole dead branches. This is especially true within a few miles of the sea, where salty air can be blown inland by the strong winds of autumn and winter.

All these clues from plants are great aids to reading the microclimate. In fact you can often make very accurate guesses about where the different microclimates will be just by looking at the landform: here a windy spot, there a sun-trap, down there a frost pocket. But to be really sure there's no substitute for being on the spot when the wind blows, the sun shines or the frost is revealed in the cold light of dawn. Your mind can predict a microclimate but only your body can really know it.

5

Wild Animals and
How to Recognise their Signs

IN THE drama of the landscape there's no distinction between actors and scenery. Wild animals both inhabit the landscape and help to form it. Herbivores, by their grazing and browsing, help to form the vegetation that is their home. Predators in their turn affect the populations of herbivores and thus also the vegetation.

All wild animals run away from us but the meetings we do have with them can be moments of delight. An unhurried fox glides over the ground, its feet hardly seeming to touch the earth, its fiery coat brilliant in the sunshine. Then at a certain distance it stops and looks back at you before going on its way. A roe deer in dense cover will sometimes have the same confidence, and a heart-shaped face will pop up among the leafy branches and peer at you curiously for a few moments before she bounds off with the rest of her family. To sit quietly with a wild mammal that's not running away is a rare experience. I've had it just once.

I was walking through a wood near my home when it started to rain. There are two huge old yew trees in the wood whose dome-shaped crowns keep out the rain like thatched roofs. I headed for the nearest one and sat in the dry, looking out through the trees to the fields beyond. A few moments later a hare came along with the same idea and sat in the dry just in front of me, unaware that I was there. For a while we sat there together, looking out at the fields. It was a rare moment of peace and intimacy. But being the fidgety, impatient person I am I couldn't sit still for long, and as soon as I moved the hare noticed me and lolloped off.

Such meetings can be peak experiences in our relationship with the land. But our indirect experience of wild animals, through their effect on the formation and functioning of the landscape, is stronger than we often think. Almost all of them are small invertebrates such as worms and insects. They work away largely unseen by us, removing debris, renewing the soil and pollinating plants. As a general rule the smaller and less conspicuous a creature the more important it is to the functioning of the ecosystem. They can manage quite well without us but we couldn't survive without them. To give even the briefest account of this diverse myriad of creatures would be beyond the scope of this book. Instead I'll concentrate on those wild animals that have the most direct and obvious impact on us, mainly by eating cultivated plants or killing domestic animals. Most of them are also key species that have a significant effect on the landscape as a whole. All of them are mammals. They are: deer, rabbits, voles, grey squirrels, foxes, badgers and wild pigs.

Deer

There have never been as many deer in Britain as there are today, either in the Scottish Highlands or in lowland Britain as a whole. The lowland landscape is ideal for them: wide fields of grass and cereals on which to feed and the occasional wood to lie up in. This is a much more productive landscape for deer than the all-pervading wildwood of prehistoric times. Most of the edible biomass in woods is in the tree leaves, which are mostly out of reach, and the ground vegetation produces little compared to grassland. In historical times the countryside was full of people, and deer are shy animals that shun human company. With the mechanisation of farming and the neglect of woodland the countryside is emptier of humans now than it's been for some four thousand years. These changes may not fully explain the deer explosion but they have certainly played a part.

The main deer species in lowland areas are roe, fallow and the tiny muntjac. One or more of them is found almost throughout the country, though there are some places that they haven't yet reached. These include parts of Wales and the English Midlands, the east of Kent and the west of Cornwall. They are lovely animals when you spot them on a summer walk. The misty white spots of the fallow and the stately antlers of their bucks suggest some medieval idyll, while the leaps and bounds of the chestnut-backed roe have the grace of an African gazelle.

They find most of their food in the fields but they do little damage there. They graze over a wide area, taking a bite here and a bite there. When they graze young cereal crops they may have no effect on the yield of grain because neighbouring plants compensate for the ones they eat by putting on extra growth. On grassland they do lower the yield because everything they eat could otherwise be eaten by farm animals but as the effect is spread over a wide area it's not very noticeable. It usually causes less concern than rabbit damage, which is more obvious because it's concentrated in small areas.

Although the food that deer find in the woods is a small part of their overall diet it can have a major impact on the woodland itself. The kind of impact depends on the density of deer. Where the population is moderate they gradually change the species composition by selectively grazing the most palatable plants, both woody and herbaceous. In general the most palatable trees are ash, elm, hazel, pussy willow and birch. The least palatable ones include oak, chestnut and aspen. These preferences are shared by most browsers, including farm animals, though sheep will eat aspen. At ground level, selective grazing can turn a diverse cover of woodland wildflowers into a sward of tough, unpalatable plants such as pendulous sedge. But where the deer population is heavy they will eat everything in the wood, less favoured species along with favourites. They can reduce the herb layer to bare earth and prevent the natural regeneration of trees altogether.

They also make coppicing extremely difficult. When trees are planted they can be protected from deer with individual plastic guards. Once they outgrow

This valuable hazel coppice has been fenced against deer. Cranborne Chase, Dorset.

the guards they are safe from deer and can grow on to become mature trees for timber production. Self-sown seedlings can be protected this way too. Coppicing, on the other hand, involves cutting the trees down every few years and allowing them to regrow. They don't regrow as a neat single stem that can easily have a guard slipped over it but as a multi-stemmed spray of tasty young shoots. These coppice stools are hard to protect individually and the most effective remedy is to put a deer fence right round the newly coppiced area. It needs to be two metres tall, so it's expensive and is only used when the coppice is highly valued.

Red deer are found in various parts of Britain but in the Scottish Highlands there are hordes of them. In fact they are encouraged, because deer stalking is a profitable business in an area where it's hard to make a living from the land by other means. In some places they're even fed silage in winter in order to boost their numbers. Death by starvation over winter is the main control on the population of most wild animals, including deer, so a little feeding at the coldest time can make a big difference. Warmer winters due to climate change must also be having an effect on the survival rate, as it is for all wild herbivores. The extermination of the wolf, their only natural predator, is probably also a factor, though this happened long before the present population explosion.

It's the high numbers of deer, along with sheep, which keep the Highlands in their moorland state. Newly planted trees are particularly vulnerable. New plantations and natural regeneration alike must be deer-fenced if the trees are to survive and grow. Sometimes the effect can be spectacular. One of the most visible examples of this lies beside the road and railway that lead up from the head of Loch Lomond into the western Highlands. Towards the end of the 1980s someone put a fence up around a small group of lonely old Scots pines that stood to the east of the railway, enclosing a hectare or so. Within a year or two you could see the dark triangles of young pines poking up through the heather and moorgrass. Among the little pines grew slender birch seedlings, their light seed blown in on the wind from further away. In a few years the land inside the fence began to look more like a young wood than a patch of moorland and another fence was put up enclosing a much larger area. I haven't been up that way for years now but no doubt there's now a flourishing pinewood where once there were a few forlorn old trees.

Rabbits and Voles

Rabbits are not native to Britain. The Normans brought them here from their home in the Mediterranean lands and farmed them for meat and fur. At first the rabbits had a hard time in their new northern home and had to be mollycoddled. They couldn't dig and had to have burrows constructed for them. Slowly, slowly they adapted to the climate, till some time around the beginning of the nineteenth century they were able to survive independently and they began to escape from their artificial warrens. As time went by they adapted more and more and bred 'like rabbits' till by the 1930s they dominated great tracts of countryside. They destroyed cereal crops and ate the grass so avidly that there was little left for farm animals in some places. Large areas around their burrows were reduced to bare earth.

Then in the 1950s the disease myxomatosis was introduced and in a few short months rabbits almost became extinct in Britain. Much land that had been kept as grassland or heath by rabbit grazing succeeded to woodland. But a few individuals had enough immunity to survive and gradually numbers built up again. Now they are an almost universal pest but very rarely a plague of pre-myxomatosis proportions. As readers of Beatrix Potter will know, they are partial to vegetables, and they harm young trees and shrubs by eating the bark, mainly in winter when herbaceous food is short. Vegetable gardens need to be rabbit-fenced if there's a warren nearby. Newly planted trees always need to be protected, either by a fence or with individual guards, except in those mountainous areas where there aren't any rabbits at all.

Unlike deer, rabbits don't graze evenly over the landscape. Instead they 'farm' the grass: they graze it down tight over a limited area near their burrows and leave it more or less untouched elsewhere. They do this for two reasons. Firstly, they like eating short grass. Keeping it short keeps it in the young, vegetative phase of growth in which it's much more digestible and nutritious than it is in the tall, yellowing gone-to-seed stage. The second reason is defence. Every predator in the countryside is partial to a bit of rabbit and rabbits have developed a whole lifestyle around running away. Short grass gives them good visibility and hopefully a head start when one of them sounds the alarm.

Like rabbits, voles mainly eat grass. They live in a network of above-ground tunnels that they make in tall, dense herbaceous vegetation. Wherever grass is left uncut for a year or more there will be a thriving population of voles, which in turn supports owls, kestrels and foxes. Their main food is the grass that they can access from inside their tunnels, but they are partial to the bark of young trees and shrubs too. They can kill newly planted trees and may play a part in preventing natural regeneration. Where voles are likely to be a problem special little plastic tree guards need to be used. Occasionally they have a population explosion and then they can wreak havoc in any garden that lies next to their grassy habitat.

Grey Squirrels

While deer are the biggest problem for coppice production, grey squirrels can wreck a timber crop. Timber trees are tall, single-stemmed ones grown for planking, in contrast to the multi-stemmed coppice, which yields a crop of small poles. Squirrels do their damage by stripping patches of bark. Being mainly nut eaters, their hungry time of year is not the winter but the summer. In autumn they eat their fill of nuts and bury some to tide them over the rest of the year. But their buried stores can get a bit thin by summertime and one alternative food supply is tree cambium, a thin layer of tissue which lies just underneath the bark. To get at it they strip off the bark and this kills the wood underneath. They go for youngish trees and most often strip bark off the trunk about two-thirds of the way up the tree. If most of the circumference of the trunk is stripped it dies at this point. The tree goes on growing from side branches, and one of these may take over and become the new leader. But that gives a crooked tree that is useless for sawing up into long, straight planks. Even if the trunk doesn't die, bark stripping leaves a patch of dead wood in the trunk that will spoil its value as timber.

Typical squirrel damage. They usually perch on a branch and strip the bark immediately above it.

Grey squirrels are probably the biggest limitation on growing broadleaved trees for timber in Britain. They are an introduced species, originally from North America. They have steadily spread from their points of introduction and are now found virtually all over England and Wales south of Cumbria and in a few places in Scotland. The trees they damage most are beech, sycamore, oak and sweet chestnut, though they will go for others if their favourites aren't there. Wild cherry and ash are hardly troubled.

Though bark stripping has economic importance, the biggest effect squirrels have on the landscape is on the reproduction of hazel trees. In some areas they have virtually made it into a relict species, one that can no longer reproduce and will die out when the present generation of hazels comes to the end of its life. They completely strip the trees of nuts and they often do it when the nuts are unripe, so any that they bury and then forget are too immature to germinate and grow. Where nuts are unusually plentiful some will escape the squirrels and have a chance of becoming new trees. This can happen in a big wood with a high proportion of hazel in it. The squirrel population doesn't go up directly in proportion to the number of hazel trees in the locality because nuts aren't the only thing squirrels need in their habitat. Where hazels are superabundant some other factor will limit their population. A big hazel wood can have enough nuts left over by the squirrels to support a population of dormice. In the same way, a good-sized hazel orchard, or platt as they are known, will only lose a proportion of the crop to squirrels. But if you have two or three hazel trees in your back garden you'll be lucky to harvest a single nut in most years. However, in years when there's an unusually heavy nut crop the squirrels can't keep up with it. Then there can be nuts left over both on garden trees and in woods and hedgerows. But whether these are enough to keep hazel going as a wild tree is not clear. There are many more pitfalls between nut and mature tree, from rodents to browsing deer.

Foxes

Foxes can make a living in any terrain, rural or urban, including the most inhospitable. No wonder they have such a special place in our folklore. Reynard is admired for his cunning but also condemned for his cruelty. When a fox gets into a hen coop he usually kills every one of the hens, not just the one or two he can carry home with him. This, some people say, proves that he takes delight in killing. But this is to judge foxes as though they were human beings. A fox is not a sadistic human but a wild animal. Hunting is a difficult way to win your food and by no means every attempt ends with success. Foxes that lack the instinct to make every kill they can don't survive. In the chicken coop the fox meets a totally unnatural situation: a bunch of birds bred for production rather than survival, trapped in an artificial box with no way out. The fox can hardly be expected to suddenly turn off its instincts.

Their main food is mice and voles. They do take lambs, though probably most of these are the weak or sickly ones that wouldn't survive anyway, and of course chickens. Some people reckon that they only take these larger prey items when one of a pair has been killed. When they are raising a litter both the vixen and the dog fox hunt to feed the cubs. The two don't meet. The dog fox leaves food at a hand-over point and the vixen comes and retrieves it later. If the vixen is killed the dog fox finds his gifts rejected. He reacts to this by bringing larger and larger prey items in the hope that they'll be accepted. Conversely, a vixen deprived of the help of her mate may be forced to take larger prey in order to get enough food for her cubs in the time available to her. If this is true, killing foxes is counter-productive. In fact foxes may on balance be the farmer's friend, as every vole they kill means more grass left to be eaten by the cattle and sheep. It takes a lot of voles to feed a fox and the constant toll they take must have a significant effect on the vole population.

Badgers

Badgers seem big and formidable compared to foxes, but they get most of their food from an even smaller prey, the humble earthworm. At night, when the badgers are out and about, the worms are above ground too. In the humid night-time air the worms can pop the top half of their body out of their burrows to find grass and other leaves to drag below for their food. The badgers snuffle the worms up wholesale. If the soil is dry and firm the worms can put up quite a resistance, and then the badgers have to dig a little hole to get them out of the earth. Badgers also dig for other soil-living creatures and plant foods. Pignut, a small plant of the cow parsley family with carrot-like leaves, has tasty tubers and where it's abundant badger feeding holes can pock-mark the ground in spring. But earthworms are their staple.

A badger feeding hole.

If the soil is so dry that the badgers can't dig the worms out they may have to go in search of other foods. One of their favourites is maize and this is often just at the tasty sweet-corn stage when a summer drought makes worm hunting difficult. In some places they raid people's gardens for the super-sweet varieties, which they can reach from the ground. The kind of maize grown for silage is much taller and they have to knock the plants over to get at the cobs. The present fashion for maize silage is at least partly responsible for a rise in the badger population. They can take it right up till it's harvested in October and it can give a boost to their diet just before winter when they need supplies of fat to see them through.

Occasionally badgers take poultry. This seems to be a very local habit. Badgers live in families and it may be that once they acquire a taste for poultry they teach it to their offspring and it becomes a family tradition. Where they do get the habit it can be a strong one. I know a farmer in Devon who is simply unable to keep free-range chickens because of badger predation. Shutting them up at night is no help as the badgers will come out during the day if needs be. The farmer solved the problem by keeping the birds out on the pasture in a series of movable arks – an ark being a combined chicken house and enclosed run. This way he can give them fresh ground each day though their freedom of movement is restricted.

Wild Pigs

Wild pigs were exterminated in Britain in late medieval times but in recent years people have begun to keep them as a speciality meat animal. Inevitably some of them have escaped and established themselves in the wild. There are now populations on the Kent-Sussex border, in west Dorset and the Forest of Dean. Like badgers they have a great love for maize. I've heard that in France, where they have never been eradicated, they can be a problem for farmers who grow it. One farmer in central France whose land is surrounded by extensive woodland reported losing a third of his maize crop to them. Whether they could be such a problem here in Britain, with our much less wooded landscape, is hard to tell. They also root up the ground for food, especially for pignut where they can get it. In a well-wooded part of west Dorset I was told that they'd rooted up about an acre of pasture one springtime. It had greened up again by June, from regrowth of the existing plants, but a lot of grass production was lost. Where wild pigs have established themselves farmers have made strenuous efforts to exterminate them, but they are shy and secretive animals and some always survive.

ANIMAL SIGNS

Since wild animals go out of their way to avoid us you can't rely on actually seeing them to find out about the local populations. You have to look for their signs. Footprints, droppings and the homes they make can all be distinctive, but the most common and most visible signs are usually those of feeding.

Browsing

Deer leave little sign of grazing in the fields but their impact on woodland is easily recognised, though the first sign of deer in woodland may not be browsing but rubbing. Stags and bucks rub their antlers against trees and bushes for two reasons. Firstly, they need to rub the velvet off the new set of antlers which they grow each year. Velvet is a thin layer of skin and fur and any small tree or shrub makes a good rubbing post. Red stags often use a small shrub, which they can more or less demolish in the process. Secondly, roe bucks mark their territory by rubbing a scent gland at the base of their antlers against young trees or coppice shoots. This can wear away the bark in a vertical slash with shaggy edges. You may see these rubbing posts in a wood where deer have recently arrived before any browsing becomes noticeable. In fact it's not inevitable that they will take up residence. It may just be the sign of a tentative exploration.

Light browsing by deer shows up in damage to young trees and coppice shoots. Browsing the same shoot again and again can give the characteristic shape shown in the drawing. Whenever the terminal bud is bitten off regrowth comes from a side bud, giving the repeated curves. The shoot has every chance of eventually growing out of reach of the deer but it will make a crooked stick. If it's a coppice pole it will be useless for craft purposes. If it's being grown for timber the crookedness can be lost in the centre of a much larger trunk but such a setback to its early growth will probably mean the tree never makes it to timber size.

rabbit or hare

sheep or deer

Tree shoots can also be nibbled by rabbits and hares, and if there have been winter snow drifts they can reach the same height as deer. But rabbits and hares have two rows of teeth and make a clean bite, whereas deer only have a bottom row and make a ragged bite. Sheep also have one row of teeth so it can be hard to tell the difference between sheep and deer browsing.

In general the presence of farm animals in a wood masks the signs of wild animals. Farm animals may be deliberately let into a wood for shelter or they may get in because of bad fencing. You can tell if cattle or horses have been there because their droppings are much bigger than those of deer and quite different in shape. You may also be able to see their tracks. (See page 66.) Sheep tracks and

The browse line on the ivy shows that deer are present in this wood but the absence of a browse line on the shrubs shows there's not very many of them: they go for their favourite food first.

droppings are very similar to those of deer. But when sheep are in a wood they always leave their calling card: little wisps of wool stuck on thorns or on the wire of the boundary fence. If farm animals have been in the wood it doesn't mean that deer haven't, just that it's hard to tell.

The most characteristic sign of a resident deer population is a browse line, which they make by eating all the leaves and small twigs they can reach. Above the line there may be dense foliage, below it nothing but bare poles and trunks. The more deer there are in the wood the clearer the browse line is. Roe and fallow deer make a line about one and a quarter metres above ground. This is below the line of sight of an adult person and you may not see it as you walk through the wood. But go down on your haunches and it comes sharply into focus. It's quite unmistakable. Deer particularly like ivy and there will often be a browse line on ivy where there's no general browse line. It usually makes a crisp line on the trunk of a tree at the height where their necks are fully extended. If you can see a browse line on ivy but not on the surrounding shrubs that indicates just a moderate population of deer.

Other animals can make browse lines too, but the height will vary. Rabbits and hares can make one at just over half a metre high, the little muntjac deer at one metre, cattle at almost two metres, and ponies, with their long necks and agile heads, even higher. Sometimes you can see two distinct browse lines in the same piece of woodland.

You can tell which animals are responsible for bark stripping by the height at which it's done. Squirrels climb and they typically strip bark three to four metres above ground level, usually just above a branch which they perch on while

The way this cone has been taken apart is a sign that squirrels are around.

they are doing it. Some ponies strip bark but it's lower down and the area stripped is bigger. Also ponies usually leave the marks of their large incisor teeth while squirrels leave a smoother surface. Both squirrels and rabbits strip bark at ground level, so here the picture is less clear.

If you don't see any signs of bark stripping it doesn't mean there are no squirrels around, but they may leave clues in the remains of nuts and cones that they have eaten. Various species of mammals and birds eat hazelnuts and they all have their own way of opening the shell. Some rodents make a neat little hole, others gnaw the shell half away. Birds wedge them into crevices in tree bark and punch holes in them with their bills. Only squirrels split them roughly from end to end. Their treatment of conifer cones is also distinctive. Birds get at the seeds inside by prising open the scales of the cone but not removing them. Mice gnaw the scales off neatly. But squirrels rip them off, leaving a rough and ragged central core, quite unlike the more methodical work of the mice.

Grazing

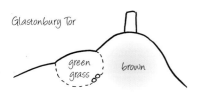

Glastonbury Tor

green grass

brown

Deer leave no distinctive signs on fields of grass or cereals. But rabbit grazing, being intensive and limited to a small area, shows up clearly. Sometimes it can be seen at quite a distance, as this sketch from my notebook shows. The hill is a famous local landmark. It's usually grazed by sheep but for some reason it wasn't that year and by the end of the summer the effect of the rabbits was revealed in the unaccustomed contrast between a small green grazed area surrounded by the brown of ungrazed grass.

Rabbit lawns have a distinctive kind of turf, usually very short and springy. Where there's high grazing pressure from the rabbits there's often a lot of moss in it because moss is more resistant to close grazing than grasses and herbs. In places moss can get close to a hundred percent. But where the population of rabbits is more moderate a rich sward of grass and sun-loving wildflowers can develop. Where the rabbit-grazed area extends under trees or a hedge there's usually bare soil. The combined effects of rabbit grazing and shade have more impact on plant growth than either one on its own.

In a field of cereals the grazed area is usually a narrow strip along the boundary, often crescent-shaped. This shape is all about insecurity. Safety lies in the hedge, so they don't venture far into the corn field. Ultimate safety lies in the burrow, which is usually in the middle of the grazed strip, and here they venture a little further out into the field, giving the strip its crescent shape. They eat the corn plants when they are young and green but the effects can still be seen in the mature crop as a strip of sparse, stunted plants.

Knocked-down maize plants are a sure sign of badgers, except in those limited areas where there are wild pigs. The number of plants knocked down is not just a measure of the number of badgers living in the area but also the dryness of the summer. The harder it is for them to take earthworms the more they go for maize. But the little holes they make to take earthworms and other ground-living prey are far and away the most common sign of badger feeding. The holes are usually narrow, eight to ten centimetres deep. Rabbit scrapes, which are a territorial mark made by the males, can be similar but they are wider and shallower. Wherever there are rabbits you'll see their droppings but finding their droppings beside a little hole doesn't necessarily mean it was made by a rabbit. If both animals are living in the same area there's no reason why rabbits shouldn't leave their droppings where badgers have been feeding.

Wild pigs also dig the ground to find their food but rather than making individual holes they root it up over wider areas. In recent years the roadside verges of the Forest of Dean have been rooted up almost everywhere. Within the woods the signs of rooting may be less obvious as it's often more a matter of moving dead leaves to find the acorns beneath than breaking the turf to dig up roots. Rooted ground in grassland soon grows back again and in spring it may stand out as a splash of bright green against the duller hues of the old pasture.

Droppings

While rabbits scatter their droppings indiscriminately, badgers have special latrine areas. They deposit each turd in a little hole not unlike their feeding holes and the latrine area becomes honeycombed with them. A badger latrine can't be mistaken for the work of any other animal. Foxes have quite the opposite habits. They leave their droppings singly, usually on prominent high spots such as an anthill or a tussock of grass. Both are territorial signals and perhaps the different dunging pattern of each species reflects the different lifestyles of the family-oriented badger and the solitary fox.

Burrows

Equally unmistakable are badger setts. Usually dug into sloping ground in woods or wide hedges, they are major earthworks. The holes are wider than they are high and piles of fresh spoil jut out from the entrance if they are in active use. Elder trees and nettles often grow near the entrance to a sett. These two plants are usually the sign of a high level of plant nutrients in the soil. Maybe badgers are in the habit of urinating near the sett.

Rabbit holes are much smaller and often taller than they are wide. In sandy soils they can be found anywhere but in clay soils they are usually in a hedgerow that runs across the slope. Here there's usually an accumulation of friable topsoil, washed down from the uphill slope, often making a distinct terrace. (See page 198.)

This is much easier to dig than solid clay subsoil, and the drainage is good. Foxes are not enthusiastic diggers and prefer to take over an unused rabbit burrow or badger sett, so there's never much sign of earthworking at the mouth.

Tracks and Paths

You rarely get to see a complete, clear print like those in the drawings and it can be hard to distinguish between, say, sheep and the medium-sized deer species. But the number of prints you see is an extra clue: sheep go around in flocks, while deer go in small family groups or alone.

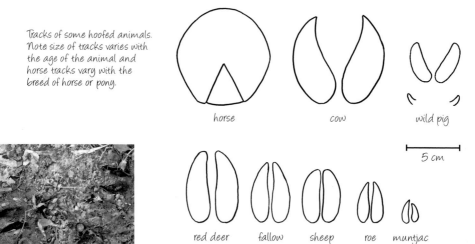

Tracks of some hoofed animals. Note size of tracks varies with the age of the animal and horse tracks vary with the breed of horse or pony.

horse   cow   wild pig

5 cm

red deer   fallow   sheep   roe   muntjac
            deer   deer   deer

Roe deer tracks.

Paths are a clear sign that some animal is about but it's not always easy to tell which. Badger paths tend to be direct and very well used. Badgers are creatures of habit and will go on using the same path determinedly, year after year. If you're lucky enough to see a footprint it's easy to tell a badger's from that of a fox or a dog. A badger has five toes in a row along the front of the foot while the fox and dog have four. The badger also has long claw marks. Unless there's snow, or you find a print in the clear smooth mud where a puddle has recently dried, you'll be lucky to see a whole footprint. But you can often recognise a badger print just by the claw marks left where it's scrambled over the bare soil under a hedgerow.

Follow the path and you may come upon another clue. I know a place on the Mendips where a badger path crosses a drystone wall. The broad brown stripe made by their muddy tummies where they climb over the wall could not have been made by any other animal. It may be that the badgers established a path here when the wall had tumbled down and refused to give it up when it was repaired. But it is just possible that this is an ancestral path that dates back to before the 1790s when the Mendips were enclosed from open common. They are very persistent animals.

Where a path goes under a wire fence there may be a few hairs caught in the barbs of the wire. Coarse grey hairs caught on the underside of the fence indicate a badger and soft red ones a fox. Red or brown hairs caught on the top strand may indicate a young deer that couldn't clear it easily. Once, walking through some woods on the edge of Dartmoor, I saw a little tuft of red hairs caught on the upper side of a top wire that only came up to my knee. It was the remains of a fence that divided the old woodland from the recently sprung up woods around it. I followed the path on quietly till I came upon a doe and fawn, grazing peacefully in a small patch of grass, surrounded by the green willows of the new wood.

badger   fox   dog

Tracks of some claw-footed animals. Note dog tracks vary greatly in size according to breed.

A badger print.

6

Niches: How Plants and Animals Make their Living

Tall, medium short, early, mid-season, late, climber, nitrogen-fixer and semi-parasite are just some of the roles that plants can take in the grassland sward.

EVERY PLANT and animal in the landscape is the centre of a web of relationships with other plants and animals. Take a grass plant in a field. The most obvious relationships it has with other plants are competitive. It competes with every neighbouring plant, whether of the same species or another, for space, water, light and mineral nutrients. But some of its relationships may be more co-operative than competitive. Clovers, for example, fix atmospheric nitrogen, that is they take nitrogen gas from the atmosphere and change it into a mineral form that can be used by plants as a nutrient, and the grass plant may be able to share some of this nitrogen if its roots intermingle with those of a clover. Bracken, on the other hand, may actually harm a grass plant with the poisonous chemicals it uses to suppress the growth of competitors. A whole range of herbivores, from caterpillars to cattle, will eat it and it will play host to parasites and diseases.

The plant also has relationships with its non-living environment. As a grass, it will be pollinated by the wind rather than by insects. It will tend to grow in one kind of soil or another, according to its species. It will have a tolerance for a certain level of shade and a certain range of temperatures. Unless the field is a monoculture, sown with just one kind of grass, you'll see a different mix of grasses and herbs in each part of it, reflecting the changes in physical conditions. Some plants will be found all over the field. Others will be concentrated in specific parts of it, perhaps under the shady branches of a hedgerow tree or in a wet patch of soil. Some will be more common at the top of a slope and others at the bottom. You can see this clearly at buttercup time in many sloping fields, where the green sward on the top of the slope gradually fades to bright yellow at the bottom, reflecting the increase in soil moisture as you go down.

If you get on your hands and knees and look at the sward in profile you'll see that there are differences in the vertical distribution of plants just as there are in the horizontal plane. Some are tall with upright stems while others are short and bushy. The tall kinds have to devote some of their energy to a strong internal structure which will hold them up, while the short ones have to suffer the lower light levels in the understorey. Tallness and shortness both have their advantages and disadvantages. There are differences in annual cycles too. Some plants do most of their growth early in the season, others later on. The early growers enjoy the moister soil of springtime while the later ones take advantage of the warmer days of summer. By specialising in these ways the different species of plants in the field avoid head-on competition and so are able to co-exist.

The web of relationships doesn't stop at ground level. Some plants have deep roots, others have shallow ones, some a single taproot, others a fibrous mass. This means they reduce competition below the ground as above. They also link up with other organisms in the mutually beneficial relationships we know as symbiosis. For instance, although we say that the clovers fix atmospheric nitrogen, that's not strictly true. What they do is trade some of their own organic food for nitrogen fixed by bacteria that live in nodules on their roots.

The relationship between clovers and these bacteria is fairly well known. What's less well known is that almost all plants have a similar beneficial relationship with fungi. The roots of the plant join up with the slender threads that make up the vegetative body of the fungus. These fungal threads are only one cell thick, thousands of times thinner than a root. So for the same expenditure of energy a fungus can produce a network that can penetrate a vastly greater volume of soil than a plant and thus garner more water and nutrients from it. The plant exchanges some of the organic food it produces by photosynthesis for some of the water and nutrients gathered by the fungus. One very visible example is the relationship between the fly agaric mushroom and birch and pine trees. The showy red mushroom with the white spots is just the fruiting organ of the fungus. By far the larger part of its body is below ground, a network of microscopic threads like cotton wool that can occupy great volumes of soil.

Fly agaric.

It's a good deal for both partners but the trading doesn't necessarily stop there. Different plants, indeed plants of different species, can be linked up with the same fungus and so foodstuffs can be passed from one plant to another. It's not impossible for nitrogen fixed by one plant to end up benefiting an unrelated plant living nearby. The fungal network is like a bustling market where mutually beneficial deals are being done every day. In the soil of a mature ecosystem there's a wide and intricate web of fungal connections that we're only just beginning to understand. It's hard to see what's going on under the ground but bit by bit a whole new picture of how ecosystems work is emerging from below.

Niche Defined

The sum total of the relationships that each species has with its neighbours and its non-living environment is known as its niche. The niche of a species is the way it fits into the ecosystem, the way it makes its living. To make an analogy with human beings: if the habitat of a plant or animal is its address, its niche is its occupation.

That analogy may at first seem to apply more to animals than to plants. An animal eats a certain range of foods and going out to find these foods each day looks very much like ourselves going off to work. Badgers and foxes, for example, although they both eat much the same range of foods overall, are specialists within that range: badgers mostly eat earthworms and foxes mostly rodents. Although there is some overlap, the difference in their occupations is clear. Plants, on the other hand, all make their food in the same way, through photosynthesis. But food is only one resource among the many that are needed for life. Just as animals specialise by eating different parts of the total food resource, so plants specialise in their use of other resources. As we've just seen in the case of the grassland, they share out the resources of space and time by their differences in shape and annual cycle.

Eating food is one side of the coin; being eaten is the other. The relationships a species has with predators, grazers, parasites and diseases are very much part of its niche. This isn't just a matter of which species are trying to eat it but also how it avoids being eaten. Plants may discourage grazers or browsers by: having thorns, stinging, being poisonous, tasting unpleasant or bearing their leaves up out of the reach of browsers, as trees do. Or they may be able to rebound from being eaten by growing especially fast or by bearing their buds safely below ground so their potential for regrowth is not diminished by the grazing, as grasses do.

Niche and Diversity

In all these ways and others, each species carves out a unique niche for itself. Having a unique niche isn't just an advantage. It's essential. Ecologists have observed that no two species can live together in the same ecosystem if they occupy the same niche. Sooner or later one or the other will lose the competition and die out.

This is just what's happening now with the two species of squirrel in Britain, the native red and the introduced grey. The grey is slowly spreading through the country and wherever it's taken up residence the red has died out. There's no direct confrontation between the two. It's just that the grey is better suited to the squirrel niche in Britain than the red is. Exactly why this is so isn't fully understood but two aspects of it are probably food and disease. The red squirrel is in fact a conifer specialist. This may seem strange for the native squirrel in a country with so few native conifers, but Britain is only part of its range and some other parts of Europe have more conifers than broadleaves. The branches of conifers are thin and flexible, so reds have evolved a light weight, adapted for moving around in a world of whippy twigs. Broadleaf branches are stiffer so the greys have been able to evolve a heavier weight. This extra weight probably gives them the edge when it comes to surviving the winter. The reds are also quite incapable of digesting acorns, one of the most abundant foods available to a squirrel in this country. But perhaps the decisive factor is a disease called parapox virus. It seems that the greys carry it without suffering from it but it's fatal to the reds.

In contrast to the squirrels, the three British woodpeckers live alongside each other quite happily. All three climb trees, picking insects out of the wood

Green woodpecker.   Greater spotted woodpecker.   Lesser spotted woodpecker.

as they go, and all three excavate holes in the trees for their nests. But there are significant differences in their niches. The green woodpecker, much the biggest of the three, also feeds on the ground, both in the woods and out in open country. It's the one you're most likely to hear and see, with its raucous laughing call and characteristic undulating flight. The other two woodpeckers only feed in trees, but the lesser spotted tends to forage higher up the trees and on smaller branches than the great spotted. There's also some difference in the choice of nesting sites, the green lower down, the great spotted at the middle level, and the lesser spotted towards the tree tops. Overall there are enough differences to reduce competition to the point where they can live side by side.

It's this differentiation of niches that makes possible the diversity of species we see around us. Without it there would be only one kind of tree in the woods with one kind of shrub, one herbaceous plant, one bird and so on. The difference between niches is the very key to the diversity of species.

It's interesting to compare a diverse ecosystem with a simple one. Take, for example, a semi-natural meadow and a bed of nettles. The semi-natural meadow may have a hundred species of plants living in it, all avoiding competition by occupying different niches. But nettles don't avoid competition. They meet it head on and carve their niche in life by being more competitive than other plants, given an abundant supply of nutrients. This is why there are so few of these competitive species, because they all occupy much the same niche, based on consuming a lot of resources and growing faster than their neighbours. It's a game of winner-takes-all that in extreme cases ends up with a pure stand of one species. That's why soils that are low in nutrients support much more biodiversity than fertilised ones.

Broad and Narrow

Niche is a theme that runs right through landscape reading. In fact much of this book is about niches. Right at the beginning of Chapter 1, I used the niche of bracken as an example of some of the fundamentals. The soil indicator plants described in Chapter 3 are useful to landscape readers because they have a 'narrow' niche, at least in respect of soil. That's to say they only grow in a narrow range of soil types. Most plants tell you much less about the soil because they grow in a broader range of soils. Hawthorn and ash trees are examples of plants with a broad soil niche.

In Chapter 5 I described the niches of several mammals, concentrating on those aspects of their niches where they interact with ourselves. Mammals tend to have relatively broad niches in most respects, but not so all animals. For instance many butterflies can only feed on a very narrow range of plants at the caterpillar stage of their life cycle. An example is the brimstone, that pure yellow butterfly that's the first on the wing in early spring and probably gave us the word 'butter'fly. Its caterpillars are entirely restricted to buckthorn bushes. Considering how uncommon the buckthorn is it's surprising how often you see brimstones.

In general the narrower the niche a species occupies the more it can tell us about the landscape. Butterflies are choosy about both microclimate and food plants and they are sensitive to chemical pollution. In other words their niche is fairly narrow all round. Because they are so exacting they are sometimes taken as indicators of the ecological health of a landscape.

PIONEERS AND STAYERS

Another way to characterise niches is according to whether the species in question is a pioneer or a stayer. The distinction is more obvious in plants than in animals. Pioneer plants are good at occupying new space whenever it becomes available. A typical pioneer produces large numbers of seeds, each one very small, and disperses them far and wide in search of unoccupied soil. It grows fast and has a short life. A typical stayer puts much less effort into reproduction. It produces fewer, larger seeds and has no special method for dispersing them. It grows slowly, has a long life and is good at holding on to whatever space it occupies. Most plants fall somewhere between the two and have some characteristics of both pioneers and stayers. Nonetheless there are some extreme types and a good illustration is the contrast between the birch tree, an extreme pioneer, and the beech, an extreme stayer.

Three Trees

Birch trees produce masses of tiny, light seeds, winged like little butterflies to help them fly on the wind. They are so abundant and travel so far that birch seedlings can pop up almost anywhere there's a bit of bare soil for them to germinate in. Being so tiny they must have that bit of bare soil, however small, because the little seedlings can't compete with established plants. Birch is quite intolerant of shade and can't grow where there's already a canopy of other trees. So while it readily forms new woods it can't go into a second generation on the same site, though it can jump into gaps in existing woods. Quick to spring up and quick to disappear, pure birch woods are temporary affairs. But they can leave a more permanent wood behind them if other, more shade-tolerant trees become established within the wood during its lifetime.

Beech has rather heavy seeds that fall to the ground and germinate near the mother plant, so it's slow to colonise new territory. In fact it rarely grows spontaneously outside existing woods. It seems to need the preparation of other trees before it can get established and it has no problem growing beneath their canopy because it's extremely shade-tolerant. In its turn it casts a very heavy shade so other trees find it impossible to get going underneath it. This means that once beech has occupied a site it can be hard to shift.

The oak has an image of a stayer. It certainly is a very long-lived tree. There's no symbol that better evokes stability, longevity and continuity with the past than an old oak. But they are not tolerant of shade so they rarely regenerate within existing woods and find it hard to compete with shade-tolerant trees like beech, lime and sycamore. They can only compete with these trees if a poor soil or a tough climate gives them the edge. In other words they can take the role of stayer where conditions are hard but not where they are easy. They do dominate most semi-natural woods in the soft, fertile lowlands of Britain. But that's because they have been favoured by the woodsmen of the past, not because of their own competitive ability.

Despite its image oak often takes the part of a pioneer. The key to this lies in its relationship with the jay, the smallest and most colourful member of the crow family. Jays eat acorns, and what they can't eat immediately they bury for later use. They have a preference for burying them well away from the parent tree, outside the woodland, and of every four they bury they only recover one. All large tree seeds, such as hazel and beech nuts, are taken by birds. But it's the special habits of jays and their preference for acorns that give the oak its ability to spread, if not as far as a birch, at least as surely.

Once sown by the jays, oaklings are well adapted to survive in grassland. An acorn is enormous compared to most seeds and the seedling can live on its stored food for a long time before it has to rely on its own photosynthesis. This means it can compete with the resident grasses. It also means that it has the opportunity to put down a deep taproot before it sends up its shoot. This enables it to survive the occasional browsing by grazing animals, as the root is able to grow a new shoot from its own reserves.

Seedlings of beech, left, and oak, right. Both have a large store of food from the seed, but note how the oak's is less vulnerable to grazing – another advantage as a pioneer.

So oak is well adapted to getting going in grassland, the most abundant pioneer habitat for a tree in Britain.

Another pioneer characteristic of the oak is that it's not tolerant of shade. Acorns that fall to the ground from a woodland oak and germinate there have little chance of growing into a tree. In times past the occasional one would make it and this was enough to maintain the oak as a component of most kinds of woodland. But in the year 1908 oak mildew disease arrived in Europe from North America. Oak seedlings growing in the open are able to survive it and grow into mature trees. But in the woods the combined stresses of shade and mildew are too much for them and these days oak almost never regenerates inside woods.

Herbaceous Plants

Herbaceous plants can be annual, biennial or perennial. That is they can have a lifespan of one, two or more than two years. The niche of a herbaceous perennial can lie anywhere along the spectrum from pioneer to stayer, just like the trees. But for annuals and biennials it's different. Annuals live for one year and biennials, though they live for two, only produce seed in the second year. Both groups of plants have to reproduce by seed every year or they die out. They have to be pioneers.

Annuals

In a totally natural landscape annuals must have been rare but in a cultivated landscape they are common. Most of our important food crops are annuals or biennials, including cereals and root crops. Those broad landscapes of arable crops that cover much of the east of Britain represent a powerful symbiosis between our crop species and ourselves. The crop plant offers us abnormally large edible parts: seeds in the case of cereals and roots in the case of carrots and sugar beet. In return we provide the bare soil they need and look after them throughout their life cycle. We've changed our crop plants so much by selective breeding that they could no longer survive without us. But as long as humans are around being a crop plant is one of the most successful niches on the planet.

Weeds are just as dependent on us as crops are. In fact most of the annual plants in the British landscape that are not crops are weeds of arable fields, gardens and other disturbed ground. Some are dependent on arable fields for their existence and these have become very rare, as weed control on farms has been revolutionised by seed-cleaning machines and herbicides. Other weeds have alternative habitats. Herb Robert, for example, is a wildflower that grows, usually in ones or twos, in whatever bare soils it can find on woodland edges and hedgebanks. Sometimes one of its seeds will germinate in the bare soil of a vegetable garden. If that plant is allowed to flower and set seed its progeny will come up in masses the following year. Like the fox in the henhouse, it's genetically programmed to struggle for every piece of bare ground it can find. When it finds bare soil in unnaturally large quantities it grabs as much as it can.

Goosegrass, or cleavers, is an annual with a successful niche. Anyone who spent their childhood in the country will remember the endless games you can play with it. The whole plant, including seeds, leaves and stems, is covered with minute velcro-like hooks that stick to people's clothes. Seeing someone walk along unaware of the green tail stuck to their back is a never-ending source of amusement for children. What sticks to clothing sticks equally well to the fur of wild animals and this stickiness is the mechanism goosegrass uses to spread its seeds.

Another important aspect of its niche is its tolerance of cold. It can germinate at lower temperatures than most other plants, which means it can start growing in the middle of winter. There's more bare soil around in winter than in summertime, when everything is in leaf. There's usually some under a hedge, where it's too shady in summer for perennials to grow but well lit in winter, and you can often see the two-lobed seedlings of goosegrass spring up there in January. As summer comes on it can scramble away from the hedgerow and into the field, climbing up the crop plants and dropping its seeds into the fertile soil below.

Goosegrass makes its living by doing something which most other plants can't do, growing at low temperatures. The others don't do it because it comes at a cost. All the tissues of a goosegrass plant need to contain anti-freeze chemicals and it takes energy to produce these, energy which could otherwise be used for extra growth, more seeds or some other useful function. Each species invests its energy in a different enterprise, an enterprise that enables it to avoid competition with its neighbours.

Teazel is a typical biennial:

year one,

year two.

Biennials

The two years of the biennials' life cycle means they can grow bigger than annuals. In the first summer they only grow leaves. The food they produce is passed down to the roots where it's stored over winter, often in a single large taproot. This means they start their second year with a capital sum of energy to spend on reproduction. Many of our root crops, such as carrots and beetroot, are biennials. We harvest them at the end of their first growing season, before they can use the stored energy for their own purposes.

Many biennials use part of their stored energy to send up a tall stem, as much as two metres high in some species. This gives the seeds a head start in long-distance dispersal, whether by clinging to the coat of passing animals or by flying on the wind. Burdock and spear thistle are two biennials that do this. They also invest part of their energy in specialised dispersal mechanisms. In burdock this is the burr, a mass of seeds equipped with big, barbed hooks. They take longer to remove from fur or clothes than the little balls of goosegrass, so they probably travel further before they are released. The large purple flowers of spear thistle mature into thousands of small seeds, each one equipped with its own parachute, which can float for miles on the warm air currents of summer.

Perennials

The other common thistle, the creeping thistle, also sends out thistledown to colonise bare ground but it doesn't have the same sense of urgency about it. It has shorter stems and smaller flowers and produces much less seed. It can afford to relax, not just because it's perennial but also because seeds are not its only means of reproduction; it also reproduces vegetatively. Vegetative reproduction means that part of the plant's vegetative body can become detached from it and form a new plant. Creeping thistle does this by means of vigorous horizontal roots that spread out from the parent plant and give rise to new vertical shoots, known as suckers. Each of these can become a new plant and eventually a single plant can expand vegetatively into a wide-spreading clump. After a couple of years the horizontal roots may die away, leaving independent daughter colonies. As sexual reproduction has not taken place the whole clump is genetically identical. A group like this of any suckering species is referred to as a clone.

No annuals or biennials can reproduce vegetatively and only a minority of perennials can, but those that do tend to be quite successful. Couch grass and creeping buttercup are two garden weeds that do it, couch by means of root-like rhizomes under the ground and creeping buttercup by above-ground runners. Unlike the annual weeds, which are successful because they produce masses of seed, these two succeed as weeds because they are difficult to eradicate. Just a tiny piece of couch rhizome or buttercup stem left in the soil can regrow into a new plant and from that into a whole new population without a single seed being shed. Trees and shrubs that reproduce vegetatively mostly do so by means of root suckers. Wild cherry, most elm species and blackthorn are examples of suckering species. Above-ground runners are less common in woody plants but

Rosebay
willowherb.

one example is the bramble, which forms a new root system wherever one of its arching canes touches the ground.

One of the great advantages of vegetative reproduction is that the new plant is much better able to compete with the existing vegetation. Unlike a seedling, supplied with only what it could bring in the tiny knapsack of its seed, a sucker can call on the energy resources of the parent plant. New suckers of creeping thistle and blackthorn can come up through a dense grass sward with no problem. This is an efficient way of colonising new ground but it's not real pioneer stuff. Compared to the widespread dissemination of thousands of tiny seeds, the slow but steady spread of a blackthorn clump is modest. In fact clonal plants can be either pioneers or stayers. An example of a suckering pioneer is rosebay willowherb while dog's mercury is a typical suckering stayer.

Those clumps of tall purple-red flowers that brighten the roadsides in high summer are rosebay willowherb. It's a plant of urban demolition sites, railway banks, clear-felled plantations and even newly coppiced woodland. But wherever it grows it must have plenty of sunlight. A single plant can produce up to a hundred thousand seeds, each one borne on a feathery sail that carries it far and wide in search of a suitable home. The large number of seeds means that they can come up thickly where they find such a site.

Dog's mercury, by contrast, is a plant you could easily miss. Although it's common and abundant in some woods it's a drab plant that acts as a background to the more colourful wildflowers. It's about shin-high with dark, 'leaf-shaped' leaves and inconspicuous greenish flowers. It's very shade-tolerant and is rarely found outside of woods and old hedgerows. It produces very little seed, most of which is sterile, and has no special mechanism for dispersing it. But it does quietly reproduce by means of underground rhizomes.

Dog's mercury in spring.

Like a miniature beech tree, it casts a heavy shade. The plants emerge early in the year and die down late so they cast this shade throughout the growing season. On its favourite soils – of medium moisture content and slightly alkaline – it forms a pure stand, while on less ideal sites it's usually mixed with other herbs. Under a lightly-shading tree canopy it can grow especially vigorously. The ash tree casts a light shade and in pure ash woods mercury can grow so densely that it actually suppresses ash seedlings and prevents the tree reproducing. Other trees, such as wych elm, yew or beech, are more shade-tolerant as seedlings and are not completely suppressed by it. A pure ash wood with an understorey of mercury can change into a mixed wood by this means. Thus a humble herb can decide the fates of mighty trees just by quietly holding its own.

Animals

Among the animals, herbivores tend to lie towards the pioneer end of the scale and carnivores towards the stayer end. Rabbits and mice grow faster and breed more prolifically than foxes and badgers. Song birds, most of which are omnivorous, raise more clutches per year and more chicks per clutch than birds of prey. In the garden the herbivorous pests recover their population much more quickly after being sprayed with an insecticide than their insect predators do – a good reason for not using broad-spectrum insecticides. But plant-eating invertebrates can be stayers too. In fact some of the most extreme species at both ends of the spectrum are herbivores. Two examples are aphids and stag beetles.

Aphids have incredible powers of reproduction and dispersal. In the summer time when food is abundant they speed up their reproductive rate by cutting out both sex and the egg stage of their life cycle: females reproduce without mating and give birth to ready-hatched young. The cycle can speed up so much that these young already have the embryo of the next generation in them when they are born. There can be several generations during the growing season, and in a few short months a single female may give rise to thousands of descendents. When this massive rate of reproduction begins to overwhelm the food supply they divert some energy from reproduction to dispersal and produce a generation with wings. Like birch seeds or thistledown, they can ride for miles on the wind in search of a new host plant. When autumn comes some males are born, mating takes place and the resulting eggs wait quietly for the following spring.

Stag beetles are curious little creatures with antlers like male deer, and they are real stayers. While aphids support their extravagant lifestyle by tapping into the rich flow of food below the soft surface of sappy young plants, stag

A male stag beetle.

beetles eat dead wood. There's not much nutrition in wood and it's hard to digest, so they are slow growers. The females lay their eggs in rotting logs and the larvae can take as much as five years to mature into adults. The adults live for a brief summer of mating, enlivened by the occasional jousting between males using those magnificent antlers. They can fly but they are heavy and clumsy flyers and rarely travel far.

The stag beetle is now a rare and endangered species. How can this be if it's supposed to be a 'stayer', so capable of holding its ground? The answer is that the stag beetle evolved in the world of the wildwood, where dead wood was always at hand. There was no-one to harvest the trees, so when they died they slowly rotted where they fell. A creature that needed nothing more than a reliable supply of dead wood was secure. If its reproduction rate was slow and its powers of dispersal negligible it didn't matter at all. There was always another log nearby.

Not so for aphids. Each species of aphid is restricted to a narrow range of host plants, some to a single species. In the diverse ecosystem of the wildwood there was never a guarantee that there would be another host plant at hand. In the constant hunt for new hosts an abundance of highly mobile young was the key to these aphids' survival. If most of them failed to land on the right plant it didn't matter. Just one aphid that did so could rapidly multiply into a new colony, which could provide thousands of new young to seek out the next host plant.

Past and Future

Plants also reveal their wildwood origins by their behaviour. It explains why plants which need light are pioneers and those which tolerate shade are stayers. Rosebay willowherb and birch are both light-lovers. In a world where woodland was the norm they had to constantly migrate or die out. Dog's mercury and beech, on the other hand, were surrounded by their favoured habitat. Energy spent on producing thousands of seeds and sending them far and wide would have been energy wasted. It's more worthwhile for a stayer to produce fewer seeds and invest more energy in each one. This equips them to compete with the established vegetation, which is always a feature of a stayer's stable habitat. Vegetative reproduction represents even more investment of energy in each offspring and the chances of each one growing to maturity are correspondingly greater.

In Chapter 2, I mentioned that there is some disagreement over whether the wildwood was predominantly woodland or a landscape that alternated between trees and grassland. (See page 11.) The niche differences between pioneers and stayers, lends a lot of weight to the view that it was predominantly woodland. The fact that pioneers are mainly species of open country and new woodland while stayers are creatures of mature woodland suggests that mature woodland was the norm. Pioneers needed their powers of reproduction and dispersal to find a habitat that was infrequent and stayers didn't because their habitat was always close at hand. It's not a conclusive argument because it's possible that the conditions that reigned during the past few thousand years are not typical of the much longer time span over which the plants and animals have evolved. But it certainly tips the balance in favour of the prehistoric landscape being largely wooded.

Today the situation is reversed. Aphids, which once needed extraordinary powers of reproduction just to survive, are now presented with monocultures of host plants. This makes them formidable pests. Annual plants, which once struggled to produce enough seeds to find that elusive patch of bare soil, are now surrounded by acres of it every year. In the wildwood they must have been rare but now we know them as weeds. The stag beetle, which never needed to bother about finding new habitat, has had a rude awakening. It's just one of a whole suite of dead-wood-eaters which are either rare or already extinct. In the humanised landscape they are the ones which need to be able to breed and fly like an aphid. But evolution works on a much slower timescale than human history and they are stuck with the traits and abilities that suited them in the wildwood.

In addition, the stayers now have to cope with a rapidly changing climate. As the world warms it's most unlikely that complete, mature ecosystems will steadily migrate north. Pioneer species move fast and they'll have little problem colonising new territory as it becomes warm enough, but not so the stayers. In most cases the speed at which they can migrate is slower than the rate at which the climatic belts are migrating northward. They'll be left behind. They are also ill-adapted to cross seas, cities and areas of intensive farming and forestry. Stuck in a climate that is becoming too hot for them, it's likely that most of them will go extinct.

As climate change intensifies, many of the more diverse ecosystems, like semi-natural woodland and unimproved grassland, may hang on for a long time. Though they will lose some of their species, their very diversity makes them resilient, maybe resilient enough to keep going in temperatures which are really too high for them. But eventually they will succumb. Landscapes with less resilience will probably break down much sooner. What will replace them will be pioneer communities made up of the most mobile species from the south. Like all pioneer communities they will be low on diversity. They will wait for the stayers to catch up and turn them into mature ecosystems, but they will wait in vain.

Diverse eco-systems, like this semi-natural grassland, have more resilience than simpler ones.

7

Succession: How Landscapes Change Through Time

LANDSCAPES ARE constantly changing. Sometimes people are the cause of change but landscapes also change in spite of us. Mostly we try to keep things more or less as they are, as arable fields, pasture, gardens and so on. But all the while natural succession is waiting in the wings, ready to take the vegetation forward to a more mature stage as soon as we relax our grip. The whole gamut of succession runs from bare soil, or even bare rock, at one end to mature woodland at the other.

Imagine a field that is ploughed and then abandoned. The bare soil will be seized upon by pioneer plants, including many annuals and biennials, eager as ever for any unoccupied space to seed into. These form the initial vegetation that for simplicity's sake we call the annual stage. Once all the available growing space is taken up, the annuals and biennials find it increasingly difficult to re-seed and then perennials have the advantage. This brings on the herbaceous perennial stage. There may be trees and shrubs present from the start, small and insignificant among the herbaceous vegetation, or they may become established later. Either way, when they begin to emerge above the canopy of herbaceous plants succession moves on to the scrub stage, a mixture of herbaceous and woody plants. Once the tree canopy closes the land has reached the woodland stage. At first the woodland is composed of pioneer trees but eventually these are replaced by stayers, or climax species as they are sometimes known. Shade-tolerant woodland herbs are slow to colonise and their presence in a wood can usually be taken as a sign that succession is well advanced.

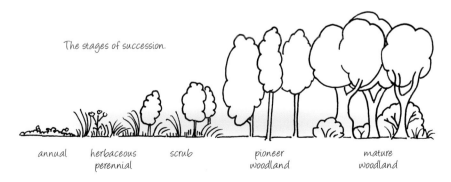

The stages of succession.

| annual | herbaceous perennial | scrub | pioneer woodland | mature woodland |

That's a simplified picture of succession. In practice there are lots of variations on it. For a start, not every succession begins with bare earth and not every one makes it as far as mature woodland. But the general trends are always the same: from bare soil to plant cover, from annual to perennial, from herbaceous to woody, from smaller plants to larger, from short-lived to long-lived, from light-demanding to shade-tolerant and from pioneers to stayers. Just as the plants change so do the animals, with a general trend from pioneer species in the earlier stages to stayers in the later ones. Many animals are quite dependent on one stage of succession. The stag beetle is an example. Others, like the fox, make use of a variety of different ecosystems within their range, from open fields to ancient woods, each one representing a different stage of succession.

Since the plants of each stage are longer-lived than those of the one before, succession slows down as it goes along. The change from annual to perennial usually takes no more than a couple of years. The changes from grassland to scrub and from scrub to woodland are much slower, though quite fast enough to be witnessed in a single lifetime. But the change from pioneer woodland to mature woodland is measured in the lifetimes of trees rather than people, centuries rather than decades. Finally, succession can go into reverse, as when overgrazed woodland gradually becomes grassland.

FROM BARE SOIL

We usually regard exposed soil as an affront to good management and plant it up as soon as possible. But for wildlife the odd patch of it is no bad thing. Many solitary bee species, which are important pollinators of flowering plants, make their nests in tunnels that they dig in bare soil. Seed-eating birds also benefit from

a hands-off approach. The annuals and other pioneers that colonise bare soil are copious seed producers. They are the kind of plants that used to be common in any field corner but have become much less so in these days of herbicides.

Along with the annuals and biennials there are some light-seeded perennial pioneers, such as the lowly coltsfoot. Its small, pale dandelion-like flowers come straight out of the ground in early spring, before the leaves, which are shaped like the sole of a horse's foot and give the plant its name. In a more mature ecosystem

Coltsfoot.

coltsfoot is an indicator of moist or heavy soils but in the open conditions of a denuded site it can grow in any kind of soil. Later, as the space is taken up and the plants start competing with each other, it will gradually die out on drier, lighter soils where other plants have the edge. Early colonisers can't be used as soil indicators because the main selection pressure on them is not their soil preferences but their ability to colonise. A common pattern at this stage is a mosaic of single-species patches, each centred on a single plant that got in early and spread while there was no competition, either vegetatively or by seed.

The more time passes the more a plant's suitability to the conditions tells. Even the slightest advantage over a neighbour with a similar niche will tell with time. A tough, persistent plant like coltsfoot may hold on for quite a few years in a soil where in the long run it will die out. But eventually the melee of competition will be fought out to its end and the mosaic of patches will give way to a mix of plants which varies from place to place according to soil conditions and microclimate.

Urban Succession

Successions which start from bare ground are less common in the countryside than in urban areas, where there's often a gap of a few years between the demolition of old buildings and the redevelopment of the site. The late Oliver Gilbert made a study of the plant and animal communities that develop on these sites and gave them the name 'urban commons'. Where other people saw wasteland he saw a unique type of ecosystem, unique because they are made up of a mixture of native and exotic plants that can be found nowhere else on Earth. They also follow their own distinctive path of succession.

The first stage consists of a mix of annuals, perennials and light-seeded trees, and usually lasts some three to six years. Gradually the taller perennials shade out the lower-growing ones, bringing on the tall herb stage, which may last some five years or so. This is succeeded by the grassland stage, which gradually gives way to scrub, as brambles, bushes and trees gain the upper hand. Urban commons can develop into woodland but they rarely get that far because sooner or later the site is redeveloped. How soon this happens depends on the state of the economy. When it's buoyant not many urban commons get past the tall herb stage but in the Thatcher years, when much of British industry went to the wall, there was a big increase in urban woodland.

Urban commons make play space for children that's far more interesting than a park, one with an edge of freedom and adventure. They can also make an interesting study for anyone interested in wildlife. Like any kind of semi-natural vegetation, no two of them are the same. One of the strongest influences on their plant composition is the raw material they grow on. Bricks and mortar are the most common materials but sometimes it's industrial wastes. In extreme cases these can be so toxic in their raw state that they only become habitable for plants after the leaching action of rain.

Pulverised fuel ash is an example. It's a waste product of coal-fired power stations. Initially it's highly alkaline, toxic and sterile. In the 1960s it was routinely dumped in heaps near power stations and to begin with these heaps were as bare as a moonscape. The first plants to colonise were salt-marsh species from the coast, even on sites far inland. After more leaching, alkaline-loving legumes such

as clovers and vetches were able to move in. These nitrogen-fixing herbs play a significant role in the succession because at this stage the soil contains very little organic matter, and nitrogen only comes from living things, not from the mineral soil. The legumes were followed by orchids. These also do well on infertile soils as they have a specially strong symbiotic relationship with fungi that provide them with nutrients in exchange for organic food. By the 1990s a whole range of herbaceous plants had colonised and some sites were developing into orchid-rich woodland. Although they are botanically important, sites like these rarely get any official protection. It's hard for people to recognise that something so urban, so industrial in its origin, is a jewel of biodiversity.

FROM GRASS TO SCRUB

Most often the starting point for succession in the countryside is grassland. Steep fields may be allowed to scrub up simply because they are too steep to drive a tractor on. They can't be fertilised, manured or harrowed, let alone cut for hay or silage, so it's impossible to farm them intensively and get a high yield. Even if the farmer is content to use steep land for extensive grazing, he can't go round with a mower once a year to cut whatever herbage the animals haven't eaten. This is called topping and it doesn't only cut uneaten grass and thistles, it also catches any tree or shrub seedlings that come up in the pasture. In the days of cheap labour it was done by hand on steep slopes but these days the value of the grazing would be less than the cost of the labour.

Much depends on the intensity of grazing. Most young woody plants can survive the odd nibble now and then but none of them can stand being repeatedly

The flat land is farmed intensively while the steep slopes are allowed to succeed to scrub.

bitten down to the ground. How often they get eaten depends partly on the pattern of grazing. If a large number of animals are put on the land for a short time then taken away and put back again when the grass has regrown, they'll eat everything that's growing there each time. But if a smaller number of animals are left there continuously they can pick and choose. Unless they happen to be goats, they'll eat the grass rather than the shrubs and the field is likely to scrub up.

Scrub formation isn't necessarily a continuous process. A few shrubs may get going one year, perhaps when there are fewer animals on the farm than usual or grass growth is particularly good. Then if grazing returns to normal no new shrubs may appear for years. The existing shrubs will stay there, their growth restricted by browsing, but they can't be got rid of by browsing alone. Once it's started, succession to scrub usually carries on to its inevitable end, however slow and interrupted the process.

Another place you may see the beginnings of succession from grassland is on the edges of towns where fields are bought up for development. A few years often elapse before construction begins and the land isn't usually grazed during that time. With the hedges no longer trimmed and the grass no longer cut the landscape can look like an idealised vision of the countryside, with billowing, curvy hedges and tall, waving grass. But it doesn't stay like that for long. Soon any large, vigorous herbaceous plants in the sward begin to take over from the grasses. The great advantage that grasses have is their ability to regrow vigorously after being defoliated. When the field's no longer grazed or mown they lose that advantage. The plants that have the edge now are the ones that can cast the most shade on their neighbours. These are mainly plants that are tall, have broad leaves, or both, such as stinging nettles and docks. Usually these plants will have been there in the grassland but kept in check by regular defoliation.

Priddy Mineries.

Nettles and creeping thistle can spread vegetatively and if they are present they'll start to form clumps that grow ever larger and progressively exclude other plants. Wet fields can become dominated by rushes. Hedge bindweed may weave its way out from the hedgerows. In high summer it will cover the drab, gone-to-seed thistles and grasses with a layer of bright green leaves, dotted with its white trumpet-shaped flowers. If bracken is waiting in the wings it may rapidly take over the whole field. But otherwise an abandoned field often develops into a mosaic of patches, each dominated by a different herbaceous plant.

It's interesting to note that this change from grass to broadleaves is just the opposite to what Oliver Gilbert observed in urban commons, where the tall herb stage comes before the grassland stage rather than after it. Just why urban successions should work the opposite way round to rural ones at this stage, I haven't the faintest idea.

Speed of Change

The time it takes for the herbaceous stage to give way to the woody stage on ungrazed grassland can vary enormously. I first realised just how long it can take one day when I was walking on Priddy Mineries, on the Mendip Hills. It's fifty hectares of rough grass and heath on former lead workings. Although willows have sprung up in boggy places and on the edges of the two ponds, on the grassland there's hardly a tree, just the very occasional pine or hawthorn.

The Mineries are not grazed, because the lead content of the herbage would poison the animals. No-one I've spoken to can remember a time when it was grazed and there's no reason to suppose it ever has been since lead working stopped over a hundred years ago. It's not the lead that's halting succession, because most trees are quite indifferent to it. It's not the lack of seed parents either. A species-rich woodland has seeded itself on the ruined buildings of the lead works nearby. At least part of the answer is that the grass itself is preventing the trees from taking root.

It's predominantly purple moorgrass, a tough, tussocky grass that produces a thick mulch of dead leaves and stems at its feet. It prevents tree seeds that fall from above getting to the soil where they could germinate. Any seed that did manage to reach the soil would be unable to grow through the thick mulch above. It also seems to be capable of preventing the succession to the broad-leaved herbaceous plants I described above. This is an infertile upland soil and none of those plants would grow well enough to challenge the purple moorgrass on its own ground.

No grassland can keep the trees at bay like this forever in our climate. Eventually something will happen to expose a little soil and once a single shrub gets going it starts to shade the grasses around it, creating the conditions for other shrubs or trees to germinate. But the rate at which this happens varies greatly and Priddy Mineries, with its dense sward of tough, tussocky grasses, is definitely at the slow end of the scale.

An example of the fast end of the scale is what happened when the rabbits were virtually wiped out overnight by myxomatosis in the 1950s. On many of the chalk downs of southern England there had been such overpopulation of rabbits that there was bare soil on every hand. This gave plenty of opportunity for trees and shrubs to germinate and once germinated there was little to stop them growing. Large areas of the downs scrubbed up rapidly.

Slope

This entry from my notebook illustrates the influence of slope. The scene is a small field adjacent to our town cemetery. One half of it is occupied by a strip lynchett, both 'step' and 'riser', while the other half is more generally sloping.

Glastonbury, Somerset

The lynchett field just below our house has been bought by the cemetery and not grazed for four or five years. It soon grew over with brambles and a few trees. Now they have strimmed the brambles but left the trees. In the generally sloping part of the field the trees are scattered, but on the lynchett part they are entirely confined to the riser. This doesn't seem to be because they cut the trees on the step, as there's no sign of stumps. It seems to be because the riser is the only place they have managed to grow.

This could be because a) the sward was more open on the riser, as it often is on a steep slope; or b) the trees got started before the end of grazing and were successful on the riser because animals tend to graze less on steep slopes. Of the two (a) seems less likely because trees have regenerated on gentle slopes in the *other half of the field, slopes which wouldn't have a noticeably open sward. (b) fits the case well because the trees are thick on the lynchett riser, scattered on the gentle slope and absent on the flattest land, the lynchett step. In other words, the steeper the slope the more young trees.*

Animals graze more intensively on the flat because it's more comfortable for them to stand or walk there, with all four feet at the same level. The steeper the slope the less it gets nibbled and the more chance trees and shrubs have to get going. This reinforces the tendency of farmers to farm the flat land intensively and let the steeper land scrub up. On some steep slopes you can see the scrub accompanied by one or two mature trees, the relic of a previous episode of succession.

Pioneer Shrubs

Hawthorn is the most widespread woody pioneer in Britain. You can see it all over the country, coming up in grassland and bracken in almost any soil and climate. It's spread by birds that eat its bright red fruits and excrete the seeds. This gives it long range without the necessity of a very small seed. But even more importantly it has a special ability to compete with grasses. Why this should be so is not fully understood but the crucial factor may be competition for water. Grasses have a finely branched, fibrous root system that is very efficient at extracting water from the soil. Tree seedlings have far fewer roots but hawthorn is something of an exception, with a more fibrous root system than most others.

Two other shrubs that often colonise grassland by seed are gorse and brambles. They are almost as successful at seeding into grass as hawthorn, though their niches are somewhat narrower. Gorse is commoner on dry, light soils and bramble on more fertile clays and loams. Brambles have the added advantage of vegetative reproduction. Wherever a seedling comes up it can quickly turn into a spreading blob of bramble, while other brambles spread out from the hedge, bounding further into the field each year and joining up with the ones that have grown from seed. In a few years the field can be turned into nothing but a mass of brambles two metres high or more. But almost always there will be the tip of a tree here and there, poking above the dark green pillows of bramble, harbingers of the next stage of succession. When these trees grow up and their branches spread, their shade will shrink the thorny pioneers back down till they become no more than a minor component of the woodland floor.

Blackthorn rarely spreads by seed but its powerful suckers make seeding almost superfluous. It will spread out inexorably from a hedge into pasture, even in the face of quite heavy grazing. Only regular topping or mowing for hay or silage will keep it in check. Otherwise it will form a dense, impenetrable thicket, armed with dangerous thorns.

It's no coincidence that these four pioneers are all thorny, but it doesn't give them total protection from browsing. Blackthorn only produces thorns on twigs in their second year of growth so its first-year shoots are unprotected. Hawthorn, bramble and gorse do form thorns on first-year twigs but the thorns take some time to harden and become sharp, so the shrubs have a vulnerable period each

spring when their shoots are quite tasty. This is why hard grazing can prevent scrub increasing but can rarely get rid of what's already grown.

The Scrub Ecosystem

On the whole farmers hate scrub. Even though present-day economics may mean that sometimes they can't help letting go of the steepest land, it goes against their deepest instincts. For thousands of years they and their ancestors have struggled against natural succession and scrub represents failure in that struggle. But it is good for biodiversity. Insects and other invertebrates benefit from the combination of shelter and sunlight that the semi-wooded structure provides. The shrubs give nesting sites for song birds while the rough grassland provides food for seed-eating birds and habitat for small mammals. Most shrubs, including the ubiquitous hawthorn, only produce flowers and fruit on second-year twigs. In a hedge that is trimmed every year they never flower or set fruit. But in scrub they are left alone and provide a rich store of pollen and nectar for insects and berries for birds. There are several species of orchid, some very rare, which tend to crop up just at that moment in succession when grass succeeds to scrub.

Scrub is essentially a changing ecosystem and these plants seem to thrive on change. So do some animals, including some invertebrates that need a variety of early-succession habitats for different stages of their life cycle. All of these need to be present at the same time but all of them are transient. This presents a problem for nature conservation. The nature reserve approach to conservation works against change. It's based on identifying the best wildlife sites and preserving them as they are. But you can't put a fence up around scrub and preserve it. It just turns into woodland.

FROM NEW WOODS TO OLD

Competition in nature is very obvious. You can see it where plants compete for space to grow and hear it when territorial birds fill the spring air with song or the roar of stags echoes round the glens in the autumn. But underneath this showy exterior there's a quiet world of co-operation, without which life could not exist.

Gorse sits at the centre of a web of co-operative relationships. Although a shrub, it's a member of the same plant family as the clovers and like them has a symbiotic relationship with nitrogen-fixing bacteria; insects, which in return receive nectar and pollen for their food, pollinate it and its seeds are dispersed through another symbiotic relationship, this time with ants. The seeds are borne in a pod, like a pea pod, which snaps open when it's ripe, catapulting the seeds away from the plant, but the ants take them that bit further. Each seed has a little package of highly nutritious food attached to it. The ants bring the seeds back to their nests in order to share this food with their fellows and then leave the seed in the nest. So they not only disperse the seeds but sow them too.

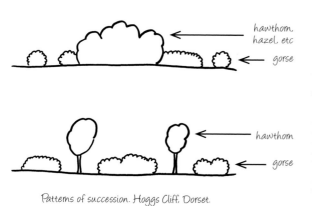

hawthorn, hazel, etc

gorse

hawthorn

gorse

Patterns of succession. Hoggs Cliff, Dorset.

All these relationships are mutually beneficial but gorse's relationship with trees could be described as self-sacrificing. It helps trees to get established and grow but, as a sun-loving plant, the gorse will die out once the trees grow up and their canopy closes. It does it, firstly, by suppressing grass. Young trees survive better and grow faster in gorse than they do in grass, as long as they keep their heads above the gorse canopy. Secondly, it protects them from browsing with its thorns. Thirdly, it improves the soil for them. The sandy soils where gorse usually grows tend to be acid and poor in nutrients. Gorse helps to counter this, both by fixing nitrogen and by bringing minerals up from the subsoil, which can enrich the topsoil when its leaves fall and decompose. Among the minerals it accumulates is calcium, the element in lime that is so important in countering acidity.

Of course terms like 'self-sacrificing' are anthropomorphic and have no place in a discussion of the habits of plants. Gorse is only doing what's good for itself. If trees take advantage of that it's presumably because the shrub hasn't devised a means of preventing them. Gorse isn't the only shrub that performs this role in succession. Brambles grow on richer soils than gorse and don't have its soil improving functions but they do protect trees both from grass competition and from browsing. In my part of the country a very common sight on lightly-grazed pasture is clumps of bramble with ash saplings growing up through them. Ash is perhaps the foremost pioneer tree round here but you rarely see it growing directly in grass.

Bracken is another plant that can act as a nurse to young trees, either alone or mixed with bramble. This isn't necessarily as 'self-sacrificing' as it is for gorse because both bracken and bramble can survive in the shade. Like gorse, bracken can bring minerals up from the subsoil with its deep root system and it adds a generous helping of sweet humus to the soil surface as its fronds die down each autumn. It's a great soil improver. A walk I took on the hillsides near the Highland village of Kinlochleven illustrates the role of bracken in succession.

Kinlochleven, Highland

The ravines on the hillside are full of a variety of trees: birch, oak, ash, beech, holly, rowan and wild cherry. The slopes around them are either treeless or pure birch. The birch is growing mostly in the bracken-covered parts of the hillside rather than the grassy parts. There are tiny birches in the grass but few saplings or larger trees. As they grow the trees tend to shade out the bracken, which slightly obscures the pattern. The grassy areas seem to be wetter than the bracken.

I don't think the wetter soil of the grassy areas directly affected the establishment of birch trees. It wasn't that wet. It affected it indirectly because bracken can't stand poor drainage and on this site the young birch trees needed the protection of bracken. They could germinate in the grassy areas but they couldn't escape the attention of the sheep and deer. The tall, inedible bracken saved the trees simply by hiding them from the eyes of the animals. As so often, grazing was the dominant factor. This is reflected in the contrast between the open hillsides and the ravines. The ravines are difficult to access. I know because I tried to cross one of them, climbing from crag to crag, and failed. Over the years this has been enough of a deterrent to grazing animals to enable woodland to survive in the gullies and develop to maturity.

Diversity

The diversity of trees in the ravines makes a stark contrast to the pure birch of the newly-forming woods on the open hillsides. It's the richest mix of trees I ever saw in that district, where the harsh climate and poor soils restrict the range of tree species. The ravines have a sheltered microclimate and a richer supply of mineral nutrients than the surrounding slopes. (See pages 170-171.) But another reason for the diversity of trees in them is the length of time that trees have grown there. In general, a new ecosystem of any kind is simple and it becomes more and more diverse as time goes by. It's quite normal for a new wood to consist of just one species of tree. As the years go by more and more are added, and diversity on its own can be taken as an indicator that the wood has been a wood for a long time.

The trees you can most often see forming new woods in pure stand are birch, ash, sycamore, alder and pussy willow. To some extent these pioneers prepare the way for the stayers that will come later. Birch, like bracken, improves the soil by bringing minerals up from the subsoil and adding them to the topsoil through its leaf fall. The light soils that it naturally favours tend to be poor in minerals and acid. Alder and willow can pump water out of an excessively wet soil. In general the pioneers create the woodland conditions which stayers like beech need. This may well include introducing the fungal partners which are so important to trees and it seems likely that the absence of these fungi is one reason why beech doesn't often reproduce spontaneously outside woods. (See page 69.)

Young woods aren't always single-species. If they are next to an existing ancient wood the species mix may be very similar to that in the existing wood or it may not. Much depends on what happened in the year when tree colonisation got started. It could be that one kind of tree had a really good seed year or weather conditions might have favoured one kind over the others. A more diverse mix of species may indicate that the trees got established over a number of years rather than all at once.

Animals can have an influence on species composition too. I know a place where sycamore and ash self-seeded directly into the bare soil of a former pig paddock. There are far more mature ashes nearby than sycamores and at first most of the seedlings were ash. But there are also rabbits there and they much prefer the taste of the ash. Every ash seedling has had its bark eaten. Not many of them have been killed outright but they have all been weakened and the sycamore has suppressed most of them. Now the saplings are past the age where they are vulnerable to rabbits but only one ash has survived and the old pig pen is on its way to becoming a pure sycamore grove.

Herbaceous Plants

It's not just the trees in a wood that become more diverse as time goes by but the whole woodland community, including herbaceous plants, animals, microbes

and fungi. At first there's little in a new wood but the trees, as very few grassland species can survive the change from light to shade. It can seem an almost sterile place. New colonists must come from other woods and, since most of the species that fill woodland niches are stayers rather than pioneers, colonisation can be a very slow process indeed.

The first herbaceous plant to colonise the little wood I planted some thirty years ago is lords and ladies, the wild arum. It's more a hedgerow plant than a woodland one and has migrated into the wood from the adjacent

Lords and ladies. The leaves don't always have black spots on them.

hedge. Behind it the creeping shoots of ivy are spreading out from the hedge. Ivy is typical of new woods. On the whole it's uncommon on the ground in ancient woods, except around the edges. In recent times this distinction has been rather clouded by decreasing light levels in woods where no trees have been felled or coppiced for many years. Ivy, being very shade tolerant, has begun to appear among the woodland wildflowers in some of these dark old woods. But pure ivy covering the ground can still be taken as an indicator of a recently formed wood.

Much depends on whether the new wood adjoins an old one or not. Most wildflowers will spread slowly over the boundary into suitable new habitat, though the speed of their advance is very variable. I know an ancient bluebell wood that has a recent extension on one side. By looking at old editions of the Ordnance Survey map I reckon the new part is around seventy-five years old. The bluebells have spilled over the small bank that marks the boundary and spread a metre or two into the new. By contrast, I know another place where a small plantation of native trees was made some hundred metres away from an ancient wood with bluebells in it. Little more than a decade after it was planted I saw a clump of bluebells growing in the new wood. Could it be that a bluebell bulb was brought here by a squirrel in the way that jays spread acorns? Or was it a perhaps a two-legged mammal who wanted to enhance the new planting? Maybe the bluebells were already there before the trees were planted, growing under a canopy of bracken as they sometimes do. There is bracken in the little plantation.

Mature Woodland

In tracing the course of succession from young woods to old we're bedevilled by the twin problems: the process takes too long to observe directly, and all our woods have been managed for centuries. We can't observe a natural succession. We can only infer it from the glimpses of the process that we can observe, such as this one from my notebook.

Bach y Gwydel, Ceredigion

The wood has a canopy of oak with a few beech. Under the canopy the regeneration is entirely beech. In the ungrazed pasture outside the wood there are oaks coming up through the matted mulch of last year's grass.

The ability of beech to regenerate in the shade suggests that in the end any wood will end up being dominated by it, the ultimate stayer among European trees. A simple theory was built on this observation. It stated that all successions, whatever their earlier stages, ended up with pure beech woodland. This end point was called the climax. Where the soil or climate is unsuitable for beech there would be other climax trees. But the vision for lowland Britain under a purely natural regime would be a narrowing down of diversity to this single species.

That's more or less what ecologists used to think. But the glimpses we can catch of the later stages of succession suggest that it's really not as simple as that. One of the best places to catch such glimpses is Lady Park Wood, a large ancient wood that lies in the gorge of the lower River Wye. Since 1944 it's been kept as a non-intervention nature reserve, untouched by human hand, just observed. So it's reasonable to suppose that what happens there reflects what might happen in a truly natural wood.

Lady Park Wood.

It's one of the few places in Britain where you can almost imagine yourself back in the wildwood. Many of the trees do still show signs of its past as a coppice wood by their multi-stemmed form, but the wood is also beginning to acquire some of the characteristics of a wild wood, notably an accumulation of dead trees, which lie where they fall and gently decompose. The opposite bank of the gorge is also covered with native woodland and wherever you look you can see nothing but trees and woodland. For a moment you can believe you're in a primeval landscape, wooded from coast to coast. Then you catch a glimpse of the meadows at the foot of the opposite slope, or hear the voice of a holiday-maker wafting up from the cycle path below, and the illusion is broken.

Typically for an ancient wood on limestone, there's a wide range of tree species, including beech. Parts of the wood haven't been touched since 1870 and these are full of big, old trees. Other parts were felled in the early 1940s and these have regrown with a strong coppice structure. The topography is also varied. The lower part of the wood, beside the river, is very steep, with patches of vertical cliff. The middle and upper slopes are gentler and on the upper slopes the soil becomes thinner.

The lower slopes make a dramatic landscape. The tallest ash trees I've ever seen reach up to the sky, drawn up by the cliffs that deny them light on one side. With such a length of clean, branchless bole they look like trees from a tropical rain forest. The steep slope gives them shaky foundations and their crowns grow away from the cliff, making them one-sided and unbalanced. Every now and then they come crashing down and you can see them lying there like giants slain in a battle with the gods. So this part of the wood is open-canopied, dynamic and full of shrubs and young trees. It's not the sort of place where beech would ever dominate. Frequent disruption gives the advantage to pioneers.

By contrast, the rest of the wood seems to be just the sort of stable environment where the contest of shading would be played out to the very end, with beech the winner. At least that's how it looked during the first three decades after the wood became a nature reserve. Then came the drought of 1976. In the old-growth part of the wood the big, old beeches were hard hit on the thin soil of the upper slopes. Some died, others weakened and died over the next few years and the survivors grew very slowly. Moderate-sized gaps appeared which allowed other trees to grow, particularly oak. Meanwhile on the thicker soil of the middle slopes the canopy stayed intact.

Of course beech was still there on the upper slopes, still ready and able to produce seed for a new generation which would one day make the drought of '76 seem like no more than a blip in the steady march towards its destiny. Beech reproduction comes in pulses at intervals of five to fifteen years. Some ten years after the drought one of these pulses of regeneration had grown into saplings about a metre tall and showed every sign of being the canopy trees of the future. Then there was a population explosion of voles, which love to eat the bark of young trees. All the young beeches were killed. Although other species were hard hit too, this episode put off the dominance of beech by a generation. The 'inevitable' destiny of beech to dominate began to seem more doubtful.

Meanwhile the part of the wood that had been felled in the 1940s had developed a mixed structure. The felled trees had regrown in multi-stemmed form. Some had not been felled and these now formed an over-storey of big single-stemmed trees. There were also young single-stemmed trees that had got started at the time of the felling. By the 1980s beech and ash were becoming the dominant species. But 1983 was a particularly bad year for grey squirrels. Beech is one of their favourite trees and they stripped the bark of most of them in this part of the wood, killing their leading shoots. The beeches were reduced from potential dominants to understorey bushes. This left the way clear for ash, which squirrels don't touch, to become the dominant species in the current generation of trees.

So Lady Park Wood today is a patchwork of different stands with a variety of structure and species that shows no sign of becoming more uniform with time. It's not a natural wood. Some of the influences on its present condition are human-made, such as the fellings of the 1940s and the introduction of grey squirrels. But others are wholly natural and they serve to illustrate how the simple vision of a steady march towards climax is in practice disrupted by a whole series of accidents. We can imagine a purely natural wood as being a dynamic ecosystem with frequent change as the only constant.

REVERSE SUCCESSION

Upland Woods

Woodland can be grubbed up and turned into arable or grassland but much more often succession is reversed by excessive grazing in woods. This can happen anywhere but it's most common in the uplands of Wales, northern England and Scotland. In the past these woods were valuable as sources of firewood, timber, or oak bark for tanning and they were carefully preserved. They would also occasionally be used as winter shelter for cattle and sheep but at a level that didn't interfere with the ability of the wood to reproduce itself. Now even the function of winter shelter is less important as more animals are kept indoors or trucked off to lowland areas for the colder months. It's no longer worth repairing the fences, hedges or walls that once restricted the animals' access. Now the woods are open to the surrounding grassland and grazed along with it. In time this turns woodland into grassland.

The first part of the wood to go is the ground layer. Woodland herbs aren't tolerant of grazing or trampling. If the wood has a dense canopy they will be replaced by bare soil. If more light reaches the ground they will be replaced by grasses, which tolerate both. The shrub layer is next. Shrubs are difficult to kill by browsing alone but in a wood they have the added stress of shade and the combination is lethal. Any saplings will be swept away with the shrub layer and once this happens the wood is dying. The existing trees can live out their lives but as long as grazing continues they can't reproduce. By this stage the value of the wood as shelter is greatly reduced. It will still be a warmer place on a frosty night, as the canopy acts like a blanket that reflects back the warmth of the ground and of the sheltering animals themselves. But when the wind blows it whistles through the bare trunks of the trees, funnelled between the canopy and the ground. The trees may survive for a long time like this. A sadly common sight in the uplands is a windswept wood of gnarled oaks standing in a sea of short grass that merges seamlessly with the surrounding pastures. Fortunately, fencing out the animals can bring the wood back to life and there are grants available for doing this.

Nature Conservation

Sometimes reverse succession is carried out intentionally by nature conser-vationists. This may seem strange. If woodland is the natural vegetation of this country surely letting trees grow wherever they will is good for biodiversity? But it's not necessarily so. As we've already seen, a new wood is very low in biodiversity. A semi-natural grassland, on the other hand, can be home to a whole range of sun-loving wildflowers and insects, all of which will be lost if a new wood springs up there. Like woodland, grassland can acquire great biodiversity if it's been grassland for a long time.

Semi-natural grasslands are very rare now and unfortunately they are often just the ones that are allowed to succeed to woodland, as they are usually in places that are difficult to farm intensively, such as steep slopes. In some

Native ponies play a part in bringing former plantation back to semi-natural grassland. Note the drawn-up shape of the surviving tree. Dundon Beacon, Somerset.

places conifers have been planted on semi-natural grassland for much the same economic reasons. There's a clear gain to biodiversity from removing the young woodland or plantation and allowing the diverse grassland to reassert itself. Seeds and bulbs of many wild flowers can remain viable in the soil for decades and sprout again when the sunlight returns. Sometimes there are also odd corners of grassland left among the self-sown woodland, or along the rides in a plantation, and these too can recolonise the newly exposed ground when the trees are taken away.

Removing the trees is straightforward enough but getting back from the scrub stage to grassland can be more difficult. Without the added stress of shade the shrubs are hard to kill by grazing alone. Also, the soil may be full of the seeds and suckers of recently removed shrubs, and there's plenty of bare ground for these to germinate in. A combination of grazing and topping can do the trick. But on a cleared plantation site the ground may be too rough for topping, especially if the land was 'ploughed' before planting (see page 126) or if the trees were grubbed out rather than merely felled. Another problem is that grazing which is intensive enough to prevent shrubs from growing may be too much for the wild plants that are the object of the whole exercise. Both of these factors operate at Powerstock Common in Dorset, where nature conservationists are trying to bring back former semi-natural grasslands. It's a large and complex nature reserve with a great diversity of habitats, including patches of cleared conifers and ancient woodland. The pride and joy of the grassland that is re-establishing in the wake of the conifers is the devil's-bit scabious. It's quite a rare wildflower and it's also the sole food plant of the marsh fritillary butterfly. Since the plant can't stand heavy grazing only a few cattle are kept on the reserve, not enough to prevent the growth of gorse where conifers have been grubbed out.

Some of the other patches of conifer were cleared by volunteers when the trees were still small enough to cut by hand. There were some self-sown oak saplings among the conifers, and the volunteers insisted on leaving them. The oak has an almost sacred status in the hearts of many people who care about nature. The professional conservationists would have much preferred to clear away all the trees but it's hard to argue with people who are doing the job for free out of their own good will. Those little oaks, released from the competition of the surrounding conifers, have grown tall and wide. Already after only a few years their canopies are reaching out towards each other and in some parts they will surely meet before long.

It seems to me that the reserve is slowly heading towards a future as a wood pasture. The cattle have access to the woodland as well as the cleared ground. In the long run they'll open out the lower layers of the former coppice woods, leaving the mature trees more isolated. Meanwhile the supposedly open areas will become more wooded as the young oaks grow and the occasional new tree gets established among the gorse. This would make for a varied mosaic of more and less wooded patches, probably very rich in wildlife. But it will surely be quite different from what was envisioned in the management plan that was drawn up before the first conifer was cut. Nature conservation is not a precise science and landscapes can have a will of their own.

CASE STUDY: JOSH'S WOOD

Although we can't live long enough to see a single place pass through all the stages of succession, sometimes we can see several different stages in one place simultaneously. Over the past few years I've got to know just such a place at Ragmans Farm in Gloucestershire, where I do much of my teaching. It centres on a little wood, only some hundred metres long by fifty wide, known as Josh's Wood. In the wood itself and its immediate surroundings you can see various types of woodland, scrub and grassland, all representing different processes of succession.

The wood itself is clearly ancient. Its trees are ash, maple, hazel, hawthorn, spindle, elder and wych elm. There are a few weak brambles and the wildflowers include wood anemone, lesser celandine, dog's mercury and bluebell. Such diversity of trees and the presence of the woodland wildflowers are sure signs of great age, as is the absence of ivy in the interior of the wood. You can clearly see why this little patch has long been left as woodland: it's the steepest part of the slope and also very stony.

The hedge on the eastern boundary of the wood shows signs of being even older than the wood itself. It contains three massive coppice stools of small-leaved lime, a tree that is absent from the rest of the wood. Lime is an extreme stayer with very little ability to colonise new woodland. It's most often found in woods that have never been cleared from the days of the wildwood to this. Its presence in the hedge suggests that the hedge is a relic of the wildwood rather than one that has grown up on open ground at some time in the past.

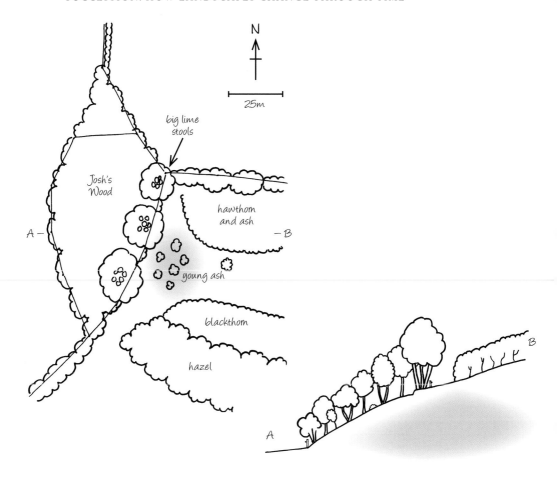

The absence of lime in the rest of the wood suggests that at some point in history the wood disappeared for a while. Given the stoniness of the ground this would have been due to grazing rather than deliberate clearing for cultivation. The diversity of trees and wildflowers in it suggests that it re-established itself a long time ago, in the Middle Ages or before.

The hazel coppice to the south-east of Josh's Wood is also on a stony slope. It has a similar range of wild flowers to the wood but the trees are much less diverse, being almost entirely hazel with a few wild cherry and ash. It's likely that hazel has been encouraged here at the expense of other trees. Historically hazel was an important tree in the rural economy. The slender coppiced wands were ideal for making hurdles and the wooden staples known as spars that are used in thatching. It's many decades now since the coppice was cut and the stems have grown thick and crooked. It's a magical place, floored with mossy stones. The occasional wild cherry tree, bright in its shiny striped bark, stands out among the gnarled hazel like a princess among peasants.

Growing out from the north edge of the hazel coppice is a dense thicket of blackthorn. Even if you didn't know that blackthorn is a pioneer shrub you could tell this thicket is a recent development. The boundary between the hazel and

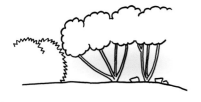

the blackthorn gives the clue. While the hazel stems in the middle of the coppice grow up more or less perpendicular, those on the margin with the blackthorn grow out at a low angle. The perpendicular ones grew up surrounded by other trees on all sides and needed to go straight up to get at the sunlight. The low-angled ones were on an edge and reached out into the field where there was no competition.

Opposite the blackthorn a similar thicket has grown out from the hedge to the north, but this one is composed of hawthorn and ash. Chance must surely have played a part in this segregation between blackthorn on one side and hawthorn and ash on the other. There's no logical reason for it that I can see. In the decade I've been working at Ragmans I've seen the thicket of hawthorn and ash develop. My earliest note describes it as 'hawthorn with a few ash' but today it looks like a young ash wood with a hawthorn understorey. Over the short time I've known it you could say it's stepped over the boundary from scrub to young woodland.

These thickets, both blackthorn and hawthorn-ash, are very young. Their lives are hardly to be measured in decades, compared to the centuries that differentiate the ancient woodland from the even older hedge. Their youth is evident in the small number of woody species and the lack of herbaceous plants beneath. The grassland plants have all been shaded out and the wildflowers of the ancient woodland have not yet started to move in.

Between the two thickets, on the eastern side of the wood, is an area that has succeeded from grassland even more recently. I've also seen this area change. At first it was a fairly thick stand of bramble and bracken with a few ash saplings just raising their heads above it. Now it's a group of young ash trees with a few wisps of bracken and bramble beneath, weakened both by shade and by the trampling of cattle.

These three patches of young woodland – the blackthorn, the hawthorn and ash and the pure ash – have established themselves on three sides of an old pasture. The grassland that is left in the middle of them is very diverse, with a full suite of typical limestone wildflowers. The whole area is a classic example of the most diverse grassland being the first to scrub up. It contrasts strongly with the grass field on the downhill side, to the west of the wood, which is much less diverse, much more productive and lacks any scrub. The main reason for this is simply that the two fields are in different ownership. The ancient hedge with the limes in it is the boundary between Ragmans Farm to the west and Glasp Farm to the east. Ragmans, although an organic farm, is in the business of food production while Glasp is more of an informal nature reserve. The Ragmans field has been grazed more intensively than the Glasp field, with regular manuring and topping.

So succession is arrested at the grassland stage on one of these fields while on the other it's going ahead. Meanwhile, in part of Josh's Wood succession has gone into reverse. This is the northern part, which is unfenced and open to the cattle that graze the Ragmans field to the west. It's a very small area of woodland so when the cattle come and take shelter in it they have a heavy impact.

This is most obvious in the ground layer, which is mostly bare earth. Almost the only survivor among the woodland wildflowers is the lesser celandine, which is particularly resistant to soil compaction and trampling. (See page 211.) In the spring it makes a cheerful splash of yellow against the dull brown of bare soil and stones. At present this small piece of unfenced woodland is a benefit to the welfare of the animals in the field but in the long term, if it stays unfenced, it will disappear.

Josh's Wood and its surroundings are a microcosm not only of succession but of the eternal dance between human and natural factors that goes to make up the landscape. The underlying rocks have fixed the location of the wood. The steep slope it stands on is caused by the outcrop of a hard limestone over the softer shale to the west. Within this framework determined by the rocks, the idiosyncrasies of human behaviour have had free play. The two landowners have very different approaches to the land. All the examples of forward succession are on Glasp and the single example of reverse succession is on Ragmans.

In that sense the most important feature in this little landscape is the ancient hedge that marks the boundary between the two farms. I wonder how long it has been a property boundary. Boundaries are often the longest-lived of all human features in the landscape. Could it even have been the boundary between two farms down all the long ages since the fields were first carved out of the wildwood?

8

Trees as Individuals

ONLY SOME of the difference between the shape of one tree and another is down to their species. External influences can have at least as much effect, if not more. Coppicing makes a tree that would normally have a single stem grow with multiple stems, so there's more difference between a maiden ash and a coppiced one than there is between a maiden ash and a maiden maple. Other ways a tree's form can be moulded by its environment include: browsing, wind flagging, competition from other trees and pollarding.

FREE-GROWN TREES

These are trees that grow far enough from others so that their branches don't touch. This doesn't mean that they aren't affected by any external influences at all. In fact trees that have grown completely undisturbed are rare, rare enough for a colleague to tell me in some detail about some examples he found.

> Phil Corbett tells me he knows three apple trees, grown from discarded cores, in a place with full light, no grazing and no water stress. They are very wide and low, with branches at the edge of the crown going up vertically 'like osiers'. The crowns are very dense. The only competition is from herbaceous plants and he sees this shape as a competitive response. Some nearby oaks are growing in a similar shape.
>
> A thought: there's no such thing as the natural shape of a plant. A tree grown entirely without competition or browsing and with no climatic stress will adopt a certain shape. But that's not a natural situation.

If Phil was right, even those apple trees were not entirely free of external influence. He reckoned their wide, low form, which would shade out the herbaceous plants below, was a response to the only possible source of competition. On the other hand it may just be that a tree with nothing to interfere with the growth of its branches will assume a more or less hemispherical shape with its branches reaching the ground on every side. I once saw an oak in a churchyard that had grown without any significant influence on its shape and it was almost hemispherical, though slightly taller than it was wide. It was a fairly young oak and the more upright shape compared to Phil's apples may be a sign of immaturity.

Age

Younger trees tend to have a more upright shape than older ones. Many species have a conical shape when young which rounds out to a broad, spreading crown when mature. Most conifers do this. The familiar Christmas-tree shape indicates that they are still growing. Because timber trees are harvested before they stop growing you rarely see a mature one, except for the native Scots pine. The broad crown of a mature pine, shaped like passing clouds, contrasts with the tight cone of the young tree. Among the broadleaves, alder and ash are two that follow this pattern. The drawing shows three ashes that I sketched one day along the same hedgerow. Notice how the shape changes with age.

Another sign of age is a stag-headed tree, one with some dead branches among the living ones. It gives the tree a sickly look and some people think a stag-headed tree is dying. But oaks can live happily for hundreds of years like this. In most cases it probably results from the tree's response to a serious drought in years gone by. Shutting down some of its branches by allowing them to die reduces a tree's need for water, enabling it to survive a drought which otherwise might be fatal. Oaks aren't the only trees to do this. Ashes do it too but the evidence quickly disappears because ash wood soon rots away when it dies. When an oak branch dies, the bark and the outer layer of wood rot away fairly quickly but the heartwood at the centre of the branch will last for a hundred years.

The outer layer is the sapwood, the living wood that moves water from the roots to the rest of the tree. The heartwood consists of dead wood and the tree uses it as a depository for unwanted waste products of metabolism. When a branch or the whole tree dies these waste products act as a preservative and the heartwood is slow to decompose. But while it's still alive sapwood is equipped to defend itself from rot while the heartwood eventually succumbs and many old trees become hollow. Being hollow is no disadvantage to an old oak. A healing layer is formed on the inside of the shell of sapwood and this hard layer, though thin, is actually stronger than the solid mass of the heartwood. Hollow trees withstood the great storm of 1987 better than solid ones.

Oaks are normally felled for timber at around a hundred and fifty years old, when the vigorous growth of their youth starts to slow down. But they can live for hundreds of years more, just as we can live for several decades after we stop growing in our late teens. It's during these centuries of middle age and decline that oaks become stag-antlered, rotten and hollow. Although by now they are useless for timber, from a biodiversity point of view they are priceless. There are many insects and other invertebrates that are completely dependent on this decaying wood and many of these creatures are now rare and endangered. The occasional old tree may still have a value for forestry, because such a richness of invertebrates will support a good population of woodpeckers and other predators, that can then move on to the crop trees and control any pests which are there.

The oldest trees are not necessarily the biggest ones, though they do usually have very thick trunks. As a rule of thumb you can estimate the age of a free-grown oak by measuring the circumference of its trunk in inches and taking

Oliver Rackham inspects a very old tree.

each inch (2.5cm) to represent one year. For smaller trees, like crab apple and hawthorn, half an inch represents a year, as it does for woodland trees, whose growth is slowed by competition with each other. But this is only a rough guide. For big old oaks it more often underestimates the age than overestimates it, as there are more things that can slow down a tree's growth than speed it up. These two pollard oaks, both growing at Middlemarsh in Dorset, have trunks of the same circumference. But, by Oliver Rackham's estimation, the larger one is about five hundred years old and the smaller one a thousand. The large one, with its tall, wide crown can clearly put on plenty of growth each year and probably has done so throughout its life. The small one has a much smaller crown and there's no sign that it ever had bigger branches, so its annual growth rate has probably always been less.

It's the same with young trees: you can't assume that the smallest ones are younger than their larger neighbours. A tree in a wood only has to fall slightly behind its neighbours for them to start suppressing it. Usually this results in the death of the smaller tree, but if it still receives enough light it can stay alive as a virtual bonsai. This can happen both in semi-natural woods and in plantations but it's much more obvious in a plantation because you know that all the crop trees are the same age. I once saw a Norway spruce that had the misfortune to be planted in the compacted soil of a tractor rut. It hardly came up to my knee while the surrounding trees were a good five metres tall.

Microclimate

Severe microclimates can also keep trees small. Those contorted little oaks you often see on hilltops and mountainsides are often far older than you might think, especially where the soil is thin and poor. Salty sea winds are the worst climatic conditions for trees. They can prune them into fantastic shapes that hug the ground. The most extreme windflagged tree I ever saw was an apple.

Oswald Beach, Dorset

On the path down to the beach I saw an apple tree, probably grown from a discarded core.

The seaward side was a hedgehog of dead vertical twigs with a few leaves growing under it. The lee side was full of leaves and blossom. Nearby was an elder, very similar but more upright.

The 'hedgehogs' on these two trees, although made up of dead material, were functional parts of the plants. It was the shelter they gave that enabled the rest of the tree to bear leaves and blossom. The fact that the elder was more upright may have reflected some subtle difference in microclimate or that elder is a tougher tree than the domestic apple. These were extreme examples of wind flagging, which is a great aid to reading the microclimate and has been described in Chapter 4. (See pages 53-54.) Most free-grown trees show some sign of wind flagging, however slight.

Browsing

Another influence that is almost universal on trees grown out in the open is browsing. Any tree growing in a field will have a browse line on it, with nothing but bare trunk up to the height to which the farm animals can reach.

The classic parkland tree has a rigid browse line at the base of its crown, the height of the line depending on the kind of animals grazing the park. Horses reach higher than cattle, which in turn reach higher than fallow deer, the usual deer of parks. Above the browse line parkland trees have no restriction on their shape and the influence of the tree's species shows up more clearly than it does in a wood. The towering column of common lime contrasts strongly with the broad sweep of beech, while the gangling ash can often be distinguished at a distance from the more compact walnut. But these species differences are

This field was shut up for hay when the picture was taken but the browse line on the trees shows it is grazed from time to time as well.

less than that between free-grown and woodland trees, regardless of species. While the woodland tree typically has a tall, branchless trunk, the open-grown tree has a shorter, thicker trunk and big branches growing both high and low.

Compare the parkland tree (left) with the trees in the sketch on the right, which I came upon one spring day in a field in Wiltshire.

It was obvious that they hadn't grown up as the isolated parkland trees that they now are. Their form shows that they spent most of their lives in a wood, competing with close neighbours to get at the light above, and the wood had been cleared in recent years.

A completely different browsing effect can sometimes be seen on evergreens. Where the deer population is very high, young conifers can be restricted to a cylindrical shape by constant browsing. But when a free-grown holly is browsed by ponies it develops a curious skittle shape. The unbrowsed tuft at the top is presumably out of reach and below that browsing is more intense at head level than lower down. I've seen something similar on gorse bushes in the New Forest. The rounded part of the bush is rather more spherical than in the case of the holly, perhaps reflecting the natural shape of gorse bushes.

A skittle-shaped holly.

Hedgerow Trees

Traditionally, free-grown trees in hedgerows were sometimes pruned for timber: removing the lower branches gives a longer length of straight, knot-free timber that can be sawn up into planks. Pruning needs to be started when the tree is young and done regularly every few years. But people have rather lost the habit of pruning and unskilled attempts can have comical results, like the two trees on the next page. They are sycamores that grow in a hedgerow near where I live. When they were pruned a few years ago they had far too much taken off at once, leaving crowns that were

This hedge has recently been laid. The shape of the tree indicates that the hedge had been allowed to grow very tall before it was laid.

too small for the amount of energy in their roots and trunks. All that excess energy burst out in regrowth of the side branches. The tree on the left is the more extreme case. The crown that was left was ridiculously small and the regrown branches are now actually longer than the uncut ones.

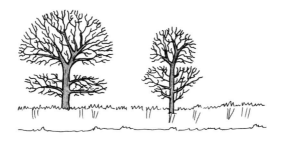

WOODLAND TREES

Single Stemmed

Much the more common way to grow timber is to put the trees together in a wood so they draw each other up. The job of the pruner's saw is done by the shade each tree casts on its neighbours. They all reach up to the light above and their lower branches are progressively suppressed as the trees grow, giving tall, straight trunks like the beeches in the picture on the left. The single oak on the right has grown up on its own, with no neighbours to interfere with the growth of its branches. It may be rich in wildlife and a delight to the eye but it wouldn't interest a timber merchant.

These beeches have been grown close together and have tall, branch-free trunks that will make good timber.

This oak is a fine tree in many ways but it has grown up with space around it, which has made it branchy and it has no value for timber.

Drawing up doesn't necessarily mean that all the trees in the wood will be uniform. It may do in a well-managed single-species plantation but in an unmanaged and mixed woodland there will be a variety of tree shapes. This is partly due to irregular spacing and occasional gaps but also to the differences between species.

Yew is a very shade-tolerant tree that hardly gets drawn up at all. The only other tree which comes close to it is the holly, which sometimes gets drawn up and sometimes doesn't. In some parts of the New Forest you can see yew and holly forming an understorey, indifferent to the shade while the deciduous trees all around them reach up to the light above. Their shade tolerance may be partly due to being evergreen, which means they can make use of spring sunshine before the deciduous trees come into leaf.

The yew in
Lady Park Wood.

The oak in
the New Forest.

Ash, wych elm and wild
cherry in the Top Wood
at Ragmans Farm.

As a general rule the most shade-tolerant trees also cast the densest shade, and that's certainly true of the yew. The sketch above left shows a group of trees in Lady Park Wood. The remorseless outward growth of the yew has caused the young oaks and beeches to lean away from the deep shade of its boughs till now they form a cup around it.

The most extreme case I've seen of a tree being bent by competition was an oak in the New Forest, so crowded by a yew and a couple of hollies that it grew almost horizontally. It looked perfectly healthy despite its bizarre shape. On the upper side of the elbow where its trunk changes direction there's a small scar like a branch scar. This marks the position of the original trunk. When the dense shade cast by its neighbours suppressed the trunk a branch took over and eventually became the horizontal trunk we see today.

Even where trees are all drawn up more or less vertically there can be differences between the forms of different species. The less shade-tolerant ones grow straightest and are less likely to have any lower branches. The Top Wood at Ragmans Farm contains ash, wych elm and wild cherry. The ash and wych elm both have smooth boles leading up to a crown of upward-reaching branches. The only lower branches that remain are occasional big forks. These lower branches are more frequent on the wych elms, which are more shade-tolerant trees than the ash. Wild cherry has a different branching habit altogether, as the sketch shows. When wych elm and ash branches die they rot away leaving little or no trace on the face of the trunk. But dead cherry branches stay there. Wild cherry can make valuable timber but to get the highest quality the trees need to be pruned even if they are grown close together. Otherwise the wood of the trunk grows round those dead branches, leaving deadwood knots that will fall out and leave a hole in the timber.

Trees can get excessively drawn up by their neighbours. Sometimes a young tree is so drawn up that it only stays standing due to the support of its neighbours. If any of them are lost, by felling or some accident, it will bend over into a curve with its crown brushing the ground. If it survives like this, vertical branches will

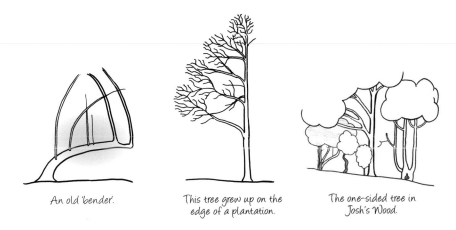

| An old 'bender'. | This tree grew up on the edge of a plantation. | The one-sided tree in Josh's Wood. |

sprout up from the curved trunk and it may go on living in this shape for many years. I've seen this happen to pussy willows and ash but no doubt it can happen to other trees too. I call trees like this 'benders'.

Trees that grow on the edge of a wood are hybrids between free-grown and woodland trees: branchy on the sunny side and clean-stemmed on the shady side. Sometimes you come across a tree with this form standing on its own with space all around it. Then you can deduce that the neighbouring trees that made it that shape have been felled. Sometimes you can find the tell-tale stumps among the undergrowth. The tree in the sketch above centre stands on the side of a ride in a large plantation. The compartment behind it has been felled. Apparently the forester decided to leave this one to grow on and become a veteran.

A tree can grow one-sided for other reasons apart from being on an edge. In a wood on a steep slope almost every tree will have more branches on its downhill side, as the tree above it shades its stem and the one below doesn't. In a mixed wood a tree can grow one-sided if there's a big difference in the size of the trees on either side of it. The sketch above right shows an example of this from Josh's Wood. If all the trees around the large one in the middle were felled it would look very much as though it used to be on the edge.

Coppice

A tree which has been coppiced has multiple stems. Hazel grows in a multi-stemmed form naturally, so it can be hard to tell if an individual hazel has been coppiced or not. But for any other tree it's a virtually certain sign of coppicing. The shape of a maiden tree, especially a young one that is growing vigorously, is ruled by the leading shoot. It produces a hormone that flows down by gravity and slightly inhibits the growth of lower shoots. This is known as apical dominance and it's the reason why many trees have a conical shape while they are still growing in height. When the tree is cut down there's no longer a leading shoot. Instead there's a ring of dormant buds around the circumference of the stump, between the wood and the bark. Now that these are the highest buds in the tree they are all equally free to sprout and grow. The resulting multi-stemmed tree is known as a coppice stool.

Almost all broad-leaved trees respond to felling like this. Beech is a bit of an exception. Some beeches regrow well enough after coppicing but others grow weakly or even die. Suckering trees, such as wild cherry and aspen, rarely coppice. Felling the tree stimulates a mass of suckers to sprout from the roots but the stump usually dies. Very few conifers will coppice and the one or two exceptions aren't important in the landscape. The produce of coppicing is a crop of poles, which can be used as fuel or for various crafts. This is in contrast with single-stemmed trees which produce timber, a single log which can be sawn up to yield planks, beams and so on.

The stems on a coppice stool follow nature's typical pattern of regeneration: a large number of offspring followed by a high death rate. A cut stump usually produces a mass of little shoots in the first year but by the second year as many as half of them may have died by mutual competition. The rate of loss slows down after that but a tree that started out with a hundred shoots may end up with a dozen by the time it's ready to be felled again. The number of stems varies, depending on the species of tree and the length of the coppice rotation, that is the number of years between fellings. Hazel is both naturally multi-stemmed and cut on a short rotation of about seven years. When coppiced it produces a large number of thin wands that are just right for making hurdles and thatching spars. All other woodland trees are naturally single-stemmed and are cut on a longer rotation than hazel, so they have fewer stems by the time felling time comes round.

These days very few woods are still coppiced and the stools you're most likely to see are old, overgrown ones. This big ash stool is typical.

Eventually old stools can be thinned down to a single stem, but when this happens there's usually a tell-tale sign of its

An old ash stool. Note the signs of former stems which have died and rotted away.

origin as a coppice stem. This may be a bulge at the base of the tree, the vestigial stump of another stem or a curved base to the trunk, known as a swept butt.

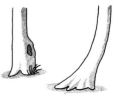

signs of former coppicing.

Oak was often coppiced right down to ground level and the stems grow up from the roots rather than from an above-ground stump, so the trees can look deceptively like maidens. But if you look carefully you may be able to see that they stand in small groups and that all the members of each group strongly resemble each other.

A swept butt on its own doesn't necessarily indicate that the tree was once coppiced. Trees can also acquire this form in a wood on an unstable hillside where the soil creeps downhill. Nor do all coppice stems have swept butts. Whether they do or not mainly depends on how close together the stools are. If they are closer together the stems are drawn up like the trees in a timber plantation. Swept butts are a sign of understocking.

In its lifetime a coppice stool will be cut many times. In fact coppicing can greatly increase a tree's lifespan because every time it's cut down its above-ground parts are rejuvenated. An ash tree can live for up to two hundred years as a maiden but as a coppice stool it can live for a thousand. A very rough guide to the age of an old stool can be had by measuring its diameter. An ash stool four feet wide may be four hundred years old and one of eight feet wide, eight hundred. (1ft=30cm.) On a waterlogged or infertile soil they will be much smaller for their age. This rule of thumb probably holds true for lime, oak and hazel as well. Maple stools grow a bit faster and sycamore and chestnut perhaps twice as fast. The age of the oldest stool in a wood gives the minimum age of the wood itself.

There are three distinct time cycles in the life of a coppice stool: the annual cycle, the coppice rotation and the lifespan of the stool. In an actively coppiced wood you may come across a stool whose roots and stump are several hundred years old while its stems are nothing but slender young wands. As the centuries go by the stump grows wider and wider, producing more and more stems. Eventually the centre of the stump breaks up and the individual stems become isolated, often with little clue to their common origin.

This big oak stool which I saw in a field in Pembrokeshire gives some clues to the history of the little valley where it grows. It almost certainly started life in a wood because trees in fields are never coppiced as the regrowth would be mercilessly browsed by grazing animals. It could possibly have grown in a hedge, but there's no sign of a former hedgebank under it and in this area hedges are grown on substantial banks. The wood it grew in must have been an old one because the width of the stump indicates that the tree was coppiced many times in its life. But the wide spread of its branches shows that for most of the time since its last coppicing it has grown out in the open, so the rest of the wood must have disappeared not long after it was last cut. The size of its stems suggests that this was over a hundred years ago.

Standards

In a traditional coppice wood there are almost always some trees that haven't been coppiced: scattered among the coppice stools are a number of single-stemmed trees, originally grown for timber and known as standards. Their form is quite distinct from that of the trees in a wood that is grown purely for timber because they are not close enough together to draw each other up. They are drawn up by the coppiced trees but as these never reach the same height as a timber tree only the lower part of a standard's trunk is free of branches. The height of branch-free trunk depends on the length of the coppice rotation. The longer it is the taller the coppice grows and the higher the clean trunk. Above that the branches grow out, often at a low angle, unimpeded by any competition. The standard in the sketch below left is growing in a mainly hazel wood that is still coppiced. Note the short length of clean trunk. This is an outsize tree and would have been harvested for timber long ago in a traditional coppice wood. (See drawing on page 118.)

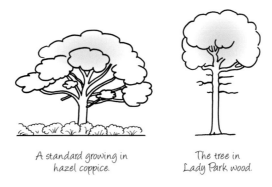

A standard growing in
hazel coppice.

The tree in
Lady Park wood.

In a neglected coppice wood the coppice will have grown up taller than it used to. The lower branches of the standard trees, which were formed when the coppice was shorter, are now shaded by this new growth and they often die. As the standards are usually oaks the dead branches can stay on the tree for a long time, preserving something of the history of the wood in the form of the old trees. The example in the sketch above right comes from Lady Park Wood.

POLLARDS

Pollarding a tree means coppicing it some two or three metres up the trunk instead of at ground level. This makes it possible to get regular crops of poles in a place where there are grazing animals. A large proportion of trees growing in hedgerows and wood pasture used to be pollarded. But pollards are not normally found in coppice woodland, except on the bank that encloses the wood.

Those brush-headed willows that you see along riverbanks are pollards. They used to be pollarded every three years to get thin sticks for making thatching spars. Crack and white willows are the species used for pollarding. These are larger trees than the rather shrubby pussy willows. They have narrow leaves and lack the catkins that turn from silver to gold in the spring and give the pussy willows their name. But when the crown of a white willow pollard gently bends to a summer breeze the silver undersides of its leaves sparkle in the sunshine like a shoal of little fish in the current of the wind.

Not much pollarding is done these days. Most of the old pollard trees are left to quietly grow on, their branches becoming fewer and larger over the years, like the stems on an old coppice stool. Eventually they reach a stable condition with just a few large branches and will live on like this with little change. Neglected pollards are quite easy to recognise once you get your eye in. Usually all the branches start at the same height above the ground and there's often a ring of bosses at that point where previous generations of branches have grown and been cut.

A maiden tree.

An old pollard.

Sometimes this basic pattern is confused because a tree has been pollarded at two different heights. Lower down you can see the point where it was first pollarded and up above you can see where the big old branches have been pollarded individually at a later date. This indicates that pollarding was stopped and then restarted. Repollarding the thick old branches at their base would have been too much of a shock to the tree and might have killed it.

A variant on the pollard is the stub. This is a tree that has been pollarded low down, usually at about chest height. Stubs are often boundary markers, especially inside a wood. Where all the other trees are either coppice or standards a stub makes an unambiguous landmark. In a wood there's no need to make it as high as a pollard, just high enough to stand out.

The tree that is most often still regularly pollarded is willow. There's still a small demand for thatching spars and willows are also sometimes pollarded just to keep them in good condition. Willows can sometimes reduce their branches to a stable few as other trees do. But willow wood is both fast growing and weak, so the weight of the crown often becomes too much for the tree and the branches break off. This not only looks untidy and gets in the way of farm work but the resulting wound lets in rot and this can kill the tree.

A riverside willow pollard.

Old pollards can grow into fantastic shapes.

This magnificent
old willow needs
repollarding soon,
or its branches
will start to
break off.

Pollarding, like coppicing, increases the life of trees by constantly rejuvenating them. If you see a large maiden tree and a smaller pollard, don't assume the maiden is older. A maiden oak may live for five hundred years but a pollarded one can reach a thousand or more.

Old pollards often grow into fantastic shapes and they can be among the most beautiful of trees. They are also usually rich in the dead wood habitats that are so valuable to invertebrate life. The bole frequently rots and becomes hollow while the tree is still producing regular crops of fresh young poles. In the crown a miniature ecosystem develops. Organic debris collects on the top of the bole and turns into humus-rich soil, where plants, including other trees and shrubs, take root and grow. Wild roses and brambles are common in willows, which is a nuisance when you come to pollard the tree. But elder, hawthorn and even ash are fairly frequent too.

The most extraordinary example of this kind of relationship that I've seen was a sycamore growing in an ash. Many years ago the ash had been a pollard and the sycamore grew in its crown. Eventually the sycamore's roots found their way down, through the rotten wood in the heart of the pollard, to the ground. Now the pollard's trunk is hollow and the sycamore fills it. The sycamore is growing much more vigorously than the old ash and one day it will surely supersede it.

114

9

Woodland

Location

A wood is part of the wider landscape and a key question is why it's located where it is. If it's an ancient wood the answer is usually that the land is unsuitable for farming. It's not that woodland was less valuable than farmland in the past. In fact medieval records show that it was often worth more than arable land. It's that trees, being the native vegetation, are much less demanding than other crops. So in a farmed landscape woods are not sited where trees grow well but where farming is difficult. In hilly regions woods are usually sited on the steepest slopes, and this is the commonest pattern you can see in most parts of the country.

Exceptions are made due to soil fertility. In chalk country, for instance, the escarpments are usually grassy sheepwalks while some of the hilltops are covered in a drift deposit called clay-with-flints. The abundant flints make for a

A hilltop wood in chalk country almost always indicates clay-with-flints. Note the steep slope scrubbing up in the foreground. Salt Hill, Hampshire.

soil which is acid and very difficult to cultivate, and these areas are usually left as woodland, reversing the usual pattern.

In flatter country ancient woods are often sited on poorly-drained land. This doesn't mean alongside the rivers, where the land was valuable meadow in medieval times, but on flat clay land, often a low plateau well away from any river. There's also a tendency for woods to be relatively far from villages, near the parish boundary. Woodland needs less frequent attention than fields so this placement made good sense in terms of people's time and energy. By no means did every parish have woodland. Those without it could get firewood from hedges but there was also a constant trade in wood.

In recent times woods have sprung up in places where other activity has declined. As grazing has lapsed on commons many of them have succeeded to woodland over the past couple of centuries, while on enclosed farmland steep fields are usually the first to be let go of. Conifer plantations tend to be on land that was cheap to buy. In lowland areas this means they have replaced heath and ancient woodland, both of which had lost their traditional functions by the mid-twentieth century. In upland Britain, where all the land is unfavourable for farming, it can mean anywhere and often the choice of sites seems to be based more on the location of a landowner willing to sell some land for forestry than on any physical reason.

In farmed landscapes woods are discrete parcels of land with definite, permanent boundaries, but in the Highlands of Scotland they can be much more mobile. Also, in these harsh conditions they are found in places that are good for trees rather than ones that are bad for other things. The alternative land use here is not farmland but moorland, which is less demanding than trees rather than more so.

North Side of Loch Leven, Highland

There's much more regeneration of young trees outside the wood than within. Does this mean that woods change location cyclically? But the woods here seem to be sited predictably rather than randomly: a) on land too steep for intensive grazing, b) on the land which is best for trees, the burnsides and lower slopes.

In posing my question I assumed that Highland woods must behave in one of two ways: either they wander round the landscape at random or their location is determined by slope, soil and microclimate. In fact the answer is that both are true. The country is big enough and the woods few enough that they can migrate from one site to another while staying within a general area that favours trees. Birch pine and oak are all pioneers that regenerate better in the open than inside woods.

As in any other region, grazing pressure is less intense on the slopes than on the flat. What is different from the south is that the harsh climate and poor soil are limitations on tree growth. Rainfall is very high so soil drainage makes a significant difference. Slopes are better drained than flat ground and, contrary to expectation, the banks of a burn are usually well drained because the burn itself acts as a drain. The soil by a burn is also better supplied with mineral nutrients. (See pages 170-171.) In terms of microclimate, lower slopes are usually less exposed than upper ones and, although the burns may not carve deep valleys, even a little dip in the ground is a help to a seedling.

Stands

With the exception of the large-scale plantations of the uplands it's unusual to come across a tract of treed land that's the same all the way through. It may be partly semi-natural and partly plantation. If it's all plantation it will probably be made up of various compartments containing trees of different species or different ages. If it's semi-natural the tree species will probably vary from one part of the wood to another and there may be differences in the structure of the trees too, as in Lady Park Wood. (See pages 93-95.) There can be more variation within a single wood than there is between one wood and another, so the unit of observation is not so much the wood as the stand. A stand is a distinct part of a wood that differs from other parts in species, age or structure. It can be any size from a few square metres to many hectares. It can be the whole wood but this is unusual. One of the first questions to ask about any wood is how many stands there are and how they differ.

ANCIENT WOODS

The Wildwood

Although there is some debate about whether the wildwood was solid woodland or not, we have a good idea of what tree species it contained. We get this from distinctive pollen grains that have been preserved in permanently waterlogged places such as the mud at the bottom of ponds. In its most developed phase at the dawn of the Neolithic there were three broad regions, which for convenience we can call the Lowlands, the Uplands and the Highlands. These regions have some relevance for woodland right down to the present day and I'll use them throughout this chapter.

In the Lowland region the commonest tree was lime. Beech had arrived in Britain but still hadn't spread very far, so lime was the most extreme stayer. Oak, hazel, ash, elm and alder were also common and could be dominant in some places. In the Upland region oak and hazel were the commonest trees, probably with oak dominant on the poorer soils and hazel on the richer. The central Highlands were the stronghold of pine. To the north of this birch was the main tree, dwindling down to treeless tundra on the north coast and the outer isles.

highland
upland
lowland

The three regions of the wildwood.

This was the general picture but within it there was more complexity, with different species and mixes occupying all sorts of different soils and microclimates. In general there was, as there is now, a wider range of tree species in the softer south than in the harsher conditions of the north.

We can't be nearly so sure about the structure of the wildwood. Certainly there would have been a lot of dead wood and some very big trees indeed. But how did regeneration happen? Young trees need a break in the canopy in order to grow. Was this mainly a matter of individual trees dying of old age and leaving small gaps or were there more general disturbances? The great storm that struck the south-east of England in 1987 may give us a glimpse, however obscure, of the dynamics of the prehistoric woods.

When the storm came most people thought it was a disaster. Hundreds of years of tree growth destroyed in one night! In some places they rushed in with bulldozers to clear away the fallen trees and replant. This caused soil compaction and erosion and in some woods completely destroyed the ground vegetation, the woodland wildflowers. It turned ancient semi-natural woods into impoverished plantations, and it was completely unnecessary. In the woods that were left alone most of the uprooted trees survived quite happily in a horizontal position. Regrowth, both by seed and vegetatively from the fallen trees, was vigorous. The main exception was beech. In some places the dominance of beech was thrown back a generation while in others the new mix of trees was very similar to the old. The patches of windthrow varied greatly in size from half a hectare to a hundred, but in all they only amounted to a tenth of the ancient woodland in the path of the storm.

Storms as strong as that of 1987 come on average every two or three hundred years. Less violent ones that blow down fewer trees happen about once a decade. The effect is always patchy. Some places may not be touched by windthrow for a thousand years while others have been hit twice in three years. Nevertheless the average time interval isn't so different from the lifespan of trees. The wildwood may have been an irregular mosaic of patches, each blown down at a different time and each at a different stage of regrowth.

The Lowland Region

The woods first emerge into the light of history in the Middle Ages. By this time the wildwood had been gone for thousands of years and the typical wood in the Lowland region was an isolated coppice surrounded by farmland. The coppices

actively coppiced wood   neglected coppice wood

A semi-natural woodland in the lowland region. There are few obvious signs of former coppicing in this view, but the woodland wildflowers are the clue that it's an ancient wood. Honeycombe Wood, Dorset.

have a distinct three-layer structure. Topmost are the standard trees, which are almost always oaks and are grown for timber. Beneath them are the coppiced trees, harvested on a cycle of anything from five to twenty years. At ground level there are woodland wildflowers. These coppice woods were formed out of the wildwood simply by regular harvesting of the trees that were there. No trees were planted nor were less favoured species grubbed out. Many of these woods are still with us, though few of them are still coppiced.

Until quite recently these woods were thought of as oakwoods and people believed that the natural vegetation of the Lowland region was 'mixed oakwood'. Indeed the standard trees do make the most visual impact and they can make up a high proportion of the biomass in a wood. But they are a minority of the trees. In the days of the wildwood, oak was even more of a minority. Since then it has been deliberately favoured by generations of woodsmen. Being a naturally durable tree it was the best species for building, which was always the main use for standards.

Though the rise of oak is easy to explain the decline of lime is not. This is the native small-leaved lime, not the common lime, which is a modern hybrid. Once the commonest tree in the wildwood of the Lowland region, lime is now only found in a few limited areas. Where it does occur it's tough and competitive and often forms a pure stand in the coppice layer. Why such a tree has disappeared over most of its former range is a mystery. Ash, maple and hazel are now the commonest coppice trees in most of the Lowland region, while hornbeam is especially common in woods around London. Coppicing leads to a greater diversity of trees. At every felling both competitive and uncompetitive kinds get cut down together and have an equal chance to regrow. Since beech is the one broad-leaved tree that doesn't regrow reliably after being cut, regular coppicing can stop it becoming dominant.

Another puzzle is the origin of the woodland wildflowers, the violets, primroses, wood anemones and bluebells. They are so well adapted to the light-and-shade cycle of coppicing that it's hard to imagine what place they had in the wildwood, with a blow-down once in a couple of hundred years. The pollen record shows that at least some of these plants were here in wildwood times. But they can hardly have been as abundant in the wildwood as they were in the heyday of coppicing.

These old coppices are the ancient woods. Some of them have been woodland continuously since the end of the last ice age, in which case they are known as primary woods. Others have sprung up by natural succession on former farmland, heath or moor. These are called ancient secondary woods. They have been woodland long enough to have been colonised by most of the plants and animals characteristic of primary woods. It can be hard to tell the difference between primary and secondary ancient woods but it's not a very important distinction because ecologically both are very rich. An ancient wood is defined as one that was there in 1600 in England and Wales and 1750 in Scotland. These are fairly arbitrary dates, chosen mainly because they are the earliest that you can get direct evidence for the existence of a wood from maps.

On the ground, one clue that suggests a wood is ancient is a wood bank round all or part of the perimeter. (See page 23.) Big, old coppice stools are another sign. But the real test is a suite of plants known as ancient woodland indicators. These are extreme stayers, slow colonisers that are rarely found in recent woods. They were first identified in a famous study of the woods of Lincolnshire by George Peterken and Meg Game in the 1970s. They took a large sample of woods whose ages were known from historical documents and surveyed the herbaceous plants in them. They found a big difference in the herbaceous communities of old and young woods and compiled the first list of ancient woodland indicators. Since then other people have made similar studies in other parts of England, with slightly different results in each region. (As I'll shortly explain, the concept of ancient woodland indicators is less relevant in Scotland and Wales.) In the box opposite, under 'All England' I've listed plants that occur in more than half the lists and are also easy to identify.

Most of the regional variations are too complex to list here but I have included a regional list for eastern England, from Essex to Lincolnshire. The east stands out from other regions because of its dry climate. Woodland herbs are adapted to the moist, shady conditions of woods. In places with wetter climates some of them can live outside woods, in hedgerows or even in the open, and this makes it easier for them to migrate to new woods. The plants in the Eastern England list are ones that can't survive outside of woods in that region. But they are typical of ancient woodland everywhere. If you see them in a wood in another part of the country you can take it as a clue, if not as firm evidence, that the wood is ancient. In fact some of them are included in other regional lists. Ramsons, for example, is listed for the north and south-west of England and almost occurs on enough lists to make it onto the All England one.

A single ancient woodland indicator species on its own is not conclusive. Any one of them can occasionally be found in a recent wood but two or more would be unlikely.

ANCIENT WOODLAND INDICATOR PLANTS

Wood anemone.

All England

Trees
Wild service
Small-leaved lime

Wildflowers
Woodruff
Wood anemone
Common cow-wheat
Moschatel or town hall clock
Wood spurge
Herb paris

Eastern England

All those listed here plus:
Bluebell
Dog's mercury
Primrose
Ramsons or wild garlic
Oxlip

Herb paris.

This list is based on the comprehensive survey of all the lists by Oliver Rackham in his *Woodlands* (2006), Harper Collins.

Ramsons or wild garlic.

Wood Pasture

While some parts of the wildwood were being turned into coppice woods other parts were being grazed. If the grazing wasn't intensive enough to get rid of the trees this resulted in wood pasture. It can vary in density, from the widely spaced oaks of a deer park to the thick woodlands of the New Forest. But one thing all wood pastures have in common is that coppice is impossible because the animals would eat the regrowth, so the trees are either maidens or pollards.

Over the centuries the more palatable trees have been browsed out. The ones that are left are predominantly unpalatable ones, like oak and beech, or ones that can protect themselves, like holly with its thorns or the poisonous yew. Woodland herbs are unadapted to grazing and trampling and were soon replaced by grass or bracken. On the other hand wood pasture does have old trees. Constant coppicing and felling of standards meant that trees could never grow old in a coppice wood, whereas primary wood pasture has a continuous succession of old trees going right back to the wildwood. Many of them have had their lives prolonged by pollarding. Those beetles and other creatures which depend on dead and decaying wood and which have survived the demise of the wildwood have mainly done so in wood pasture. Wood pasture is also the stronghold of lichens, which grow very slowly and are even slower to colonise a new tree.

Very little wood pasture is left now. The modern trend towards monoculture has seen it converted either to plantation or to farmland. Here and there a very old pollard or a small scatter of them in farmland shows where once there was a wood-pasture common. The one place in Britain where a great deal of it does survive is in the New Forest in Hampshire. My notebook records a visit to an ancient wood in the Forest.

Ridley Wood, New Forest

The wood has a feel of wildwood about it, especially in the amount of dead wood lying around. There's a contrast between the parts that have a closed canopy and the parts where there's windthrow and regeneration of young trees. The former feel quiet, the latter full of event and movement. I saw four or five treecreepers together, working up neighbouring trees. I've never seen more than one at a time before. Maybe it's because they flock in winter and previously I've only seen them in summertime.

On the other hand, two things make it feel quite unlike a wildwood, the overgrazing and the low number of tree species. Within the wood I saw only beech, oak and holly. There's a sharp browse line and virtually no ground vegetation. Even bramble is severely browsed. There are tiny holly seedlings, but nothing above ankle height. The poor ponies have nothing much to eat. There's no grass longer than a billiard table, either in the wood or on the heath outside. They were eating beech and oak leaves inside the wood – there can't be much food value there – and browsing gorse and a rare small holly outside.

The Upland Region

Here there's less of a hard-and-fast distinction between wood pasture and coppice. Many upland woods have had a patchy history that includes both coppicing and grazing, or at least being used as a winter refuge for cattle and sheep. There's also much less distinction between ancient and recent woodland than there is in the lowlands.

The typical ancient woodland of East Anglia is an island of semi-natural vegetation in a sea of intensive cultivation. When you step outside the wood you go into another country, with a different climate, a transformed soil and hardly an inch of land that hasn't been sown or planted. The further west and north you go the more this contrast softens. In the uplands the woods merge gently into the surrounding landscape, much of which is semi-natural vegetation. The damp climate makes it easy for many woodland plants to survive outside of woods, so they are there in situ if the land becomes wooded again. Bracken can simulate the light-and-shade regime of deciduous woodland. It dies down in the autumn and comes up again in early summer, just when the trees would be leafing. As long as it's not too dense it can make a permanent home for bluebells, violets and other woodland flowers. Trees can often hang on in the face of grazing on steep slopes and in rocky places, like the ravines at Kinlochleven. (See page 91.)

The oak-hazel woods which dominated the uplands in prehistory are now mainly oak. Hazel, which favours the more fertile soils, has mostly been cleared

for farmland. The oakwoods are probably also much purer than they were. In many upland woods browsing has reduced the more palatable trees while in others oak was favoured for tan-bark production. Of course there are mixed woods in the uplands and regional variations too, such as the ashwoods on the limestone of the Pennines.

I live in the Lowland region, but from the window of my house I can see the curving profile of the Quantock Hills, the first rampart of the West Country and thus of the Upland region. The highest bump on this profile is a hill called Dowsborough.

The lack of shrubs and the grassy floor indicate that this is a grazed wood but the double-trunked tree at the left of the picture suggests a history that includes coppicing. Dartmoor, Devon. (Compare this wood with the one shown on page 119.)

Dowsborough, Somerset

The hill is covered by an old coppice wood. The trees are very stunted, some four to five metres tall, with no large ones except in a steep valley. They are almost all oak, with very occasional birch and rowan inside the woods and a fringe of birch where the wood is advancing. The advance is controlled where small patches of moor have been burned here and there.

The ground vegetation inside the woods is mainly whortleberries.* I found a few ripe berries, though the canopy is dense. There's also cow wheat, a few very small brambles and occasional bracken. Wherever there's a break in the canopy, such as under a dead tree, the bracken thickens up. There's some rather poor heather growing in the woods, possibly in spots where there was formerly more light.

As soon as you move out into the open the relative proportions of the plants change. Bracken and heather greatly increase and whortleberry decreases in proportion. Cow wheat is replaced by tormentil. I didn't see brambles in the open but I did see gorse.

* Somerset word for bilberries or blaeberries.

The Highland Region

In the Highland region the concept of ancient woodland more or less melts away, at least in the sense of a definite site with fixed boundaries. Although a particular wood may stay within the same area for centuries, it will occupy different parts of that area at different times. You can sometimes see this process in action, where a pinewood is dying away on one edge and spreading onto new ground on the other – if the deer permit it. The spread often happens in two stages. First a few scattered trees get established in more favoured places, such as where the peat is worn away by erosion, exposing the richer mineral soil, or in a rocky place that discourages browsing. As these mature they flood the area with seed and a second generation grows up. The young trees are close together and drawn up while the older generation have the broad, spreading crowns of trees which grew in the open.

The ground vegetation of Highland woods is rarely very different from the surrounding moorland, perhaps because they have a long history of grazing. Neither the cattle and goats of the times before the Clearances nor the more recent sheep and deer have ever been fenced out of the woods. Now that the deer population has grown higher than ever, regeneration of the woods is impossible in most parts of the Highlands without fencing. This is extremely expensive but the charity Trees for Life have put up miles of deer fences in Glen Affric and the surrounding area. Where once there was moorland dotted with the odd surviving tree now there are wide expanses of young woodland.

RECENT WOODS

Semi-natural

A recent wood that has arisen by natural succession is semi-natural. At first it will be composed entirely of pioneer species and the diversity of both plants and animals will be low. The species that are typical of ancient woodland will colonise it slowly and gradually diversity will increase. Being adjacent to ancient woodland speeds the process up considerably. At Hayley Wood in Cambridgeshire Oliver Rackham has observed dog's mercury, bluebell and oxlip advance from the ancient wood into a recent extension at a rate of a metre a year. Anemone and sanicle have spread more slowly. This is just one example and shouldn't be used to calculate the age of a new extension in another place but it gives an idea of what's possible. By contrast, a Lincolnshire plantation of mainly native trees, three and a half miles from the nearest ancient wood, still 'had the air of a grassland that had acquired trees' after a hundred and twenty

WOODLAND TYPES

Ancient Semi-Natural

Primary
Has always been woodland

Secondary
Became woodland before
1600/1750

These may be either:

Coppice
Trees coppiced on regular rotation

Wood Pasture
Maiden or pollard trees with
grazing animals

Upland and Highland woods
Less distinction between coppice
and wood pasture than in the
Lowland region

Recent Semi-Natural

Lowland
Has self-seeded since 1600/1750

Upland and Highland
Less distinction between ancient
and recent woods than in the
Lowland region

Plantation

Timber
Single-stemmed trees, usually
grown on the clear-fell system

Coppice
Rare, mostly chestnut in SE
England

Amenity or wildlife
Usually mixed native species

years. A few woodland wildflowers had colonised but not enough to change the character of the place.

A new wood is often a pure stand of a pioneer species – birch, pussy willow, ash, hawthorn or sycamore are typical – though it may be more diverse if there are seed parents nearby. There are no old coppice stools and usually no sign of coppicing at all. Sometimes they contain the occasional veteran tree, maiden or pollard. These will have the broad spreading branches which show that they were there before the wood grew up. A recent wood never has a big woodbank round it, though there may be the ditch and bank of an ordinary hedgerow along one or more boundaries. This isn't diagnostic, though, because some ancient woods haven't got banks either. The herbaceous plants are more typical of hedgerows or even grassland than of ancient woods: ivy, lords and ladies, goosegrass, nettles, Jack-by-the-hedge, cow parsley, hogweed and creeping buttercup. How different these plants are from the carpets of wildflowers in an ancient wood!

All these features combine to give new woods a raw feel compared to the mellowness of an ancient wood. Recent extensions to ancient woods are less raw than new woods which stand alone, and often more interesting. Sometimes it's hard to be sure exactly what you're looking at.

Rew Copse, Isle of Wight

This is an ash-hazel wood on steep chalk. In the southern part of the wood there are two distinct stands, separated by a small bank that runs across the slope. On the uphill side there's hawthorn and elder along with the dominant ash and hazel, and the ground cover is mainly ivy with some dog's mercury and bluebells. In the rest of the wood, below the little bank, there are a few spindle trees and maples among the ash and hazel but no hawthorn or elder. Here the ground vegetation is bluebells, dog's mercury, wood anemone and moschatel, with ivy only in patches. This must be an ancient wood but the upper part shows every sign of being recent. Did the upper part go through a period of grazing?

Well that's a possible explanation. The lower part of the wood is certainly ancient. The presence of anemone and moschatel indicate that. The upper part could have lost its woodland ground layer during a period of grazing that didn't last long enough to destroy it as a woodland altogether. When grazing ended it was recolonised by ivy, perhaps the most distinctive ground-layer plant of recent woods. Mercury and bluebell, both more mobile than anemone and moschatel, are slowly following.

However, if that had been the story you'd expect the mix of tree species to be the same in both parts of the wood. The upper part lacks maple and spindle which, while not exactly ancient woodland indicators, are characteristic of older rather than newer woods. Instead it has the pioneers hawthorn and elder. So the upper part could be a recent extension to the wood rather than a part that has been modified by grazing. The lack of any discernible woodbank or lynchett on the upper boundary of the wood and the presence of a little bank between the two stands supports the idea that the upper part of the wood is new. But the presence of coppice stools and a few big old ash trees in the upper part supports the opposite story. An investigation of the old maps could settle the matter.

Plantations

If you look at a road atlas of Britain, one which colours woods and plantations in green, you'll see that by far the biggest areas of green are in the Upland and Highland regions. These are mostly large-scale monocultures of exotic conifers. In sheer size they dwarf all other tree-covered land in the country, both lowland plantation and semi-natural woodland. They are grown on a short rotation of just a few decades, often not thinned, then clear-felled and replanted with the same species. Much of the land where they are grown is too wet for good tree growth. To dry it out it's 'ploughed'. This is really more of a ditching operation than ploughing. A huge machine draws out a ditch for each row and the trees are planted on the ridge of spoil. If the land later reverts to moorland these furrows and ridges leave an unmistakable record of its former life as a plantation. Many of these soils are peaty. As the peat dries out it starts to oxidise, releasing far more carbon dioxide into the atmosphere than the trees will ever remove from it as they grow.

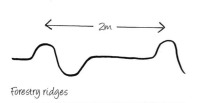

Forestry ridges

Broad-leaved trees and the more demanding conifer species can't produce an economic crop on these difficult sites so they are grown at lower altitudes where climate and soil are more forgiving. These are higher-value crops and they

A well-grown
plantation of
trees with good
timber form.
Great Breach
Wood, Somerset.

receive more care and attention. The ground is planted densely with young trees which are progressively thinned till perhaps only ten percent are left as the final crop. Growing trees this way improves the quality of the timber. Initially the close spacing draws the trees up into good timber form and suppresses lower branches. Later the increasing space allows the trees to expand into well-proportioned individuals with a good girth. Thinning also allows the forester to choose the best trees for the final crop. A plantation that is neglected will develop thin, spindly trees that are not worth much as timber and are prone to windthrow.

Although most plantations are monocultures there are mixed plantings too. Mixtures require more careful management but they also mean that more of the available niches are filled and this can make the plantation more productive. The commonest kind of mixture is that of a nurse crop along with the main crop trees. The nurse trees are of a tough species and they help the main crop by providing shelter when they are young. If the nurse crop is coniferous and the main crop is broadleaved the nurse also helps by drawing up the broadleaves with its dense shade. The conifers come out as thinnings. They can be used for fencing stakes and so on whereas young broadleaves can only go for pulp or firewood. But the final crop of mature broadleaves is more valuable than conifers would be.

A typical layout is to alternate three rows of the main crop with three rows of the nurse. Early thinning can then simply be a matter of removing whole rows of conifers. In hilly country these alternate strips may stand out clearly on a hillside. Some people disparagingly call this 'pyjama forestry' and complain that it doesn't look natural. Personally I like it. It shows that someone is doing something a little more thoughtful than simply planting monocultures. I agree it doesn't look natural – but neither do hedges, which are held to be one of the glories of the countryside.

Virtually all plantations are finally harvested by clear-felling. That's to say the whole plantation or compartment is felled together and then replanted, giving large blocks of even-aged trees. This is very disruptive to wildlife and to the visual appearance of the landscape, and exposes the soil to erosion. Just occasionally you may see a completely different kind of plantation in which there are trees of various ages growing side by side. This is known as continuous cover forestry because the trees are felled a few at a time so the land is never completely denuded of trees. It's an alternative approach that is beginning to gain ground among more progressive foresters.

Continuous cover is a commercial form of forestry. Although it lacks the economies of scale of the clear-fell system, its advocates say it's actually more profitable because small stands of trees can be treated individually to get the best from them. But there are also plantations that have no commercial purpose and have been made entirely for amenity or wildlife purposes. They are usually easy to recognise.

Slapton Ley, Devon

We passed by a typical amenity/wildlife planting of trees, perhaps ten or fifteen years old. It was oak, ash and wild cherry, regularly spaced and planted so far apart that their branches aren't yet touching. There's a high proportion of cherry and the occasional shrub of impeccable nativeness, such as dogwood and spindle. The whole effect is only slightly more natural than a closely mown lawn.

A few hundred yards further on we passed some natural regeneration of about the same age. It was a hundred percent sycamore, with the trees very close together, drawn up and already killing each other with hot competition.

Perhaps I shouldn't have been quite so sarcastic about the plantation. I've planted something quite similar myself in the past. There's always the temptation with wildlife planting to make it unrealistically diverse and include more of the rarer species than you'd find in nature. Why not? If we wanted a semi-natural wood all we'd do is leave the land alone and see what happened. A plantation is always artificial.

Almost all plantations, whether they are for timber production or amenity, are made up of single-stemmed trees. Coppiced plantations are very rare. An exception is the pure chestnut coppices of Kent and Sussex. Although some of these coppices are probably semi-natural many were planted in modern times. Chestnut is an excellent fencing wood as it's durable without the use of preservatives, and many chestnut coppices are still in commercial production. Some pure hazel coppices are still worked for hurdles and thatching spars, mainly in Hampshire and Dorset, but most of them are believed to be semi-natural.

Plantations have a bad image. They have often replaced diverse ancient woods with dark blankets of conifers. The irony of it is that many of these plantations now stand derelict and unharvested. With increasing globalisation and the opening up of the former Soviet Union the price of timber has plummeted. On large-scale upland plantations the economies of scale have kept the industry alive. But in scattered compartments on the sites of former woods, many with poor access, the cost of harvesting is often more than the value of the timber. They usually haven't been thinned, which means a high-value final crop is now unlikely or impossible.

On some sites the only clue to their past as woodland may be an irregular outline and the presence of a woodbank. Sometimes there's a 'dishonesty belt', a screen of the original trees left on the edge to give the passer-by the impression that nothing has changed. On other sites some of the woodland trees survive inside the wood. How many survive varies enormously, from the occasional one or two to a resurgence of the original vegetation which is clearly winning the competition with the conifers. Which gets the upper hand depends partly on the choice of the conifer species – the better it's matched to the soil and climate of the site the better the conifers will do – and partly on the kind of trees in the original wood. The usual procedure was to kill off the trees with Agent Orange, the herbicide once used by the Americans to defoliate the forests of Vietnam. Oak, beech and birch succumbed to it more completely than ash, hazel and maple. But lime, the small-leaved lime that was once the dominant tree in the lowland wildwood, has proved almost impossible to kill. Many limewoods have survived more or less intact, including the ground vegetation, and some are now nature reserves.

A commercial chestnut coppice. Prickly Nut Wood, West Sussex.

TREES, SHRUBS AND HERBS

The Trees

Almost all native British trees are broadleaved rather than coniferous. The broad leaf is designed to intercept the maximum of solar energy and it's the ideal adaptation to a mild, well-watered climate like ours. The narrow leaves of conifers are adapted to harsher conditions, to the drought of the Mediterranean or the cold of the far north, where frozen soil often creates a virtual drought. Conifer needles lose less water than broad leaves but at the cost of being less efficient as solar collectors. The yew, one of only three native British conifers, is most competitive in very dry situations, such as on chalk downland.

Why, then, do conifers dominate British forestry? If broadleaves are better at converting sunlight into biomass surely they must grow faster than conifers? The answer is that they do but it's the wrong kind of biomass. Firstly, it's denser than conifer wood, so you get less volume of timber for the same weight of tree. Secondly, a higher proportion of the biomass of a broadleaf is in the branches, which aren't marketable. The toughness of many conifer species also means that they do better than broadleaves on the harsh upland sites where most forestry goes on.

The greater biological productivity of broadleaves explains why the many species of conifer that have been introduced to this country for forestry have on the whole failed to become naturalised. The main exception is Scots pine, which is not a native tree south of the Highland line but has become a pioneer on the light sandy soils of lowland heaths. On less drought-prone soils it can't compete with native trees and if it's grown in a plantation it must be kept well weeded to stop it being taken over by native, self-seeded trees. "A landowner once told me his father had planted pine on a field and he'd just harvested a good crop of ash from it," says Oliver Rackham.

The key to successful forestry is to match the tree species as closely as possible to the soil and climatic conditions. In semi-natural woods this has of course been done by nature but the match isn't always very close because chance can also play a part. If a particular species has a good seed year just when space for regeneration becomes available it can become the dominant tree in the next generation even if it's not the tree best fitted to the site.

When looking at the composition of an ancient coppice wood the first thing to do is to forget about the standard trees. In most woods they'll all be oak and they are there because they have been deliberately encouraged by past generations of woodsmen. The coppice trees are the ones which differ from one wood to another and which give a wood its character. In the Lowland region oak was only coppiced where there was more than enough of it to provide the standards and it only grows in such abundance on the least fertile, acid, sandy soils. Birch, hornbeam and chestnut are the trees of relatively poor soils, while maple, ash and elms favour the richer soils. Alder is confined to wet soils but always where the water is moving, while aspen will grow where the water is stagnant. Beech is found on any well-drained soil, from light, acid sands to thin soils over chalk, though it does occasionally grow on clay. Hazel will grow on any soil except the least fertile.

In woods on poor soils the landform can have a strong effect on the distribution of trees. You can often see this in woods in the Upland and Highland regions, as this sketch from my notebook illustrates.

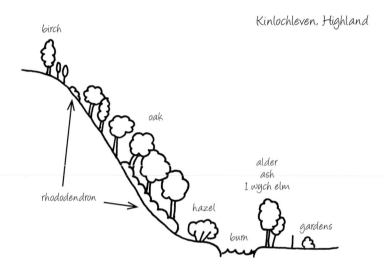

In this region of high rainfall and old, nutrient-poor rocks the soil is easily leached. There's a strong contrast between the leached, acid soil of the slope and the soil on the flat ground beside the burn, which catches some of the leached nutrients. The more demanding trees are confined to the burnside while oak rules on the slope. Rhododendron has seeded from the gardens on the other side of the burn and seems to be spreading up the slope. It's a strong indicator of acid soil and has leapfrogged the richer, more alkaline soil at the bottom. At the top, where the slope flattens out onto open moorland, conditions of soil and microclimate are harsher again and oak gives way to birch.

The Shrubs

Under a closed canopy there may be no shrub layer because there's not enough light. Where there is one it's defined simply by being lower than the tree layer. In an actively coppiced wood the coppice stools can be regarded as the shrub layer in comparison with the standard trees, though if coppicing stops they may eventually join the standards in the canopy. Hazel, whether coppiced or not, can make a distinct understorey to taller trees, although there are pure hazel woods where it makes the canopy. Saplings of the canopy species can be part of the shrub layer and in some woods they are all of it. Then there are the undershrubs like bramble and bilberry, which may be closer in size to the larger herbaceous plants.

The shrub layer can be a passing phase. In a plantation shrubs may thrive between the trees when they are still young and die out when the canopy closes, only to return later in the rotation when the canopy opens out due to thinning. In a newly self-seeded wood shrubs may remain from the scrub stage of succession. But as the trees start to cast more shade it thins out and only survives on the edge of the wood, where there's light from the side. There may be some shrubs in the interior but they are usually small, drawn-up specimens that never blossom. Meanwhile, on the woodland edge, beside a ride, on the edge of a glade or under a gap, they grow strongly, flower and set fruit, providing nectar for insects and berries for birds. These edges can be places of great productivity and diversity.

Edge vegetation can sometimes be found fossilised in the interior of a wood that has expanded. Once plants get established they may hold their ground for a long time even though conditions have long since changed, as this entry from my notebook illustrates.

Brockley Combe, North Somerset

This is a recent, self-sown wood, mostly of ash and sycamore. There's little ground cover except for occasional patches of dog's mercury, some ivy and tree seedlings. In some places there are saplings, about a metre or two high. Ash seedlings are very much more common than sycamore – they form a carpet in some parts – but almost all the saplings are sycamore. Perhaps this is due to sycamore being more shade-tolerant, or to preferential browsing. There's a visible though indistinct browse line.

As I got near to the adjacent conifer plantation, hawthorn and spindle shrubs suddenly became abundant. I hadn't noticed either of them elsewhere in the wood. This suggests that this was once the edge of the wood and the conifers are younger than the broad-leaved stand, planted on open fields rather than on a felled part of the wood.

Ancient woods usually have a hedge on the boundary, either on top of a bank or on the flat, and this is often composed of much the same species as the coppiced trees of the wood itself. These days a combination of neglect and increasing shade from the grown-out coppice will have made the hedge useless as a barrier in most woods but you can usually recognise its remains.

Herbaceous Plants

Herbaceous plants often indicate the woodland soil more accurately than the trees do. Why this should be so isn't fully understood but their smaller size and shorter lifespans would tend to even out the effects of chance events. This means there's often a poor match between the distribution patterns of the trees and the herbaceous plants beneath them. The least fertile soils are often indicated by bracken, bilberry and cow-wheat, moderately infertile by honeysuckle and bluebell, moderately fertile by dog's mercury and primrose, and the most fertile by nettles.

The two plants at the opposite ends of this spectrum, bracken and nettles, are both tall, densely-shading plants and on extreme soils can sometimes grow so vigorously that they prevent the regeneration of trees. Bracken, with its deep rooting system, thrives on a very sandy soil where other plants, including tree seedlings, are disadvantaged by the lack of water in summer. Where a patch of pure sand occurs in a wood a bracken glade can form, devoid of trees, except perhaps the occasional oak. Nettle glades can form in flat-bottomed gullies on heavy soils. This is the sort of place where nutrients collect naturally but many nettle glades are enhanced by fertiliser-rich runoff from adjacent arable fields or dungy farmyards. At most there may be the occasional hogweed or elder poking its head above the nettles.

In many woods the only difference in soil from one part of the wood to another is its moisture content. The sketch below is from a wood in the Lowland region, where leaching is not such a major factor as it is in the Highlands. The soil is much the same on both the steep bank and the flat bottom except that the bank is well-drained and the flat ground, fed by a line of springs at the base of the slope, is wet.

Park Wood, Chaffcombe, Somerset

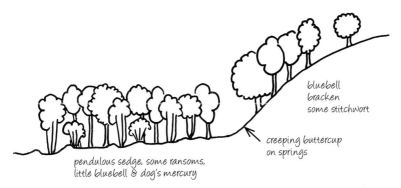

bluebell
bracken
some stitchwort

creeping buttercup
on springs

pendulous sedge, some ransoms,
little bluebell & dog's mercury

The bluebells are in full flower and there's a dramatic contrast between the electric blue of the bank and the deep green of the flatter ground below, dotted with the odd patch of white ramsons. The difference, so visible at this time of year, appears to be due solely to moisture content, which in turn is due to the landform. I did the finger test on soil from both parts of the wood but wasn't able to detect any difference in the sand and clay content.

The trees can also influence the distribution of herbaceous plants. Trees vary in the amount of shade they cast and herbs in the amount they tolerate. Ash gives light shade and a whole range of woodland wildflowers can thrive under it, whereas lime gives heavier shade and you may see a patch of the shade-tolerant ramsons under a lime. Under a gap in the canopy brambles may grow vigorously and take over from the herbaceous layer altogether.

Leaf fall can have an effect too. Beechwoods are famous for having little or no ground layer but this isn't only because they cast a heavy shade. Beech leaves are the slowest of all to decompose and they build up into a layer so deep that the little roots of germinating seeds can't get to the mineral soil below, which they must do in order to grow. Ash is at the opposite extreme: its leaves are the first to disappear. In a plantation with compartments of both beech and ash there will be a sharp contrast in the ground cover, though the mineral soil may be the same under both trees.

Mosses tend to do better under conifers than broadleaves, because they are sensitive to the smothering effect of the autumn leaf fall. Conifers do lose their leaves but it's a constant trickle through the year rather than a sudden shower. The deep shade of the conifers helps mosses too because it reduces competition from more light-demanding plants. Mosses also have the advantage of not needing soil to grow in, so in a deciduous wood they are often found on stones and logs, where they are free from competition and usually above the level of leaf litter.

An actively coppiced wood is full of edges and full of light. The dark interior of an undisturbed wood may seem a dull place by comparison but it may contain just as much diversity, though the species will be different. The creatures that shun the edge are often drab and boring compared to the bright butterflies and song birds of coppice. The stag beetle (see page 78) is top of the range for visual interest. We often wax lyrical about the wildlife of coppices but who are we to say that fritillaries and chiffchaffs have more right to exist than some greyish grub that lives in dead logs and few of us has ever seen? Everything has a right to life and wild creatures are not there purely to please us.

CYCLES OF CHANGE

The Annual Cycle

If you go to an ancient wood in late winter or early spring, when the twigs of the trees are bare, you'll see the wildflowers which spend their dormant season below the ground emerging and putting on leaf. Some of the first celandines may already be flowering. In mid-spring the herbaceous layer is in full flower and the shrubs are just beginning to come into leaf. Most of the trees don't come into leaf till late spring, when the latest-flowering herbs are in full flower. As the tree leaves open up and cast full shade in early summer some of the herbaceous plants, such as ramsons and bluebells, give up on photosynthesis and their leaves die away, not to reappear till the following spring. High summer is a quiet and uneventful time on the woodland floor.

This annual sequence is the result of a trade-off between the two niche factors, light and temperature. The plants of the ground layer leaf early in order to have at least some time in direct sunlight. It means they have to invest some of their energy in making themselves frost-hardy, but plants that live below deciduous trees have little option. The trees can save themselves this expense by leafing late and it's because they do this that the herbs have their time in the sun. The shrubs occupy an intermediate niche in this respect. How long has it taken for this beautiful piece of dove-tailing to evolve? It epitomises what an ecosystem is all about: not just a collection of plants and animals but an integrated community in which each species fits in with the others around it like the parts of an intricate machine.

Natural Regeneration

Large seeds, like those of oak and beech, make an attractive meal for seed-eating creatures, which include mice, voles, squirrels, pigeons, nuthatches and deer. These trees get around the problem by the pattern of mast years. Mast is an old word for tree seeds and a mast year is one in which a tree produces a bumper crop of seed. Usually all the trees of one species will have a mast year together. Beech has mast years at intervals of four to fifteen years, oak at two to seven and ash every other year. Without mast years some of these trees would hardly be able to reproduce at all. A steady yield of seed would support a steady population of seed-eaters and few seeds would survive. But the population of seed-eaters is kept down, at least in part, by the lack of seed in the non-mast years and in a mast year they can't eat all of it. One reason why hazel is now finding it hard to reproduce in the face of the grey squirrel is that it doesn't have really pronounced mast years.

It's late April. The bluebells are in flower, the shrubs are greening up but the trees are still dormant. Kingcombe Copse, Dorset.

Some trees are specially shade tolerant as seedlings. They can grow a little bit and then wait for years for a break in the canopy to occur. Sycamore is particularly good at this. Once a gap does occur the young sycamores have a head start on other trees and their wide, horizontal leaves cast a heavy shade on any competition. This is called advanced regeneration and foresters who restock their plantations by natural regeneration rather than by planting are always on the lookout for it. Felling a group of trees which has a good stand of seedlings under it is a much surer way of getting the next crop than felling and hoping for the best.

Seedlings have to run the gauntlet of browsing, competition from herbaceous plants, shade from older trees, drought and fungus diseases. Most die as seedlings but the initial numbers are usually so great that the survivors are enough to make a dense thicket of saplings. From now on the main cause of tree death is mutual shading. A hundred saplings may occupy the space that eventually will be taken by one mature tree. Competition is the commonest cause of death and most dead trees you will see in a wood are young rather than old. Once a tree makes it to the mature canopy it will probably stay there for much longer than it took getting there. But one day it will die, get blown over or be harvested and the cycle can start ag ain.

Wood Pastures

The oldest trees in medieval deer parks are slow-growing pollards and some of these probably date back to the woodland or hedgerow trees that stood on the site before it was emparked. Planting was very rare in medieval times. Maiden trees in parks are usually younger, planted and protected from browsing with a timber cage when the deer park evolved into the ornamental park of a country mansion.

In denser wood pasture, such as the New Forest, seedlings and saplings can find shelter from hungry mouths among the branches of a fallen tree or in a dense growth of holly. But over the ages there have also been times when grazing was drastically reduced and a major pulse of regeneration took place. This could happen, for example, when there was an outbreak of cattle disease. It seems to have happened in the New Forest in the years after 1851 when the powers that be made a determined effort to exterminate the deer.

Coppice Woods

Normal coppicing practice is to cut a small part of the wood each year, so an actively coppiced wood is a mosaic of patches in different stages of regrowth. Every cutting of the coppice gives an opportunity for trees to reproduce by seed. Conditions are so open that even oak can self-seed. (See page 73.) Coppicing also gives an opportunity to wildflowers. Some, like foxglove, survive the shady years between each coppicing as buried seed. Others, such as willowherbs and burdock, are mobile and come in on the wind or on the coats of passing animals. But most survive in situ as vegetative plants and only come into flower after coppicing. Then butterflies and other insects feed on the wildflowers and thrive in the unique microclimate that combines post-felling sunshine with shelter from the surrounding trees that have not been felled this time. As the coppice regrows a whole succession of song birds nest in the dense cover of the regrowing stools. Shade-loving herbs, such as ramsons and dog's mercury, are set back by coppicing. Dog's mercury is also sensitive to trampling so the coppicing operation itself knocks it back. A pure stand of dog's mercury is very much a feature of an abandoned coppice wood.

Only about one in ten ancient woods is still coppiced. In some of them it's done to provide pheasant cover for shooting, in others for nature conservation. Most ancient coppice woods you'll see these days are neglected and have been for a long time. As the canopy closes the mosaic of shaded and unshaded patches is taken over by uniform shade over the whole wood. The ground layer becomes less diverse and often rather dull. Woodland wildflowers may survive but without blooming and may be joined by ivy. The birds and butterflies that depend on coppicing decrease or disappear. Eventually dead wood starts to accumulate. But the bugs and beetles that thrive in undisturbed woods may not be there to take advantage of the situation. They need continuity of old trees and dead wood and will probably have died out during the centuries of coppicing.

In some woods the standards have grown to enormous sizes and reduced the growth of the coppice. In others the coppice has grown up and joined the standards in the canopy. There are some woods where an overwhelming number of standards were encouraged during the later nineteenth century and in these the coppice is now largely suppressed. In others the standards were all felled during one of the World Wars, when there were shortages of imported timber. Some of these woods are still full of pioneers such as birch, hawthorn and pussy willow that came in to fill the vacuum left by the standards. But eventually in all woods the balance swings towards stayers. Hornbeam is a real stayer, similar to beech in both appearance and habit, and coppice woods that were once a mix of hornbeam and hazel have turned into pure hornbeam.

Plantations

The young trees in a plantation are planted further apart than nature usually sows them and for the first few years there's space between them. What kind of vegetation fills this space depends on the former land use, whether moor, grassland, woodland or plantation. Often it gets cut back or sprayed to allow the trees to grow. This stage is somewhat like the scrub stage in natural succession and some of the wildlife of scrub will inhabit it. On former grassland sites voles multiply in the undisturbed grass between the trees and these in turn support owls and kestrels. When the canopy closes and the young trees start drawing each other up, the plantation moves into the thicket stage. The shade is intense, especially if the trees are conifers, and little wildlife survives. Thinning takes the place of the mutual suppression that goes on in a natural wood and eventually the plantation opens out into the high crowns stage. Now some light can once more reach the ground and herbaceous plants and shrubs can move in and with them some animals.

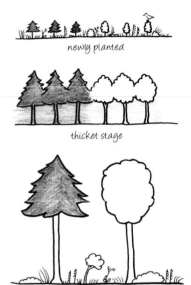

newly planted

thicket stage

high crowns

Felling brings a sudden increase in light levels. In plantations on former woodland sites this can be a stimulus to the buried-seed plants. In some places foxgloves come up in their millions. It will be decades since they last flowered and set seed but they are well adapted to waiting a long time. In the wildwood they might have had to wait much longer. The foxglove is a vigorous biennial and it invests the energy of its first year in prodigious seed production in the second. Each plant produces some three-quarters of a million minute seeds. Only a tiny proportion of these need to survive the long years of dark in order to cover the ground with new plants when the light returns. Then they can make a hillside shine purple in the distance at flowering time.

Successional Changes

The sketch below shows a piece of landscape that at first looked quite simple: all woodland on the far side of the stream and all pasture on the near side. But a closer look suggested a dynamic situation, with an ancient wood which is extending itself on the far side of the stream and has retreated from the near side.

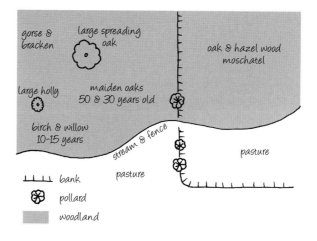

The following passage from my notebook illustrates how reading a wood can sometimes be easy and sometimes rather puzzling.

Laurieston Hall, Galloway

In the woods by the loch there's a very diverse stand with nine species of trees and a ground layer including bluebells, violets, dog's mercury etc. It's on a steep slope. As you go up, the slope flattens out and right on the break of the slope the wood changes to a stand of almost pure young birch with a ground layer of grass and a little bracken.

Further along, on a moderate slope, there's a third stand and the picture here is less clear. The trees are mostly birch with some old oak and a few others. The ground layer is moderately diverse, typically grass and bluebells. The extremes represented by the first two stands are obvious, but making sense of this third stand is less easy.

If you come upon a stand that is as hard to read as this one, don't be downhearted – it had me foxed too.

A WOODLAND CHECKLIST

Earthworks

see page

A bank round the perimeter suggests ancient woodland or a plantation on an ancient woodland site.

Internal banks: in ancient wood, property boundaries; in a recent wood or plantation, former hedgerows.

An irregular boundary suggests an ancient wood, a rounded boundary an ancient deer park.

23-24

Ridge and furrow inside a wood shows that it's been cultivated at some time and so is secondary, but it may still be ancient.

Charcoal hearth: a circular platform, which becomes a terrace on sloping ground, 2-5m diameter; the soil is black and its colour usually contrasts with that of neighbouring soil.

Small quarries are quite usual in woods both ancient and recent.

Herbaceous Plants

The herbs usually indicate the soil conditions more faithfully than the trees.	132

They are most visible from March to June.

The soil may be bare at other times but bare soil during spring often indicates excessive grazing.

For ancient woodland indicator plants — 121

For typical plants of recent woodland — 125

Grasses indicate: either a recent wood that was grassland not long ago; or an older wood with a history of grazing.

Nettles indicate: in a grazed wood, places where cattle congregate, especially a feeding place; former habitation sites – phosphorous is very persistent in the soil; a nettle glade.

Tree Shapes

Coppice usually indicates ancient woodland, especially if the stools are big. The wood may be older than the biggest stool, but not younger. — 110

Pollards: in ancient coppice woods, only found on the perimeter; in a recent wood, either the remains of ancient wood pasture or former hedgerow trees. — 112-114

Stubs: indicate the edge of an ancient coppice wood or an internal property boundary. — 113

Maiden trees, without coppice or pollards, indicate a plantation or recent self-sown woodland. Exceptions are the Highland pinewoods and some Chiltern beechwoods.

A plantation is also indicated by:
- Trees in straight lines – more visible in a young plantation than an old one
- Trees more or less the same size and evenly spaced
- Trees genetically uniform, all much the same shape – especially noticeable in oak.

Tree Species

For relationships between tree species and soils. — 130-131

A high diversity of trees and shrubs, say a dozen or more species in one wood, indicates an aid soil. — 45

Ancient woodland indicators: small-leaved lime and wild service; any tree not listed as a pioneer suggests an older wood. — 125

In a coppice wood, ignore the standards. — 130

Recent woods are indicated by pioneer species. — 125

A low level of diversity indicates one or more of the following: a recent wood; harsh soil or climatic conditions; a very competitive species, e.g. beech; deliberate simplification; or a plantation.

At first it wasn't obvious whether this stand was a plantation or semi-natural but this straight line of trees settled it. River Teign woods, Devon.

10

Grassland

I HAVE a close personal relationship with grassland. In 1983 an old field came up for sale. It had never been ploughed and reseeded or treated with chemical fertilisers and was a haven of biodiversity. I had just inherited some family money and bought it to save it from 'improvement'. For eight years I lived in the field in a tipi, experiencing its changes through the seasons and from year to year. I learnt to recognise the plants that grow there and recorded a total of seventy-three wildflower species and twenty-six grasses. Each year I arranged for someone to make hay and then graze the aftermath, as we call the grass which regrows after haymaking.

Life moved on and it became time for me to live in a house again but I carry that experience of living close to nature inside me. In my permaculture work it complements the scientific knowledge I learnt at college. Eventually I handed the field on to the Somerset Wildlife Trust and now they look after it as an official nature reserve.

Common spotted orchids, one of the jewels in the crown of my former field.

Clifftop Grassland

The origins of grassland are lost in the mists of time. In Chapter 2 I mentioned the possibility that grassland plants were introduced to Britain by the first farmers. (See pages 10-11.) There's also the theory that the primeval landscape of Britain was not continuous wildwood but alternating woodland and grassland. A third possibility occurred to me on a day I spent walking on the south Devon coast path.

Prawle Point, Devon

Today I counted sixty-four species of herbaceous plants by the sea, not including grasses or ones that aren't flowering at the moment – it's early July. They were mostly on the clifftop though a few were a mile or two inland. This is surely the highest number of species I've ever counted in a single day.

Most of them were grassland wildflowers. Clifftops are one ecosystem in Britain that has hardly been affected by human activity. Maybe these two facts are connected.

I wasn't the first person to have that idea. Salt winds and spray can play much the same role as the munching mouths of cattle. Some trees and shrubs can tolerate salty winds up to a point but on the most exposed headlands there are only grasses and herbs. Clifftops, along with some of the highest mountain tops, must surely be the only places that have been grassland continuously since the passing of the Ice Age tundra.

The sketch below shows the western bank of the Salcombe Estuary, also in south Devon. At the extreme left is the headland that juts out into the sea, with a covering of grassland between the jagged exposures of rock. A little further in the grass gives way to bracken, dotted with the occasional hawthorn and elder. Then the isolated shrubs merge into continuous scrub and that in turn grades into sycamore woodland. There's no grazing on the headland, just salt spray.

IMPROVED AND UNIMPROVED

Improved

We think of grass as being naturally green but the greenest grass of all is in fact the least natural. It's a monoculture of ryegrass, fed with fertiliser, which gives it an intense gloss-paint green. These are short-lived grasslands which are ploughed up and reseeded every few years, either to alternate with arable crops or simply because they become less productive with time and need renewing. Ryegrass is

Ryegrass flower.

Timothy flower.

Cocksfoot flower.

the only species of grass used, though usually a mix of two varieties is grown, one early and one late. The gross output of animal fodder is extremely high but the net output is another matter. It takes a great deal of energy to produce fertiliser. If you subtract the total energy input from the energy content of the grass produced the net output is not nearly so impressive. This kind of farming is only possible while we pay an unrealistically low price for fossil fuels.

A less intensive approach is to sow clover along with the ryegrass and allow the bacteria that live in the roots of the clover to provide the nitrogen. A simple ryegrass-clover mix is easy to recognise in the field, even when it's not flowering. The little round leaflets of clover contrast with the lancet blades of the grass and apart from this there's no variety of leaf shapes in the sward. Both conventional and organic farmers may use this simple kind of mixture to establish a ley, as temporary grassland is known. But some organic farmers use a much more complex mix, especially for a longer-term ley or for establishing a permanent pasture. An example is the classic Clifton Park mix, which contains nine varieties of grass plus four varieties of clover and five species of herbs. This kind of diversity means that many different niches are filled.

One of the grasses used is Timothy. It does especially well on wet, heavy land and produces plenty of leaf in early summer when other grasses are putting their energy into seed rather than leaf. Cocksfoot is another. It has a deep, well-branched root system that makes it tolerant of dry, sandy soils and occasional droughts. In a field with patchy soil conditions these two will complement each other, each taking a leading role in a different part of the field. They will also complement each other from year to year, with Timothy producing more in a wet year and cocksfoot in a dry one. The 'herbs' are plants that are neither grasses nor clovers. They mostly have deep tap roots and each has a special ability to extract certain nutrients from the subsoil. The animals consume these nutrients directly when they eat the herbs and the other plants in the sward get them in the animals' dung. Ribwort plantain is one and yarrow, with its feathery leaves and flat, white flowerheads, is another.

In Chapter 6 I emphasised how niche differentiation leads to diversity but I didn't mention that it also enables the ecosystem to have a high overall yield. This is partly because a diverse mix makes fuller use of the available resources than a monoculture can: a mix of tall and short plants makes fuller use of the resource of space; a mix of early, mid-season and late species makes better use of the resource of time, and so on. It's also because the plants in the mixture positively help each other. The clovers provide nitrogen, the herbs bring other nutrients up from the subsoil and the deep well-branched roots of cocksfoot improve the soil structure, all of which benefits the ecosystem as a whole. The result is a high yield without a high energy cost.

Semi-improved

Whatever kind of seed mixture has been sown, from pure ryegrass to Clifton Park, the composition of the sward will change in time. The species and varieties that are deliberately sown are productive ones from an agricultural point of view but they probably aren't the ones most perfectly suited to survival on that site. There will be other plants waiting in the wings which are ever so slightly better adapted to the soil, climate and other niche factors. They may be broad-leaved plants such as buttercups and thistles, or species of grass that are never sown because they are not very productive or even wild varieties of the cultivated grasses and clovers. All of them will reduce the productivity of the sward as they become established in any gaps left by the demise of the sown plants.

The resulting grassland is known as semi-improved. This is a catch-all term for any field of grass that falls somewhere between a productive new ley on the one hand and completely unimproved semi-natural grassland on the other. It can also come about simply by applying fertiliser to semi-natural grassland. Raising the level of nutrients gives the advantage to a relatively small number of very competitive grasses and herbs that will eventually out-compete their neighbours. The result is much the same whichever end of the spectrum you start with.

In springtime, when all grasses are composed mainly of leaf, a semi-improved grassland that's heavily fertilised turns much the same shade of unnatural green as a field of pure ryegrass. In summer, when the grasses are flowering, fields of ryegrass still show green but semi-improved ones turn buff or brown, because ryegrass flowers are green while those of other grasses are brownish.

Seen from close up, a semi-improved sward can seem at first sight to be more diverse than it really is. Even if the herbs aren't flowering the mix of leaf shapes gives an impression of diversity. But on closer inspection you'll find that they are a pretty limited selection, often not much more than buttercups, dandelions and plantains. In summertime a combination of red and white clover with yellow buttercup can give a vivid display which brings the phrase 'flower-rich meadow' immediately to mind. But this is really a very modest level of diversity.

A semi-improved grassland may still contain a diversity of grass species.

Unimproved or Semi-Natural

It's very easy to 'improve' a diverse semi-natural grassland by applying fertiliser but much more difficult to bring it back to its former diversity. One reason for this is that phosphorous, one of the key nutrients in fertiliser, is very persistent in the soil and remains long after applications of fertiliser have stopped. Another is that potential seed parents have vanished from the surrounding landscape. These days it's very rare to find true semi-natural grassland outside of nature reserves, except on land which is too steep for tractors. Whenever I find myself in a flattish field that supports a wide diversity of wildflowers I start to wonder where the Nature Reserve sign is. But there are some fields that have fallen through the net of improvement. If you ever come across one I strongly suggest you let the county Wildlife Trust know about it. Semi-natural grassland has a priceless ecological value and can be destroyed in the twinkling of an eye when the land changes hands. Don't assume that the Trust already knows about it.

This sketch from my notebook shows how closely the improvement of grassland can be tied to the degree of slope.

Hay Hill, Somerset

There's a gradation from improved grassland on the lower slope to unimproved on the steepest part, with a narrow strip of semi-improved between the two. The improved sward is dominated by white clover and also contains red clover, ryegrass, other grasses and a few wildflowers such as self-heal. The semi-improved strip has these and some more wildflowers, e.g. agrimony, in a matrix of mixed grasses. The unimproved grassland above contains all these flowers plus some others such as restharrow and ox-eye daisy. It's succeeding to scrub, mainly of brambles.

This site shows the loss of semi-natural grassland in microcosm. It's gone on the flatter land through being ploughed and reseeded and it's going on the steeper land by succeeding to scrub. It's a case of either too much attention or not enough. Both of these mean the end for a field of herb-rich grassland. It's all part of the on-going simplification of the countryside.

In spring, when the fields around it shine with the hard green of artificial nitrogen, an unimproved field may stand out with softer, patchier hues of green. Most of the wildflowers come out in early summer and then, though it may still look dowdy from a distance, from close to it will be lit up by a thousand blooms of all shapes and colours. By July, when most of the herbs have finished flowering and the grasses are in full flower, the predominant colours are the buffs and fawns of grass flowers, and then it may be hard to tell an unimproved field from a semi-improved one at first glance.

One plant to keep an eye out for is the ox-eye daisy, a tall herb whose flower is like a giant version of the common lawn daisy. It's by no means diagnostic but it's conspicuous and can signal that the field is worth investigating for other flowers that may at first be hidden by the grass. Another is knapweed, also tall and easily visible, with a purple flower that is usually out in July to September.

Knapweed with burnett moth feeding.

Some of the flowers you find, like the orchids, may be rare. But what makes this kind of ecosystem special isn't the presence of some rarity so much as the sheer diversity of plants, both grasses and flowers. A single visit in May or June is enough to tell you whether you've found something special and in April cowslips are a promise of floral riches to come. But to get a full picture of what's there you need to visit the field regularly over spring and summer, as many plants have a short flowering season and they are all much easier to identify when they are in flower. Then you'll find yourself delving into the intricate world of grasses with names like sweet vernal, crested dogstail and Yorkshire fog. You may get to know curious flowers like goatsbeard, also called Jack-go-to-bed-at-noon because it only opens for a short time in the morning then closes for the rest of the day. You'll almost certainly cross paths with butterflies and grasshoppers, and with improbable insects such as the iridescent green beetles that live in the miniature jungle of grass stems, and the steely burnet moth, whose red and black markings warn predators that it's poisonous.

A headcount of plant species is a rough guide to the ecological value of grassland but it does need to be seen in the context of the potential diversity on that site. The main factor is soil acidity. A species count of a dozen in a field with an acid soil may be equivalent to fifty on a neutral soil. Downland, that special kind of grassland that grows on thin, alkaline soils over chalk or limestone, has the highest potential of all. It may contain fifty species of plants not per field but per square metre.

GRASSLAND TYPES

Improved	Semi-improved	Unimproved or Semi-Natural
Sown grassland, which may be:	Improved grassland which has deteriorated	Shows no signs of having been ploughed and reseeded or of being fertilised. May be very diverse.
Ryegrass monoculture	Or unimproved which has been treated with fertiliser	
Simple mixture with clover		
Diverse mixture, e.g. Clifton Park		May be either:
		Meadow – tall grasses and herbs, or
		Pasture – short, springy turf

This field has been cut repeatedly for silage during the summer but the strip on the right was just too steep for tractor work so it was left uncut. The contrast shows how constant cutting keeps the grass at its young, leafy stage and prevents it going to seed.

USES OF GRASSLAND

Meadow and Pasture

Modern improved grassland can be used interchangeably for grazing or mowing but traditionally there was a big difference between pasture, which was grazed, and meadow, which was mown for hay. Meadow was sited on the best land because at haymaking all the nutrients in the hay are removed from the field, whereas in a pasture most of the nutrients stay behind in the animals' dung and urine. Pasture was usually the land that wasn't good enough for any other use.

The difference between meadow and pasture can still be seen in unimproved grassland and in many semi-improved fields too. Land that is only used for pasture has a short, springy turf, formed by constant nibbling, while a meadow has a tall, straight-stalked structure. Hay is left for two or three months to grow undisturbed before it's cut, and the plants reach upwards like trees in a plantation, competing for the light. To some extent this contrast is reflected in the species composition of meadow and pasture. Tall-growing species are favoured in meadows and lower-growing ones in pasture. An example is the two common clovers: the taller red clover is more common in meadow and the shorter white species in pasture.

Grass does most of its growth in spring, when it produces lots of leaf. In summer it converts this goodness to stems, flowers and seeds and produces little leaf. Intensive farmers do their best to keep it at the young, vegetative stage by repeatedly cutting it or grazing it, so it keeps starting again from the beginning of the annual growth cycle. Rather than allowing the cattle to range over the whole farm they keep them on a small area of land for a short time and then move them on. Each piece of ground gets grazed in this way several times a year, or cut for silage two or three times. It's impossible to stop grass going to seed altogether but this treatment produces the maximum of young, nutritious leaf.

If the winter feed is conserved as hay rather than silage the grass needs to grow to a more mature stage. Silage is grass pickled in its own juice whereas hay is preserved by being dried in the sun. So the first cut of silage is taken in spring, when the grass is young and juicy, whereas hay is cut in summer, when the grass is flowering and the plants are more stemmy. You can only take one cut of hay each year but the aftermath is grazed.

After cutting, whether for hay or for silage, the grass stubble is a pale, strawlike colour. This can give the countryside a dry look and just after haymaking people often remark how drought-stricken the land appears. But it's not lack of water that causes the pale colour; it's lack of light. Before mowing, the bottom of the grass plants is in deep shade and so doesn't produce chlorophyll, the green pigment that turns sunlight into food, and this is the part that's left after mowing. All grassland, whether improved or unimproved, fertilised or not, looks much the same with a short haircut. As soon as growth starts again the sward greens up.

The glory of a semi-natural meadow is its wildflowers, because a meadow is shut up for hay during the time when most grassland plants are flowering. By contrast, a semi-natural pasture can look quite drab at the same time of year, as the grazing animals munch the flowers along with the leaves and stems. In fact sheep actually have a taste for flowers and will seek them out. On the other hand pastures are better for insects and other invertebrates, as in a meadow their habitat suddenly disappears at haymaking time.

The broad-leaved plants that really do well in pasture, both unimproved and semi-improved, are ones that are thorny, like thistles, poisonous, like ragwort or unpleasant to eat, like buttercups. Ragwort and the tall spear thistle, being biennials, need bare soil to get established and this is most likely to occur when a pasture is overgrazed. The perennial creeping thistle, on the other hand, can reproduce vegetatively and is less dependent on bare soil. Cutting can help to control it but it needs to be done at the right time of year. In spring the plant puts all its energy into vegetative growth. Cutting it then only encourages it to produce more horizontal roots, which just makes the problem worse. But in summer it puts its energy into the flower buds and if you cut it then you remove those flower buds and rob it of that energy. This weakens the plants and if it's done several years running it kills them. Hence the old rhyme:

Ragwort.

> Cut them in May and they're here to stay,
> Cut them in June and they'll be back soon,
> But cut them in July and they're sure to die.

Kinds of Grazers

There are differences between the grazing habits of cattle, sheep and horses and if a field has been used predominantly for one or another you can read the signs in the sward.

147

Sheep bite the grass off with their teeth and graze it down much shorter than cattle, who tear if off with their tongues. So sheep pasture is usually shorter and can have a lawn-like appearance. They are less fussy than cattle and will eat docks, buttercups and thistles, especially when the plants are young. They normally leave rushes but they will graze them if, as a farmer I know put it, 'you keep them hungry enough'. They can even eat the poisonous ragwort. Although it's deadly to cattle and horses it's less toxic to sheep, especially in the spring, and judicious sheep grazing can play a part in controlling it. One plant they won't eat is nettles and you sometimes see a sheep pasture grazed as close as a billiard table except for the odd clump of tall nettles.

Cattle are more choosy. As well as leaving docks and thistles they avoid eating where they have dunged. The dark green patches of taller grass that grow up over their dung pats can give a cow pasture a pimply look. The dark colour of the grass is due to the extra nutrients in the dung but it's tall mainly because the cattle won't eat it until the dung pat has decomposed and disappeared. A large clump of nettles, or sometimes docks, usually indicates a place where they were fed hay or silage during the winter. Both their dung and the fodder they spill while eating raise the nutrient level and the bare, poached soil leaves space for these nutrient-hungry plants to come in.

Horses are the worst grazers. They segregate the field into two parts, one for grazing and the other for dunging. They won't take a bite from the dunging area, while in the grazing area they take the grass down even shorter than sheep with their double row of sharp incisors. If horses are kept on the same field continuously the contrast between the two parts becomes stronger and stronger. The dunging area grows tall with rank grasses, docks, thistles and nettles while the grazed area gets nibbled down almost to the bare earth. It also becomes compacted and docks, which tolerate compaction, often move in on the grazed area. Topping can help a lot and some horse-owners go to the length of removing the dung by hand, but the best solution is to alternate horses with other grazing animals.

Gateways

Gateways develop a community of plants that tolerate both soil compaction and being trampled. The part nearest the gate is usually bare soil. Moving out a little, or in a less used gateway, you come upon the most tolerant plants of all. These are greater plantain and a funny little flower called pineapple weed, a member of the daisy family with an egg-shaped flowerhead and no petals. Where trampling is a little less severe these two may be joined by the tiny annual meadow grass and knotgrass, which isn't a grass at all but a low sprawling plant with spear-shaped leaves and minute flowers. Mayweed, a medium-sized daisy flower, often comes up in the bare soil around a gateway after the trampling is over. Being an annual it benefits from the bare ground and it can tolerate soil compaction, though not trampling. You often see it in the gateway of a hayfield which was used for pasture the previous year.

Further out from the gateway there may be a zone that is less obviously affected. It may have suffered from temporary poaching, perhaps when the field was grazed by dairy cattle during a wet time. As dairy cows go in to be milked twice a day they cause much more trampling round a gateway than beef cattle or sheep. This outer zone may be dominated by couch grass for a few years afterwards. Couch is a pioneer grass that can take advantage of a new patch of bare soil but it rarely survives for long in an established sward. Creeping thistle may come up too. Its roots can stay dormant in the soil for years and then sprout when the soil is bared by poaching. The drawing shows a typical example.

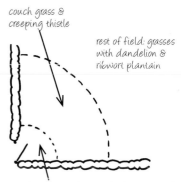

couch grass & creeping thistle

rest of field: grasses with dandelion & ribwort plantain

usual gateway plants including pineapple weed, mayweed, greater plantain, knotgrass

Mayweed flowering in a gateway at haymaking time.

Watermeadows

This term is sometimes used to mean any grassland alongside a river or stream but strictly speaking a watermeadow is a grass field that in the past was irrigated. In our wet climate they weren't irrigated for the sake of the water itself but for the warmth it brings. Springwater stays at a constant temperature throughout the year and although river water does change temperature with the seasons it does so less than dry land. So in late winter and early spring the water is warmer than the soil and if it's allowed to flood over a field of grass it warms up the soil and gets the grass growing earlier.

Watermeadows reached their most evolved form in the chalk valleys of Wessex. The whole meadow was laid out in a pattern not unlike the ridge and furrow of medieval ploughing. Along the top of each ridge ran a carrier ditch and along each furrow there was a drain. The water would flow from carrier to drain in an even sheet. The engineering had to be very precise in order to achieve this and each system was run by a skilled worker known as a drowner. Today much of this detail is lost and watermeadows may appear to be little more than ridge and furrow with a dense growth of rushes in the furrows.

In the West Country, a simpler version can sometimes be seen, often just a channel or leat that comes from a spring and appears to go nowhere. When it was in use the leat would have overflowed along its last section and flooded the land downhill from it.

Orchards

Although the fruit trees may define an orchard, the pasture in a traditional orchard was equally important to the farm economy. Orchard trees must always be widely spaced. They only produce fruit on those parts of their crown that are exposed to the light, so if you crowd them together like trees in a wood they give very little fruit. This means that there's also enough light at ground level to grow a crop of grass.

Almost all the traditional orchards are gone now. In the cider counties of Herefordshire, Devon and Somerset, the old editions of the large-scale Ordnance Survey maps show that each village or hamlet was surrounded by a dense cluster of orchards, where now perhaps one or two remain. They needed to be near the farmstead because the harvest is heavy so you didn't want to haul it too far. Also, an orchard is more sheltered and shady than an open field, so they were ideal for poorly animals and for cows and mares giving birth. Siting them near the farmstead meant these animals could get the attention they needed. Pigs could be let into the orchard to clean up windfalls and chickens could be put there in winter for pest control: many fruit pests spend winter hibernating in the soil and chickens love to scratch and peck to find them.

Although traditional orchards have little place in the modern economy they are wonderful places for wildlife, especially song birds. The old trees provide the nesting holes which tits need while the mix of trees and grass gives a diversity of food sources which keeps many birds well fed throughout the year. Some trees are thick with mistletoe and others lean over at steep angles.

They can live quite happily for decades bent almost to the ground, still producing apples as well as ever.

Modern orchards are quite a different thing. The trees are kept small throughout their lives because they are grafted onto dwarfing rootstocks. Their small size makes them easier to pick, prune and spray. They also come into fruit just a couple of years after planting, which is an important advantage when you're paying interest on the cost of buying the trees and planting them. The little trees are planted close together in rows, with alleys wide enough to take a tractor between the rows. A strip of ground directly beneath the trees is kept bare by regular spraying with herbicides because the dwarf trees can't stand the competition of grass.

A traditional orchard (left) and a modern orchard (right).

Unused Grassland

When grassland is neither grazed nor mown it eventually succeeds to scrub and then to woodland. But that takes some time and meanwhile the sward goes through some changes. At first the change may be more apparent than real. Broad-leaved plants which have been kept in a green, vegetative state by mowing or topping become highly visible as they flower and set seed. Thistles, docks and yarrow that have gone to seed can make the field look terribly weedy. You can get the same effect on a roadside verge, part of which is mown for visibility and part left to grow tall. As you drive past in a car the unmown part looks mixed and the mown part pure grass. But if you get out and have a closer look, you may find the two are composed of much the same range of plants.

After a year or two the composition of the sward does start to change. As long as it's regularly mown, the smaller, less vigorous plants are able to hold their own with their bigger neighbours because the big plants get cut down to size and, for a time at least, the don't over-top the smaller ones. But when mowing stops the small ones soon get out-competed and die out. This is especially noticeable in a semi-natural, herb-rich meadow. I've seen a diverse sward full of wildflowers reduced to just three grasses and the tall hogweed in a few years. Although there was a huge loss of biodiversity the change will have benefited small mammals such as voles, which like dense cover, and a few new plants moved in. One of these was the meadow cranesbill, a large wildflower with big, bluish blooms which, despite its name, is often found in uncut grass. Creeping thistle and hedge bindweed also came in and a clump of great willowherb, which sprang up on the site of a fire, persisted for years.

Churchyards

In many places the only semi-natural grassland that survives is in churchyards and cemeteries. You wouldn't think it when you see those close-mown lawns, but when the mowing regime is relaxed to just once a year the result can be like unlocking Aladdin's cave. The most striking example I've seen is the cemetery at Ventnor on the Isle of Wight, which lies on a chalk down high above the main town. Part of

The cemetry at Ventnor, Isle of Wight.

the cemetery is still mown like a lawn and part is treated as 'meadow' and cut once a year. In spring the meadow is covered in cowslips and in summer it explodes into the full splendour of chalk grassland.

It's remarkable how the wild-flowers have managed to survive the long years of close mowing. Yet they have, even the tall species such as knapweed and field scabious. They are there in the lawn area, kept to a miniature size and a vegetative state, but surviving.

NATURAL INFLUENCES

Improved grassland tends to be uniform right across the field. Every effort is made to do away with the variability of nature. But where the human hand rests a little lighter natural influences show through. These include the soil, the landform and microclimate.

Soil

This passage from my notebook records how a change from a clay soil to a sandy one is reflected in the grassland vegetation. It records a walk on the semi-natural pastures of the Kingcombe Nature Reserve in Dorset.

Kingcombe, Dorset

As you pass from the Gault clay to the greensand there's a sudden change in the grassland vegetation. On the clay there are rushes while on the sandy soil there's bracken and gorse. Apart from these three indicators, the same plants are growing on both clay and sand. The change in soil coincides with the line of a hedge, now grown out and no longer a barrier to animals. Both fields lie on the same gentle slope, the greensand uphill from the clay.

Further along we recrossed the boundary between clay and sand, this time at a place where the transition was emphasised by a sudden change in slope.

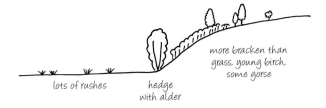

more bracken than grass, young birch, some gorse

lots of rushes

hedge with alder

Here there are almost no plants that grow on both sand and clay. On the sandy hump, tormentil and foxglove grow, in contrast to the orchids and other wildflowers on the clay below. On the better-drained parts of the clay there are clumps of bramble.

Kingcombe is an easy place to read the landscape. The whole farm is a nature reserve and among the wildlife that nature reserves exist to preserve are the very plants that tell the story to a landscape reader. On a more commercial farm the clay fields would probably be under-drained, which would put paid to the rushes, and regular topping would discourage the bracken and gorse. Indicator plants might still be there, such as buttercup in the pastures and foxglove in the hedges, but you'd have to look for them.

The next extract comes from a more mundane place, a former pony paddock. I took these notes while teaching soil observation on a permaculture course. The field had been used for pony grazing for thirty years, but recently it had changed hands and since then had been lightly grazed with sheep. From where we entered the field, at its highest point in the south-east corner, you could see a flower-spotted sward running down the right hand side of the field, a belt of dark green grass down the middle and to the left an area of paler green.

Kia's Field, Butleigh, Somerset

We dug a soil pit in each of the three areas, A, B and C.

A. Soil: clay loam, compacted, dark topsoil gradually grading to paler subsoil over 25cm. Plants: low grass, dandelion, both buttercups (mostly creeping), common daisy, ribwort plantain, red clover, black medic.

B. Soil: clay loam, no compaction, very dark topsoil grading to dark subsoil over 30cm. Plants: tall, dark green grass and not much else.

C. Soil: medium loam, no compaction, change from topsoil to subsoil at 35cm. Plants: mostly grass, medium height.

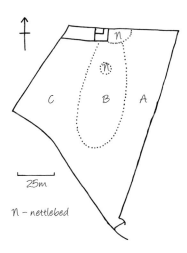

25m

n – nettlebed

This patchwork of different swards is the legacy of the ponies. The tall, dark green grass and rich, dark soil in area B is where they had their latrine area. Manure decomposes to form humus and gives the soil a dark colour. The fact that the soil there hasn't been compacted by the pounding of the ponies' hooves is testament to the power of humus to maintain soil structure. The difference between the two areas on either side is due to the difference between a heavy soil and a lighter one. The clay loam of area A is more susceptible to compaction than the medium loam of area C. Compacted soil restricts the root growth of plants and thus denies them access to mineral nutrients. This reduces the growth of the more competitive plants, such as the tall grasses, and allows the smaller ones, including the wildflowers we saw, to thrive.

Landform

The landform often causes differences in the soil. It will be thinner on a slope and deeper on flatter land due to the twin processes of erosion and deposition. But it also influences the way animals graze. Since they feel more comfortable on flat ground they graze the flat parts of a field more than the steeper parts. You can see this most clearly on strip lynchetts, those large terraces made by medieval cultivation. (See page 20.) Through much of the year the grass on the flat parts is short and green while the steep 'risers' bear the buff colour of stemmy, flowering grasses. The colour contrast is reinforced both by the dung of the animals and by summer rain, which is absorbed by the flat bits while the steep bits shed it.

You can see the same pattern in any grass field with an intimate mixture of steep bits and flat bits. But where the flat area is large and accessible it will almost certainly be improved and this will override any contrast caused by the grazing preferences of the animals. In predominantly arable areas the flat is not improved grassland but cereals and other arable crops, while permanent grassland is restricted to land that is too steep to plough. In the chalk country this often produces a sandwich landscape with arable on the hilltops and in the valleys, both of which are relatively flat, and permanent pasture on the steep slopes between.

A common feature of grassland on steep slopes is the little horizontal terraces known by the rather inelegant name of terracettes. Grazing animals find it more comfortable to walk across the slope rather than up and down. It's also easier for them to follow in the footsteps of an animal which has been that way before, so distinct paths form. The result is a whole series of terracettes running across the slope, giving it a corrugated texture.

Terracettes.

The following pair of sketches from my notebook illustrate some of the interactions between slope and grassland.

Wearyall Hill, Glastonbury

August, a couple of days after the first rain for a long time.

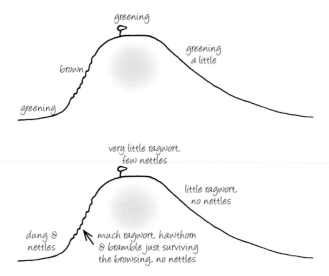

The first sketch illustrates how slope influences soil moisture. Summer rain coming after a dry spell gives the best opportunity to observe this but you need to wait at least a couple of days for the grass to green up. In this case the difference is reinforced by aspect as the steeper slope faces south and the more gradual one north.

The second sketch shows how slope affects the intensity of grazing and thus influences the vegetation. The tighter sward on the more intensively grazed areas makes it difficult for the biennial ragwort to find a place to germinate and grow. By contrast, there's plenty of bare soil on the steep slope with terracettes, and ragwort is abundant there. The lower intensity of grazing on the steep slope has allowed some shrubs to get a toehold. Meanwhile the patch of dung and nettles indicates the cattle's favourite place to hang out and chew the cud.

Sun and Shade

Anthills look like over-large molehills covered in a tight sward of grass and herbs. They are a sign of lightly-grazed permanent pasture. On a meadow or more intensive pasture they wouldn't survive the mowing, topping, chain harrowing or even the trampling of the cattle. But they are also an indicator of warm, dry soil, because the yellow meadow ants that make them are intolerant of wetness and need heat during the summer.

In some places you can see quite clearly how they have sought out the best-drained part of a field. In a steep field on a clay soil you may see them strung

*Anthills on an
old pasture.
Yarley Fields,
Somerset.*

along the little ridges on the outer edge of terracettes, like so many beads on a string. On the Mendips I've seen them seek out the line of a former wall, now just a grassy ridge a few inches higher than the ground on either side. But you'll often see them spread out across a field, usually favouring the warm, sunny south and south-west slopes. The ants will abandon their hills if a pasture is left ungrazed and the shade of the tall grass cools them down too much, though they may recolonise an old hill if conditions become suitable again.

Anthills have their own distinctive vegetation. Plants that like hot, dry conditions favour them. Marjoram sometimes grows on anthills while shunning the ground in between. Wild thyme favours the dry, sunny south side of an anthill while mosses are more common on the moister north side. On a cloudy day you could use an anthill as a compass to help find your way.

In summertime the coolest places in a field are under the trees, and animals congregate there on hot days. The trampling easily leads to bare ground as the plants are already weakened by shade from the tree. Hedgerow trees are shadier than free-standing ones because the hedge itself adds to the shade. Free-standing trees are more likely to have bare soil under them if they are the only shelter in the field and so get heavily used.

Nettles are very common under trees in grassland due to the dung of the sheltering animals. In the wood pasture of Moccas Park there's hardly a single big tree without a bed of nettles under it. Sometimes you get a 'doughnut effect' with bare soil in the shadiest zone near the trunk and a ring of nettles further out. In orchards that are no longer harvested there may be nettles round the trees because of the accumulated nutrients from fruit that has fallen and rotted in situ. Sometimes nettles grow under trees simply because tractors can't get in there to mow. Most modern fields are quite rich enough in phosphorous to support nettles. It's only their intolerance of cutting that stops them from out-competing the grass.

11

Heath and Moor

AN OPEN moor has a real feeling of wildness. With nothing in sight but mile upon mile of heather and moorgrass, and no sound but the sigh of the wind and the croak of a raven, you can feel yourself truly immersed in nature and far from any human influence. But then you see sheep quietly grazing and you know that the wildness is an illusion.

Most of the moors in Britain are semi-natural, forged from the wildwood by grazing that was persistent enough to prevent the regeneration of trees. Whether the grazing led to grassland, heath or moor, depends on the soil and the climate. Where they are favourable you get grassland. Where they are not you get that rougher landscape which we call heath when it's in the lowlands and moor when it's up in the hills.

Heath literally means heather and heather is the characteristic plant of both heaths and moors. But they also contain other plants, such as bracken, gorse, grasses and sedges, and can be dominated by them over large areas. In fact there's no hard-and-fast distinction between a rough, unenclosed grassland and a grassy moor. The distinction between heath and moor isn't hard and fast either. But heaths arise simply because their soil is poorer than that of the surrounding farmland while moors are formed both by soil and by the harsh climate of high altitude.

HEATHLAND

Heaths are usually formed on sandy and gravelly soils, which are acid, poor in nutrients and prone to drought. The heather itself increases soil acidity. Broadleaf trees, with their deep roots, bring up minerals, including lime, from the subsoil and spread them on the surface when their leaves fall. Heather, by contrast, has shallower roots and leaves which produce an acid litter when they fall.

Before the modern age farmers could do very little to remedy the deficiencies of these soils and the land was left as common grazing. The small but steady loss of nutrients from the heathland soil in the meat, milk or wool produced on it would tend to make the soil even poorer over time. Some heaths may have been cultivated during their history but this only speeded up the decline of the soil. It wasn't till the nineteenth century, when the railways could bring in lime from distant hills and steamships could bring guano and Chilean nitrate from the far side of the world, that farmers had the power to turn the heaths wholesale into permanent farmland.

Today very little heathland remains. Once-large areas of heath, such as the Suffolk Sandlings, have been reduced to isolated fragments in a sea of fertile fields. Others like Breckland and the Dorset heaths have been mostly coniferised. Small areas of heath, having no real place in modern agriculture, are often undergrazed and succeed to woodland unless they are taken in hand by a wildlife trust. The only really large area of heathland left in the lowlands is the New Forest in Hampshire. About half woodland and half heath, the New Forest is both a royal forest and a common. It still has something resembling its medieval legal structure, with a forest court and officials called Verderers and Agisters. Perhaps more importantly from a landscape point of view it still has a large and determined body of people who have rights to pasture animals on it. They are mostly part-time farmers, and grazing animals in the Forest is perhaps more a part of their lifestyle than an economic activity. Their determination to go on doing it is what keeps the heathland alive.

A Heathland Mosaic

A walk I took across some New Forest heathland provides an introduction to the relationships and processes that go on in a heath.

Broomy Plain to Slodden Inclosure, New Forest

The heath is a mosaic of different vegetation types but none of them consists of just one plant. They are all a mix, though usually with one species predominating. The size of the patches that make up the mosaic varies a lot according to the landform. On the gravel plateau of Broomy Plain the patches are large, measuring hectares. On the central, flat part of the plain heather* predominates, with bell heather, gorse and grasses mixed in with it. On the sloping edges there's bracken.

I went through Broomy Inclosure and came out in the little valley of the Dockens Water. On the south-facing slope of the valley the mosaic is at a much smaller scale, with some patches only a few paces wide. Where the soil is wet there's a mix of heather and cross-leaved heath, the latter increasing where the soil gets wetter. Where it's very wet the heathers give way to purple moorgrass and bog moss. I soon learned that these were places I had to avoid if I wanted to keep my feet dry! On well-drained loams, bracken and grass

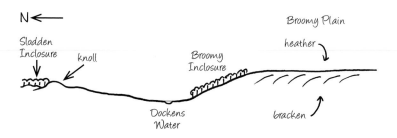

158

alternate. At the top of the slope I found a knoll where heather, bell heather, bracken, bilberry and gorse are mixed. Here the soil is pure sand. On the whole the wetter patches are further down the slope and the drier nearer the top, but not in every case. The boundaries between one patch and another are mostly clear and abrupt.

I made my way along the valley and recrossed the Dockens Water further up. Here the valley floor is a little wider and on the flat ground either side of the stream there's a 'lawn' of close-cropped grasses. The soil, a sandy loam, is well-drained here. The place has a strangely domestic air compared to the chaotic heathland vegetation, almost like a golf course or a garden.

* Here and throughout this chapter 'heather' means common heather or ling, as opposed to its cousins, bell heather and cross-leaved heath.

All the plants I saw that day were typical of poor, acid soils. But some are more tolerant of poor, acid soils than others, while some of them grow in drier or wetter soils. The interactions between these two niche factors produced the mosaic of vegetation I saw.

Dry

Broomy Plain is a typical dry heath on a gravelly soil and some of the plants that grow there are specially adapted to resist drought. Plants constantly lose water from their leaves and in gorse the leaves have been reduced to spikes so as to minimise the surface area exposed to the air. In bell heather the small, narrow leaves are curled in on themselves to much the same effect. This makes it the most drought-tolerant of the heathers. Nonetheless common heather dominates here. It's a very competitive plant and grows more vigorously and reproduces more abundantly than the other two heathers.

Common heather or ling.

The heathers are supremely well adapted to a poor, acid soil but not so common gorse, which usually

Cross-leaved heath.

Bell heather.

159

This pattern is often repeated in the New Forest: heather and gorse on the plateau, bracken on the slope and sweet grasses on the floor of the little valley. Long Slade Bottom, New Forest.

grows where the soil is slightly richer. On heaths, it's often found by roads, tracks, old boundary banks and gravel workings. In these places the soil has been disturbed and subsoil, which contains some of the minerals leached out of the upper layers by rainwater, has been brought to the surface. The few gorse bushes scattered over Broomy Plain indicate a soil that is slightly less poor than ones that support only heathers. More demanding again than gorse is bracken. It's confined to the sloping edges of the plain. Here it can find more nutrients because where there's a slope there's erosion and this exposes layers of material that are slightly richer than the flat cap of leached gravel on top.

The other dry area I saw was the knoll on the other side of the little valley and this had very mixed vegetation on it. This is unusual on heathland, where normally one or two plants dominate and the others are subordinate. The soil has a thin layer of pure humus lying over a topsoil of pure sand, so leached that it's almost white. The thin humus layer is typical of heath and moorland soils that are too acid for the soil-living creatures, especially earthworms, which would otherwise mix it with the soil. The extreme dryness of this soil may account for the diversity of plants, as it reduces the vigour of the would-be dominants so other plants can co-exist with them as equals. Bilberry is one of them. Although it's not confined to dry places it's well adapted to them, with a thick, waxy coating on its leaves that reduces water loss.

Wet

The water that drains so freely down from the plains and hillocks emerges again in the wet patches I found on the slope. For water to emerge on a slope like this there must be an impervious layer below the sands and gravels, probably of clay. (See page 175.) Here the cross-leaved heath makes its appearance. Just as bell heather specialises in drier soils so cross-leaved heath specialises in wet ones. There's only a narrow band where it's the dominant plant, between the mix of itself and heather on the slightly drier soil and the purple moorgrass and bog moss on the wetter. Purple moorgrass is a tall, tough plant that often grows in tussocks and whose narrow flowering heads are usually, though not always, purple. It's very tolerant of poor, wet soils but it's an unpalatable grass with little feed value and grazing animals will avoid it if they have the choice.

More Fertile

The sweet grasses which grow on the patches of well-drained, loamy soils are a different matter altogether. They are the most palatable and nutritious of heathland plants and the animals graze them down short. They are in competition with the bracken. If grass and bracken are left to battle it out on a deep, well-drained soil the bracken wins every time. But if you throw grazing animals into the balance the contest is much more equal. Since bracken is poisonous, animals hardly eat it but it is vulnerable to being trampled.

There's a symbiotic relationship between grass and its grazers. The more the animals eat the grass the more they trample any bracken growing along with it and the more the grass prospers, which in turn means more food for the grazers. To some extent this leads to a segregation between bracken and grass, as the animals concentrate on the places where there's more grass and shun the places where there's more bracken, reinforcing any difference which already exists.

The largest patch of sweet grasses I saw that day was the strip of lawn either side of the Dockens Water. The streamside lawns provide the richest grazing of all in the New Forest and though they make up a tiny proportion of the Forest area the animals get a large part of their nutrition from them. The streamside soils are rich and relatively alkaline because this is where the mineral nutrients which are leached out of the rest of the landscape end up. The poor Forest soils don't contain much in the way of nutrients but the area of leaching is large compared to the area where they accumulate. Good drainage is essential for the sweet grasses. Some of the lawns may flood in winter, and this is how they gain much of their fertility, but they dry out in summer. Where the water can't get away even in summer peat accumulates in the valley and a bog forms.

The lawn of sweet grasses beside Dockens Water contrasts with the rough vegetation of the heath.

Heathland Dynamics

Heaths, like any other ecosystem, are constantly changing. Much of this change centres around the life cycles of the dominant plants. Heather has a lifespan of twenty-five to thirty years. It starts out as a little conical plant that doesn't cover much ground and allows plenty of space for other species to grow beside it. But as it grows it develops a strong dome of dense foliage that excludes most other plants. When it matures it develops a more flat-topped shape and in old age the plants start to collapse, once again leaving space for other plants to grow.

The collapsed stage may be the time of greatest diversity in the life of the heath, with mosses, lichens, grasses and flowers all taking advantage of the light which is let in by the fall of the heather. But if bracken is present it may become dominant for a time. On some heaths dominance can swing backwards and forwards between heather and bracken according to which of them is in its most vigorous phase of growth, but it doesn't necessarily result in an even see-sawing down the years. All sorts of factors can swing the balance one way or the other.

Fire is one of these. Heather thrives under a regime of controlled burning. After a fire it reseeds copiously and unless the plants are too old or the fire too hot it will sprout from the rootstock too. Fire can be used as a management tool to keep the heather at a young, nutritious stage of growth. But an accidental fire which sweeps uncontrolled across the heath is very much hotter and destroys both plants and seed. Bracken, which has rhizomes deep in the soil where the heat hardly penetrates, is better able to withstand such a fire than other heathland plants and an uncontrolled fire can turn a mixed heath into one of pure bracken.

Grazing is another factor. Many heaths are now grazed only by rabbits and they give the advantage to bracken, because it's poisonous and they eat everything else in preference. Cattle and horses, on the other hand, trample out the bracken and favour the heather. The decline in grazing by domestic animals in recent years has led to the takeover of many heaths by bracken. The result is a loss of biodiversity. Bracken is so competitive that little can live underneath it. Some spring-blooming woodland wildflowers can survive if the bracken canopy is light, but most heathland plants can't and almost nothing lives under a dense stand. Some nature conservationists have resorted to spraying it with herbicides.

The bushy structure of heathland is important to some animals. Stonechats and whinchats, two little birds that are often found on heathland, need shrubs about waist height as hunting perches. It doesn't matter what the plants are as long as they are the right height. Bracken or young trees are equally suitable, though once the trees grow too tall the chats will disappear. In fact whole heaths can disappear as the trees grow, by succeeding to woodland. Scots pine and birch, and also rhododendron where it's present, are avid colonisers of heath. Burning actually favours trees by providing bare ground for them to seed into, without killing existing saplings. The occasional tree is no bad thing, though. Nightjars, those elusive and mysterious birds which haunt the evening gloom with their churring call, need trees as well as open ground in their habitat. They often live on the edge between wood and heath and these days some of them live in forestry plantations, where recently felled compartments take the place of heath.

JOHN ADAMS

Fungi

Some of the most vital members of the heathland ecosystem are the fungi. When a mushroom or toadstool pops its head above ground it's even less than the tip of the proverbial iceberg. It's just the reproductive organ of the fungus, like the flower on the holly bush or the acorn on the oak tree. Almost all of its body is below ground and it's there all the time, not just for a few days in the autumn. Fungi are everywhere beneath the surface, filling the soil with millions of threads.

As I described in Chapter 6, many of them make mutually beneficial relationships with plant roots and no plants are more dependent on this than the members of the heather family. (See page 69.) This includes heathers themselves plus bilberry, its relatives such as cowberry and cranberry, and even rhododendron. These are all plants that live in the poorest soils, soils which even gorse and bracken would find too poor. But they can only do it because the fungi are super-efficient at extracting mineral nutrients from even the most recalcitrant soils. While above ground the drama of competition is played out between plant and plant, below ground the quiet co-operation between plant and fungus makes it all possible.

A heath of heather and purple moor grass succeeding to woodland of birch and pine. Surrey.

163

MOORLAND

Microclimate

The journey from lowland to upland often goes something like this.

Cambrian Mountains, Mid Wales

Going east from Tregaron you soon leave behind the lowland landscape with its thick hedges full of hazel, their banks brightened with foxgloves and red campion. You climb a U-shaped valley and the hedges give way to fences, the frequent farms and villages to long, lonely stretches with just a rare farmstead.

Today, the blue sky and puffy white clouds over the vale have turned into a solid grey mass over the mountains. I came through a big plantation and out onto unfenced grass moor, four to five hundred metres up. It has a harsh, uncomfortable feel after the sunny lushness of the lower land. Down there the bracken is chest high, up here hardly knee high and still not fully open. Of all the plants I've seen only foxgloves are growing in both lowland and upland and at the same stage of growth in both places.

When I came back down to the valley the sun was still shining. On a dull day in the valley it would have been raining on the hills. The harsher climate that comes so quickly with increasing altitude is an important factor in the formation of moorland. (See page 49.) The rocks do tend to be the old, hard rocks that form acid soils. But the incessant rain leaches minerals from the soil so thoroughly that even a rock that would produce quite a fertile soil in the lowlands may support nothing but moorland on the hills.

The Rocks

This sketch from my notebook illustrates how rock type and climate can interact to form moorland.

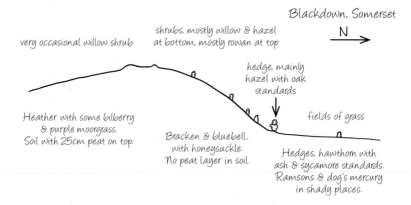

Blackdown, Somerset

N →

shrubs, mostly willow & hazel at bottom, mostly rowan at top

very occasional willow shrub

hedge, mainly hazel with oak standards

Heather with some bilberry & purple moorgrass. Soil with 25cm peat on top.

fields of grass

Bracken & bluebell, with honeysuckle. No peat layer in soil.

Hedges, hawthorn with ash & sycamore standards. Ramsons & dog's mercury in shady places.

Blackdown is the highest hill on the Mendips and the only real piece of moorland on the range. From it you have a magnificent view down into the intricate

landscape of North Somerset, with its small fields and thick hedges, bright green on the sunny May morning I made this sketch. At the foot of Blackdown, but still up in the hills, lies a strip of fields where the land flattens out before it dips down into the gorge of Burrington Combe. Blackdown itself is made of Old Red sandstone while the strip of fields at its foot are on carboniferous limestone.

Old Red sandstone can make a reasonably fertile soil where the climate's not too harsh. But up here where the rainfall is high it makes a poor, acid soil that is poorly drained unless the land has a good slope on it. The limestone that lies under the fields is richer in nutrients and alkaline, and its soil can support pasture of sweet grasses despite the high rainfall. There are other outcrops of Old Red sandstone along the spine of the Mendips but Blackdown is the highest of them and the nearest to the sea, so it has the wettest climate.

Blackdown shows a familiar pattern of vegetation you can see on many of the hills of Britain: bracken on the slopes and heather or grass moor on the flat tops. Bracken is the most competitive of moorland plants but it's limited by soil conditions. It needs a richer, better-drained and deeper soil than other moorland plants. On Broomy Plain in the New Forest, I suggested that it was confined to the slopes by the lack of nutrients on the flat plain. That may be a factor on Blackdown but here drainage is certainly important too. The Old Red is a cemented sandstone that doesn't allow free drainage, so the flat hilltop is wetter than the sloping hillside. The layer of peat that lies over the mineral soil on the hilltop suggests poor drainage.

Bracken is an unpopular plant. Farmers don't like it because their animals can't eat it and nature conservationists don't like it because it reduces biodiversity. And it's spreading. Over the past half-century the area covered by bracken

A typical moorland pattern: bracken on the slopes, with heathers and grasses on the flatter tops. The conifer plantation is located at random. Dartmoor, Devon.

has increased enormously. This is partly because of the modern drive towards monoculture. In the hills this has meant a steady decrease in cattle, who trample bracken, and an increase in sheep, who don't. It's also because bracken is no longer used for anything. In earlier times hill farmers would cut it for animal bedding and the constant cutting kept it under control. A third reason is climate change. Bracken is not a very cold-tolerant plant and its upper limit on the higher hills is determined by temperature. As the climate warms it's gradually extending upwards.

Burning

Blackdown is a small, isolated moor in an area with little living tradition of using moorland. In areas where there's more of it, moorland is more integrated into the farming system and this has its effect on the vegetation. This example from Mid Wales makes an interesting comparison with Blackdown.

Mynydd Llanllwni, Carmarthenshire

On the lower slopes of the common there's closely-cropped grass with scattered clumps of gorse and heather. The gorse is more towards the bottom of the slope and the heather higher up. Right at the bottom, against the boundary bank, I can see a bit of pure bracken. So there's a gradation in the vegetation as you go up the slope that, if you discount the grass, can be summarised as: bracken to gorse to heather. This seems to be the general pattern round the edges of the moor, though in some places it's more complex.

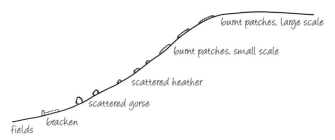

On the upper slopes, the vegetation at first looked like alternating patches of heather and grass, which I assumed reflected natural variations in the soil. But when I walked over it I saw that the mix of plants is the same in every patch: mainly heather and grasses with some cross-leaved heath and bilberry. The patches where grass is dominant are the more recently burnt ones and where heather dominates the less recently burnt. Grass regrows more quickly after burning and grows taller and more abundantly than the little heather plants. With the passing of time the heather grows up and suppresses the grass. On the patches that have been left unburnt for longest, dome-shaped heather plants alternate with tightly-grazed grass. Beside a small abandoned quarry some heaps of stony spoil are covered with a pure stand of bilberry.
    The top of the moor is a wide plateau. Here the burnt areas are much bigger and generally in a younger stage of growth, indicating that they are more

frequently burnt. The general impression is of a grass moor, until you walk out over it and see the heather coming up through the grass. The sky is full of singing larks and though it's a windy day bumblebees are working the cross-leaved heath, which is in flower at the moment. There are sheep all over the place but Sarah (a horsewoman and one of the commoners on Mynydd Llanllwni) says it's undergrazed. She's never seen it looking so green. She says that these days there are no cattle and fewer horses and sheep. The farmers are supposed to leave the moor unburnt for five years, but they are still burning it despite that.

At first the sloping edge of Mynydd Llanllwni seems to be quite different from the hillside of Blackdown. But there is an underlying similarity between the two hills. Both have heather on the top and other, more demanding plants on the slopes. At Llanllwni, intensive grazing has banished bracken to little patches on the best soil at the bottom of the hill, thus giving the competitive edge to grass and gorse. The gradation bottom to top – bracken, grass with gorse, grass with heather, and finally heather which would be almost pure if it wasn't for the burning – indicates how the soil gets less fertile as you go up the hill. It reflects the old saying, which I've heard from both Wales and England:

> *There's gold under bracken,*
> *Silver under gorse,*
> *And famine under heather.*

Burning is much more common on moors than heaths and most heather moors are managed this way. The main aim is to rejuvenate the heather, replacing the tough, old plants with tender young ones that are more nutritious. On some moors, like Mynydd Llanllwni, burning is done solely for the benefit of sheep while others are managed both for sheep and grouse. The burning regime is different in either case. Grouse need young heather for food but they also need old heather for shelter and nesting, so the interval between burnings is longer to allow it to grow bigger. As grouse territories are fairly small the burnt patches need to be small so that each territory contains both young and old heather. The result is a small-scale mosaic of strongly contrasting patches.

On moors that are managed for sheep the aim is purely to get the maximum of young heather and grass, so a much shorter cycle is used. Larger areas are burned at a time because it saves labour. The result is a much more homogenous appearance. But grouse are not the only wildlife to appreciate the longer rotation and the shorter cycle reduces overall biodiversity. Hence the ruling that Mynydd Llanllwni should be given a break of five years without burning, presumably as a condition of the new subsidy regime which links payments to wildlife-friendly practices. The old subsidies were paid on the number of cattle and sheep and the drop in animal numbers on the moor is a consequence of the ending of those payments. This is why there was more grass on the moor than ever before. But habits die hard and the farmers were still burning. The urge to 'make two blades of grass grow where one grew before' is deeply engrained in farming culture.

Moorland Dynamics

There's an interplay between burning, grazing and soil fertility. If grazing is too hard immediately after burning it can knock the heather back so badly that it fails to regenerate. Then grass, with its structural ability to withstand grazing, out-competes the heather and takes over. Whether the change from heather to grass is of benefit to the farmers or not depends on the soil. If it's very poor the heather will be replaced by purple moorgrass or matgrass, a wiry grass with a grey cast to it. These rough grasses are less nutritious than young heather, so they bring down the productivity of the moor. If the soil's not so poor the heather may be replaced by sweet grasses, which are more nutritious than the heather. Even without burning, hard grazing over a long time can turn a heather moor into a grass moor. This is probably how most grass moors have been formed.

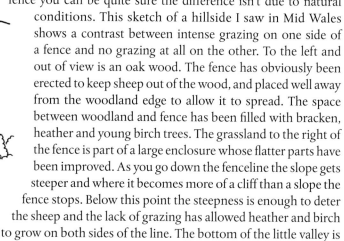

The effect of different levels of grazing can often spring into focus along a fence line. If you see a change in the vegetation exactly on the line of the fence you can be quite sure the difference isn't due to natural conditions. This sketch of a hillside I saw in Mid Wales shows a contrast between intense grazing on one side of a fence and no grazing at all on the other. To the left and out of view is an oak wood. The fence has obviously been erected to keep sheep out of the wood, and placed well away from the woodland edge to allow it to spread. The space between woodland and fence has been filled with bracken, heather and young birch trees. The grassland to the right of the fence is part of a large enclosure whose flatter parts have been improved. As you go down the fenceline the slope gets steeper and where it becomes more of a cliff than a slope the fence stops. Below this point the steepness is enough to deter the sheep and the lack of grazing has allowed heather and birch to grow on both sides of the line. The bottom of the little valley is inaccessible to sheep and some quite large birch trees grow there.

This contrast between moorland vegetation and grassland is often marked where open common land lies beside enclosed fields, with moorland on the common and grass in the fields. It's possible that the fields have been deliberately improved, with lime, fertiliser and drainage, or even ploughing and reseeding. But it's not necessarily so. It's just as often simply a matter of being able to control the pattern of grazing.

Once you have a wall or a fence round a piece of ground you can put a large number of animals on it for a short time and then move them off again. While they are there they will eat, browse or trample everything in reach. When they are gone the grasses, with their superior ability to regrow after defoliation, will bounce back at the expense of other plants. A few weeks later you can do the same again. Meanwhile on the common land the animals wander where they will and eat the plants they find most tasty, leaving the less palatable ones, like bracken and rushes, to thrive. So controlled grazing improves the pasture while uncontrolled grazing causes it to deteriorate.

Curiously, controlled grazing in fields is closer to the way wild grazing animals behave than the uncontrolled grazing on the common. Wild herbivores stick together in a tight herd to defend themselves from predators, who are always on the lookout for an isolated individual. Wherever the herd goes it eats everything down to the ground and doesn't return till the sward has regrown. Although it might seem more 'natural' to leave animals to wander around, in fact shutting them up in fields and moving them regularly from one field to another is much closer to their natural conditions.

Enclosed pasture and open common. Blawith, Cumbria.

Blanket Bogs

In the western Highlands there are tall mountains that in places rise up in a series of big steps. From a distance you can see how heather and birch trees cling to the steep 'risers' while the 'treads' appear to be clothed in grass. In another part of the country you might put this down to grazing pressure being higher on the flat ground, and indeed that may be a factor. But the rainfall here is very high and flat ground over impermeable rocks is often too wet for heather and trees. What looks from a distance like grassland is more likely peat bog covered in grass-like plants called sedges.

At the beginning of this chapter I said that most of the moors in Britain are semi-natural, formed from the original woodland by grazing. But there are some moors that were formed by a purely natural process, the growth of blanket bogs. A bog is an accumulation of peat. Peat consists of partly-decomposed plant material which forms where conditions are too wet for it to decompose fully. (See page 179.) Peat itself absorbs and holds a lot of water, so once started the process of peat formation is self-reinforcing and a deep layer of it can form where conditions are continually wet. Trees can't survive in the waterlogged environment of a bog and large areas of wildwood were overwhelmed by growing blanket bogs during the more rainy episodes of prehistoric times.

You might expect bogs to form in low-lying places where the water can't drain away easily, and indeed they do. But in the wettest hill and mountain areas the rainfall is so high that bogs can form on any flat or gently sloping land where the rock is impermeable. They are called blanket bogs because they cover whole landscapes with a blanket of peat that can be several metres deep. This is on a completely different scale to the thin layer of peat on the surface of a typical heather-moor soil. Most heather moors are found in areas of modest rainfall whereas blanket bogs are the product of rainfall which is so high that saturation is the normal condition of the soil. They are concentrated in the rainy north and west of Britain. On the Pennines they occur mainly on the wetter western side of the range and at higher altitude, while heather moors are more common on the east side and lower down. In the Highlands, most of the moors to the south-east of the Great Glen have been formed by grazing while most of them to the north-west have been formed by the spread of blanket bog.

From Bog Moss to Trees

Blanket bogs can be wonderful and complex ecosystems. The most character-istic plant is bog moss or sphagnum, which not only tolerates these conditions but is also partly responsible for creating them as it absorbs many times its own weight of water. Pick up a fat handful of bog moss and squeeze it: water pours out and you're left with a wisp of moss as thin as a feather. Cottongrass grows in both bogs and shallow water. With its distinctive seedheads like blobs of cotton wool it's a useful warning of where it's not safe to walk. The short, wiry deergrass dominates wide areas of blanket peat and in the western Highlands it's mainly responsible for the golden brown colour of those great, rounded hills in late summer. Despite their names, both these plants are sedges rather than grasses. You can tell a sedge from a grass because their stems are solid and more or less triangular in section while those of grasses are hollow and round.

The extreme poverty of bog soils has given rise to some curious plants, and some interesting folklore. Sundew is a little plant with unremarkable white flowers but very distinctive leaves. The leaves have a sweet scent and a covering of prominent red hairs, both of which attract insects. No sooner does an insect land on a leaf than the hairs, which are covered in sticky glue, curve in on it and trap it. The plant then proceeds to digest the insect, not for the organic food it contains but for the precious minerals, especially nitrogen. Bog asphodel, with its spike of yellow star-flowers, used to be called break-bone. Farmers knew that sheep that graze where it grows often suffer from brittle bones. They had no way of knowing that it was the deficiency of calcium and phosphorous in the peat that was the culprit rather than the plant itself.

Blanket bogs aren't uniformly wet and in many places they become dry enough for heather to grow and sheep to graze. In time the peat may be broken up by drainage channels. These often start out as sheep tracks or small-scale peat diggings and can end up eroding down to the bedrock. The blocks of peat that remain are called haggs and are much drier than intact bog. Much the same range of plants grows on them as before but the balance of species changes. Only the bog moss dies out entirely and heather is usually the main plant that increases. Pine and birch trees may colonise if it dries out enough and the grazing pressure is sufficiently low. But at high altitude or near the coast succession may be very slow to start. Trees find it hard to get established in a cold, wet and windy climate, especially if the wind is salty, and in some places there's also a lack of seed parents.

In areas of high rainfall and leached soils, the tree most likely to succeed on open moorland is birch, not just because of its powers of dispersal and tolerance of harsh climate but also because it tolerates very poor, acid soils. More demanding trees such as ash, hazel and wych elm are confined to places where active erosion of the rock is taking place, such as the banks of a stream or at the base of a cliff, where stones dislodged by frost action collect. As the rocks slowly weather they release some of the minerals that have long since been washed out of the tired, old soil of the open hills.

VEGETATION SUMMARY

The Heather Family

Heather	Poor, acid soil, moist to dry; tolerates thin soil.
Bell heather	Mixed with heather on drier soils, dominant on very dry ones.
Cross-leaved heath	Mixed with heather on wetter soils, dominant where it's too wet for heather.
Bilberry	Often on drier soil or boulders; shade-tolerant and also thrives in woods.

Plants of More Fertile Soils

Bracken	Deep, well-drained soil, richer and less acid than typical heather soil, usually on a slope; sensitive to trampling; altitude limited by cold.
Sweet grasses (bents and fescues)	A mix of fine-leaved grasses, usually grazed down short because the animals like them; similar soils to bracken.
Gorse, common	Slightly poorer soils than bracken, but sometimes more alkaline, well-drained; not cold-tolerant.
Gorse, dwarf and western	Much smaller plants than common gorse, with similar soil preferences to heather.

Plants of Wet Soils

Matgrass	Similar soil to heather but often a bit wetter; it and purple moorgrass may take over where heather is overgrazed.
Purple moorgrass	Similar soil to matgrass but usually a bit wetter still; often grows in big tussocks – hard going for walkers.
Bog myrtle	Wet to very wet soil, often with purple moorgrass.
Deergrass	Deep peat and bogs, very wet and acid.
Cottongrass	Bogs, wetter than deergrass and including open water.
Bog moss	The ultimate peat-forming bog plant, only found in extremely wet conditions.

12

Water in the Landscape

WATER BODIES reflect the character of the surrounding landscape, not least by the colour of the water itself. The clear water of rocky mountain pools and streams is a sign of acidity and a low level of nutrients. Mountain rocks are hard and slow to release what minerals they contain, and many are poor and acid as well. The water is clear because there aren't enough nutrients to support the growth of the microscopic plants and animals that cloud more fertile waters. As you go down into the lower hills the water gradually becomes more opaque. Even if the rocks are still nutrient-poor, the water has travelled further and has had more opportunity to pick up both nutrients and inorganic silt. Streams that flow through chalk have the special quality of being rich in calcium but, because chalk is a very pure form of limestone, clear of silt. The fast flowing water mixes in plenty of oxygen and the combination makes them ideal for trout. Trout and their cousins the grayling are indicators of clean, oxygenated water.

Not all upland streams and lakes are clear. Ones that get their water from peat bogs can range from a pale yellow to a mysterious black. Looking down into a dark, peaty pool it can be hard to tell if it's knee deep or bottomless. You don't need much imagination to see where the tales of the monster from the deep came from. Rivers are often peat-stained too. A river that rushes down the hills, Guinness-brown and topped off with a creamy foam, reveals its origins in a distant peat bog, though on either side there may be only woods and fields.

These peaty stains are quite different from the muddy colours of lowland rivers. They may be quite clear in dry weather but after rain they turn anything from milk-chocolate brown to ruby red, according to the colour of the local soil. This indicates soil erosion, the invariable companion of agriculture. Although soil does erode under natural conditions the rate is tiny compared to that on farmland.

Ponds may contain less eroded material than rivers but more nutrients and these feed a thickening soup of green phytoplankton and the resulting colour can range from muddy grey to blue green. The high level of nutrients is partly a natural effect. Throughout the ages nutrients have been leached and washed from the wider landscape and ended up in the low places from which further movement is slow. But human activity has greatly added to the flow.

Sewage is one source. Although sewage treatment is supposed to remove nitrogen and phosphorous from the treated water, in the real world things don't always go exactly according to plan. Runoff from fields is another source.

Chemical farming is not an exact science and in practice only about half of the fertiliser applied is actually taken up by the crop plants. Most of the other half eventually ends up in water bodies. The effect on the river ecosystem can be similar to fertilising a grassland field, giving an extra advantage to the competitor plants. (See page 71.) Sadly these days many lowland riverbanks are covered in a continuous bed of nettles, thriving on the nutrients left behind by enriched flood waters.

Cattle like to eat oilseed rape: the field on the left is being grazed at the moment while the one on the right is shut up for silage. Somerset Levels.

A waterside plant that has become common in recent years is oilseed rape. As a cultivated crop it's a fairly new introduction but it's lost no time in getting established as a naturalised plant. Here in Somerset it mostly grows on the banks of rivers and drainage channels. It's an out-and-out competitor and certainly appreciates the extra nutrients, both from the enriched river water and from the spoil that's dumped on the banks when the river is dredged. With its large seed, fast growth and big, horizontal leaves it's well able to hold its own against perennials such as nettles. In some low-lying parts of Somerset you can spot a river from a distance by a line of bright yellow rape-flowers, often mixed with the white of cow parsley, cutting across the deep green of the springtime grassland.

Springs

Small springs are potentially useful. Even if water only flows in the winter there may still be a usable yield all year round that is used up during summer by the surrounding plants. Clear away the plants and collect the water in a pipe and you may have enough to meet a modest domestic need.

In grassland, small springs may reveal themselves by a strip of grass that is brighter green than its surroundings, stretching downhill from the point where the water emerges. It's greener in summer because it's kept continuously moist. It's greener in winter because the water from underground is warmer than the cold winter air and this difference is enough to keep the grass growing. Patches of green like this must surely have been the inspiration for the first watermeadows. (See page 150.) In a frost the green stripe is even clearer as it stands out against the white rime. When spring comes and all the grass is green, the wet strip may stand out brown if it gets poached by the feet of cattle, turned out after spending the winter inside. Later in the year the poached area may grass over again but, if the field hasn't been rolled, the deep footprints left by the cattle will give it away. On soils where buttercups aren't common the moist patch around a spring may be thick with them and stand out a brilliant yellow at flowering time. A stronger spring or one on a heavier soil is more often marked by rushes. In woods the creeping buttercup may indicate a slight spring while golden saxifrage usually indicates soil that's too wet to walk on. Larger springs are often marked by the presence of alder trees.

Sometimes a spring can dry up in one place and reappear in another, and I've had the opportunity to observe this process in my field. When I first came to the field there was a small spring at one end. Though it ran for most of the year, the flow was weak and the water only crept a little way down the slope before it seeped back into the soil. After some years it suddenly dried up and reappeared at the other end of the field.

There was no discernable cause for this change, but under the ground there lies evidence that the stream that runs along one side of the field, and any springs associated with it, have steadily changed position over the long ages of prehistoric time. This is a layer of tufa, some thirty centimetres below ground. Tufa is a limy substance that is sometimes deposited by a stream or spring flowing from a limestone catchment. In the present stream you can see it forming as a thin surface layer on twigs and other debris in the water, a cream-coloured crust that makes the twig look petrified. Over time the organic nucleus is lost and the tufa gradually becomes a homogenous, granular deposit. Far from being confined to the present course of the stream, the underground layer of tufa is spread over several hectares, including all of the field and parts of its neighbours. All of this area must have been either streambed or spring at one time or another.

In its new position the spring flows a little more strongly and there's water on the surface throughout the year, which means that corner of the field can't be mown for hay. The change also happened around the time I found it increasingly hard to find a farmer who would graze the aftermath. The original spring had only been marked by a few rushes, which are resistant to grazing. But the lack of mowing and grazing in the new position allowed other plants to move in. The first was great hairy willowherb, cousin of the more familiar rosebay willowherb, which established itself on the new wet patch. This was followed a year later by the common reed. Over two metres high, with a feathery flowerhead which bends to the breeze, reeds can easily out-compete the knee-high rushes, but they are palatable to grazing animals and soon die out if they are regularly grazed. There were other plants, of course, but great hairy willowherb and reeds were the principal actors.

You would expect the reeds to take over in the standing water, right by the spring, as they are plants of shallow water as well as wet soil, whereas the willowherb favours moist to wet soils. But the opposite happened. The willow-herb held its ground in the very wettest part, while the reeds grew up around them in the outer area which is only moderately wet. They say that in ecology possession is nine-tenths of the law and the willowherb certainly proved that, at least for a time. I kept a record of the changing vegetation in the wet area around the spring, and it took sixteen years before the reeds finally overcame the willowherb. Now the whole area is a fairly homogenous reedbed. Just one willow tree has sprung up there and spreads its branches above the top of the reeds – the harbinger of the next stage of succession.

Spring Lines

While small springs only affect their immediate surroundings, large ones can influence the landscape on a broad scale because they attract settlement. Before the days of mains water every village, indeed every farm, had to have a reliable supply of its own. Springs often occur where hills of a permeable rock, such as limestone, stand over a valley of an impermeable one, such as clay. Rain that falls on the hills seeps down through the permeable rock till it comes to the impermeable layer. It can't go down any further so it stays there, saturating the lower part of the permeable layer and forming an underground store of water known as an aquifer. Where the junction between the two rock types meets the surface, which is usually near the bottom of the hillside, the water comes out in a series of springs. This is called a spring line. An example of a spring line on a very small scale can be seen in the sketch on page 153, where sand overlies clay. Notice the alder trees in the hedge that marks the boundary between the two. They indicate where the water is coming out of the ground.

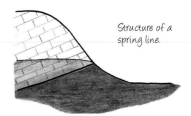

Structure of a spring line.

A second reason a spring line offers good village sites is that it gives access to both hill and vale. Pretty much every range of chalk or limestone hills in England has a series of villages along the spring line at its foot. The territory of each one extended in a narrow oblong, reaching up onto the hills above and down into the clay vale below, giving each community its share of the different kinds of land: downs for pasture, clay vale for arable and riversides for meadow. The boundaries of these territories have often been inherited by the modern civil parishes and you can trace them on the Explorer series of Ordnance Survey maps.

Ponds

A disadvantage of the downland pasture was that there was no surface water up there and the grazing animals had to walk a long way to drink. A solution to the problem was the dew pond. These days the word is often used loosely to describe any pond out in the fields but a real dew pond is a specific kind of pond designed to collect rain. Why they ever got called dew ponds I don't know, because the dew doesn't provide enough water to flow along the surface and fill a pond.

A dew pond is a shallow, circular bowl at the centre of a catchment area that naturally drains towards it. Both pond and catchment area were lined with puddled clay to make them impermeable. On the Mendips the pond itself was also lined with flagstones, perhaps to prevent the clay lining being punctured by the hooves of the cattle as they jostled to get at the water. In the rainy maritime climate of the Mendips the ponds held water for most of the year, though they did need cleaning out regularly. They were made at the time of the enclosure acts, when the land was parcelled out into stone-walled fields and the cattle could no longer walk down to the valleys for water. These days they have been superseded by drinking troughs fed by the mains.

While a dewpond needs careful construction and regular maintenance, nothing could be easier than making a pond in low-lying clay country where the water table is near the surface. All you need to do is dig a hole and it will fill with water. But you do need to be sure that the water table is indeed near the surface. The best way to find out is by digging a test pit and seeing what happens over twelve months. The twelve months are necessary because a pond that fills in winter may dry up in summer. In some places a test pit may not be totally reliable as one part of the site may be more leaky than another, for example where clay is interbedded with irregular layers of limestone.

A newly dug pond will become a thriving ecosystem of its own accord, as most plants and animals which inhabit ponds are well adapted to colonising new ones. They need to be good colonists because of the relatively short lifespan of ponds. We may think of them as permanent features but on an ecological timescale they silt up quickly. So water beetles can fly, newts can walk quite long distances and sticklebacks have sticky eggs that hitch a ride on the feet of water birds. Some plant seeds also stick to the feet or feathers of birds, while other plants, like bulrushes and reeds, produce masses of light, wind-blown seeds.

A pond that dries up in summer is not necessarily bad for wildlife. It will just have a different range of inhabitants from a perennial pond, including some creatures that can only survive in seasonal ponds because they are vulnerable to predation by fish.

Most ponds develop concentric rings of vegetation, indicating different depths of water or degrees of wetness. The photograph shows an example. In the middle of the pond where it's deepest there's Canadian pondweed floating on the surface; next come water lilies, both yellow and white; then, in the shallowest water, bullrush; and in the damp soil round the margin there's great hairy willowherb and purple loosestrife.

The pond at Ragmans Farm, Forest of Dean.

People have made ponds for various reasons. Watering animals was the most usual one but soaking the wheels of wagons was another. The wooden parts of a wheel can shrink in dry summer weather, making the wheel weak and unstable,

so every now and then they needed a good soaking. That's why the haywain in Constable's famous painting is parked in a pond. The first steps towards the mechanisation of farming actually increased the need for ponds: the steam traction engines used for ploughing needed a copious supply of water and in some places extra ponds were dug.

At the same time, ponds were being formed by subsidence in coal mining districts and especially in salt mining areas. The meres of Cheshire, which now seem so much a part of the natural landscape, were formed by subsidence of the salt workings there. Even the Norfolk Broads are the product of an extractive industry, in this case medieval peat digging. They were long assumed to be natural lakes till the botanist Joyce Lambert, while working on the ecology of the broads, discovered that they had vertical sides and flat bottoms and were quite clearly old peat workings. Once she'd pointed this out, other clues to their artificial origin came into focus, such as the remains of the baulks that were left between one set of workings and another. They survive either as narrow peninsulas or lines of little islands in a straight line. But they weren't obvious before Lambert made her discovery.

Lakes

It can be hard to tell an artificial pond from a purely natural one but natural ponds and lakes are probably quite rare. They can't be formed by water erosion because water doesn't make hollows. It cuts down ever deeper along its course. In fact a stream flowing out of a pond will eventually drain it, though this will take a long time if the rock is hard. But ice can make hollows and the great majority of the natural ponds and lakes in Britain are the result of the Ice Age. The map shows the parts of the country that have been affected by ice and those which have not.

The limit of glaciation

limit of last
Ice Age
maximum limit
of Ice Ages

Water and ice erode the land in completely different ways. A river in spate cuts down into the rock below it like a series of drills. Wherever there's an irregularity in its bed an eddy forms and the stones carried by the current whirl around and

Dartmoor lies south of the limit of glaciation and the valley of the upper Dart is formed by water erosion only. It has a V-shaped profile with interlocking spurs. Poundsgate, Devon.

ELIZABETH JACOBS

excavate a pothole. Eventually the potholes join up and the riverbed is lowered. In upland areas of hard rocks this forms a narrow, V-shaped valley. Any lump or bump in the terrain causes the river to change course abruptly and a zigzag course develops, with interlocking spurs.

If a river cuts through rock like a series of drills, a glacier wears it away like sandpaper wrapped around a block of wood. The ice picks up stones that become frozen to its bottom and sides and abrade the solid rock as the glacier moves slowly forward. Because they move slowly glaciers have to be huge in order to shift the same volume of water in a given time. So, when a young river up in the hills becomes a glacier the valley gets much bigger. The interlocking spurs are worn away and the base of the valley broadens out into a U-shape.

The lochs of the Highlands and lakes of the Lake District lie in the bottom of U-shaped valleys carved out by glaciers. The hollows in which they lie were formed towards the end of the Ice Age. As temperatures gradually rose glaciers melted at lower altitudes and only remained in the higher parts of the valleys. They continued to erode the valley floor downwards while the lower part of the valley, where the glacier was replaced by a small river, was eroded more slowly. Thus the upper part became deeper than the lower and when the ice melted altogether the upper part filled with water. Hence the characteristic long, narrow shape of lochs and glacial lakes.

Just at the point where a glacier becomes a river a dam of debris can form which adds to the depth of the lake. The debris consists of all the mineral matter, whether boulders, gravel or rock dust, which are carried in the ice and left behind when it melts. This kind of material is known as moraine and a dam at the end of a glacier is called a terminal moraine. Of course moraine is a relatively erodible material and the river that replaces the glacier can cut down into it and lower the level of the lake. You can see this process halfway completed at Tregaron Bog in Mid Wales, which started out as a lake formed behind a terminal moraine. The River Teifi, which runs through it, has eroded a gap in the moraine deep enough to partially drain the lake and turn it into a bog.

Bogs and Fens

Unlike blanket bogs, which form because the climate is extremely wet, Tregaron Bog is a valley bog, which has formed in a valley where drainage is restricted. The first stage in the formation of a valley bog is shallow water, shallow enough for emergent plants like reeds and bulrushes, which have their roots in the soil below the water and tall stems which emerge into the air above. Most plants couldn't live in such a waterlogged and therefore oxygen-deficient soil. The emergent plants manage it because they have vertical channels in their tissues, almost like internal pipes, which take air down to the roots. With this problem solved, they are able to put on prodigious growth every year, most of which dies back in winter and falls into the water. Since most of the micro-organisms which decompose organic matter need oxygen for respiration and still water contains little oxygen, decomposition is always incomplete in such conditions. Every year more dead organic material is added to the water than is decomposed. Gradually a layer of partly-decomposed material builds up in the water. This is peat.

A reedbed.

Eventually the peat builds up to the level of the water surface and the character of the reedswamp begins to change. It's no longer a body of open water but a mass of very wet peat, interspersed with pools and channels. Now different plants take over. If the water is acid, they are the typical bog plants such as cottongrass, deergrass, bog myrtle and, above all, bog moss. But if the water comes from a catchment of alkaline rocks a different range of plants will grow on the peat. Prominent among them is the great fen sedge, or sword-sedge, so called because its leaves are so sharply serrated that they can cut your fingers to the bone if you clutch them and pull. They say it's better to fall over and get a soaking than to 'save yourself' by grabbing it! There are many other types of sedge, rushes and herbs that grow along with great fen sedge, but it dominates. Alkaline peatlands of this kind are usually called fens while acid ones are known as bogs, or mosses in Scotland and the north of England.

From this point a valley bog or fen can develop in two different ways. It can succeed to woodland or become a raised bog. Trees can take root if parts of the peat become dry enough, perhaps during a run of dry years. Once the first pioneers get established they pave the way for more trees because they reinforce the drying-out process. All plants pump water from the soil and lose it from their leaves in a constant stream. Trees, being much bigger than other plants, do this at a greater rate and they can lower the water table significantly. Even so conditions remain wet and the main trees are the water-loving ones: alder, willow and white birch. This kind of woodland is known as carr.

A raised bog develops where rainfall is higher and the surface stays very wet. The absorbent nature of the valley bog or fen means that the rainwater can't flow away as it would on a mineral soil and rain-fed peat starts to form on the surface. This is similar to the formation of blanket bog (see pages 169-170) but the very high levels of rainfall which are needed to get a blanket bog going on a mineral surface are not necessary where the surface is already made of peat. Like a blanket bog, a raised bog is fed entirely by rain. Since rainwater is slightly acid, raised bogs are always acid, regardless of the kind of peat below. They contain the usual range of bog plants, with bog moss as the dominant one. Like blanket bogs, they can dry out at the surface, usually in response to a long-term drop in rainfall. Then heathers take over from the bog moss and a heath or moor is formed, and if the grazing pressure is low, trees can get established.

Types of Bog

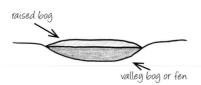

Valley	In a low place with impeded drainage acid – *bog* or *moss* alkaline – *fen*
Raised	On top of a valley bog, rain fed always acid
Blanket	In an area of extremely high rainfall always acid

The progression all the way from open water to carr woodland is a process of succession similar to the one that goes from bare soil to woodland on dry land. In fact carr is not the end point, in theory at least. Alder, willow and birch are all pioneer species. They are able to cope with wet conditions but, by lowering the water table and by themselves adding to the depth of peat when they die, they eventually make conditions much drier and allow species like ash and oak to become established. In practice this probably didn't happen very often under natural conditions. The water level in places like the Fens of eastern England and the Somerset Levels has gone through cyclical changes over the ages, periodically knocking succession back to square one. Even without an overall change, individual places must have experienced cycles of wetness as rivers changed course, sandbanks were laid down and eroded away again.

These days there are very few lowland wetlands that have not been drained for agriculture. One of the few places you can get an idea of what a natural wetland might have been like is in the Norfolk Broads. On the margins of some of the less disturbed broads you can see zones of vegetation running from open water with floating plants, through marginal reedswamp, to willow scrub and finally to alder carr. What's happening here is that the broad is gradually filling up, from the margin towards the middle, as all ponds and lakes eventually do. The further you are from the centre of the broad the more advanced the succession.

Wetlands aren't always located at the lowest point in the landscape. The nature of the underlying rock, whether it's permeable or impermeable, can have its effect too. Where a band of clay outcrops part way down the slope, with more permeable rocks upslope from it, a reedbed can form in much the same way that a spring line does. In fact you could regard such a reedbed as a diffuse spring, in contrast to the classic spring that comes out from a definite hole in the ground. A patch of rushes halfway down a sloping pasture field indicates much the same thing.

Streams

Small wetlands have a valuable role in the landscape, not least in helping to even out the movement of water. This is especially noticeable if a stream runs through the wetland. Even a small marsh or bog will absorb a great deal of water when the stream is in spate and release it slowly afterwards. I lived for a few years just below the southern edge of Dartmoor, first in one hamlet and then in another. By chance both these places lay on streams of similar size. One of the streams passed through a marsh on its way from the moor and the other didn't. Both of them could overflow their banks after torrential rain but the volume and violence of the floods were much less on the stream that passed through a wetland. Conversely, in dry times the water stored in a wetland is slowly released and this helps to maintain the flow of rivers and streams. You notice this effect especially in areas where streams are inclined to dry up altogether in summer. The New Forest, with its sandy and gravelly soils and comparatively dry climate, is just such a place, and New Forest streams which pass through valley bogs are much more reliable in the summer than the ones which don't.

A meandering stream in a primary woodland. Asham Wood, Somerset.

Another factor that may have affected my two Dartmoor streams is woodland. The second stream passed thorough more woodland than the first and this may have contributed to its more even flow. The value of woods in slowing down and evening out the flow of water through the landscape is well known but the mechanisms by which they do it are less so. Although the woodland soil and the leaf litter do act like a sponge, they are not that much more effective than the soil of permanent pasture. The thing that really makes a difference is log dams. Dead branches and even whole trees fall into streams, the gaps between the sticks are filled by autumn leaves, and sand and silt build up behind the organic debris to make a water-holding dam. These dams slow down the water and allow it to seep into the soil on either side. They also add diversity to the structure of the stream, with shallow riffles and deep pools. This gives a greater variety of habitat for wildlife and fish populations are usually higher where there are more log dams. Eventually they rot away but new ones are always being formed. Comparisons with relatively untouched woods in North America suggest that log dams were very much more common in the wildwood than they are today. Like so many other natural features in the countryside they are victims to the incessant human urge to tidy up.

Nevertheless some woods give a glimpse of what a natural stream may have looked like. Out in the fields and in most secondary woods the smaller streams have almost all been straightened and turned into ditches. But in some primary woods, places which have been woodland continuously since trees came back after the last ice age, they are still more or less untouched. You may be able to see the pattern of interlocking spurs on a miniature scale. Or, where the terrain is flatter, the stream may form those snake-like curves we call meanders, characteristic of mature rivers in lowland areas but not often seen on small streams outside of primary woods.

You can also see how a stream can act as a natural drain. The place where it rises, if not a definite spring, is often a marshy area. But once the stream is concentrated in a single channel it starts to cut down below ground level. This has the effect of draining the ground in much the same way as a ditch that has been dug for the purpose. So the banks of a stream are not always, as one might expect, the wettest part of the landscape but often the driest. Where the banks are marshy it's either because there's virtually no fall on the stream or because its flow is obstructed, perhaps by a log dam.

13

Hedges and Other Boundaries

HEDGES ARE like coppice woods in miniature. The shrubs take the role of the coppiced trees and the hedgerow trees the standards. A regularly cut hedge is like an actively coppiced wood while a hedge that is left to grow has much in common with a neglected wood. Britain has less woodland than almost any other European country, but more hedges. Is this a coincidence or are the hedges to some extent a compensation for our lack of woodland? Although their main purpose was always to keep animals in the fields, hedges used to be an important source of firewood in districts that lacked woodland. They also compensate for the lack of woodland both visually and ecologically. In some parts of the country the abundance of well-treed hedges can give the illusion that somewhere not far in the distance there's a wood amongst the fields. But as you move through the landscape you find nothing but a succession of hedgerow trees that combine to fill the view and hide the open fields that lie between them. Perhaps this is where the word 'woodland' comes from in the old distinction between woodland and champion countryside. (See page 17.)

In fact hedges are more like continuous woodland edges than complete woods. Like woodland edges they are rich in shrubs that flower and set fruit in the abundant light. They usually have a bank, or at least a strip of herbaceous vegetation at their

There's no woodland in this view, only hedgerow trees. Priddy, Somerset.

foot that doesn't get farmed along with the rest of the field, in effect a narrow belt of semi-natural grassland. Many hedges also have a ditch, a linear wetland. So hedges are to some extent a microcosm of the semi-natural landscape. In many parts of the country they are about the only semi-natural vegetation left. Despite the grubbing out of thousands of miles of hedges during the past half-century, they are the largest single wildlife habitat left in lowland Britain.

Hedges and Farming

Whether they are a net benefit to farming or not is a moot point. Their main function is to contain animals and that can also be done by a wire fence. The question is which does the job better and cheaper. Both need maintenance: regular trimming for a hedge versus complete replacement every decade or two for a fence. Most hedges also need a bit of fencing to make them a hundred percent effective but this is often minimal compared to the full paraphernalia of a stand-alone fence. The hedge probably wins on cost grounds, especially as it's usually already there. In terms of usefulness it also wins because it has the added benefit of providing the animals with shelter.

As evidence of this, look at how few of them have been replaced by fences in the grassland areas of Britain. Although some hedges have gone in the west it's mainly been a matter of amalgamating small fields. In the arable east, as farms have become more specialised and the animals have gone, most of the hedges have gone with them. Bigger fields mean tractors spend more time working and less turning at the end of a row. Hedges also take up space that could be growing crops and they need maintenance, which is a cost. Although arable farmers may see hedges as worth preserving for visual amenity and wildlife they generally see them as a dead loss in productive terms. But hedges also play a part in the ecology of arable farming. They have both positive and negative effects and the question is which are the greater.

The hedge casts shade on the crop, especially if there are hedgerow trees, and competes with it for water and nutrients. Slugs live in the hedgebank and venture a little way into the field to eat the crops. The strip of crop affected by shade, root competition and slugs can stand out clearly on the edge of the field. But the positive effects are spread more widely and less easily seen. The shelter effect increases crop yields over a long distance downwind. Beetles live in the hedgebank over winter and range widely over the field in summer, eating pests as they go. Wildflowers in the hedge provide food for flying insects that lay their eggs on the crop, where their larvae feed on caterpillars and aphids. The hedge also protects the land from erosion by wind and by water but the effect may only be revealed after the hedge has been removed. So the negative effects are concentrated and highly visible while the positive ones are spread out in space and time and are not visible, though on balance the positive are greater.

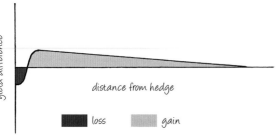

distance from hedge

yield difference

loss   gain

The positive effects of hedges are also easily masked by the quick fixes of chemical agriculture. The benefits of pest control won't show up in a landscape that is regularly sprayed with pesticides. Nor will reduced soil erosion be appreciated where any loss of topsoil can be countered with an extra dose of fertiliser. But in a sustainable landscape, where chemical remedies aren't available and the health of both soil and crops is founded on biological diversity, hedges are an economic asset to arable farming.

KINDS OF HEDGES

Just like woodland, hedges can be ancient or recent. In the case of woods the division between the two is fairly arbitrary. (See page 120.) But with hedges a step change came with the parliamentary enclosures of the eighteenth and nineteenth centuries, which transformed the open fields of the planned countryside into the hedged fields of today. Suddenly there was a need for millions of shrubs to make thousands of miles of hedges and the nursery industry was born. In truly modern fashion it churned out a monoculture of hawthorn, which is quick and easy to grow and has the benefit of being thorny. Before that time people used whatever shrubs were available, probably digging up young plants from the woods rather than growing them from seed. So ancient hedges are usually a mix of shrub species while recent ones are mostly hawthorn.

There are some ancient hedges in the planned countryside, often on parish boundaries, and you may see the odd recent one in the ancient countryside. But the level of diversity of shrub species in the hedges is one of the prime clues to which kind of country you're in.

An old, mixed hedge. The tree with the yellowish fruits is a crab apple, an uncommon tree that indicates an ancient hedge. Allaleigh, Devon.

Ancient

The most diverse hedges of all are usually ones that were carved directly out of the wood. In the planned countryside these woodland relict hedges contrast strongly with the straight hawthorn hedges of enclosure. They often came about when a wood, already enclosed with a bank and hedge, was grubbed out to make more fields, and what was the wood-hedge became the field-hedge. It usually has a crooked course and contains a similar mix of tree and shrub species to that in local woods. It may also have woodland wildflowers growing in it, such as dog's mercury, yellow archangel and bluebells. But these plants aren't sure indicators of a woodland relict hedge, since they can also gradually spread into recent hedges that abut onto woodland or a former wood-hedge. It's a slow process and the clue may be that the woodland plants only reach part of the way along the hedge. Dog's mercury is often the most rapid colonist and may reach further along than the others.

In ancient countryside woodland wildflowers are more common in hedgerows generally, especially in the wetter west of the country. The most spectacular displays of wildflowers I've seen anywhere in Britain are on the high hedgebanks of the English West Country. In late spring and early summer they come alive with a mix of both woodland and grassland flowers. There are flowery hedgebanks in other parts of the country and drab ones in Devon and Cornwall but the overall contrast with the rest of England is dramatic. Why should there be such a difference? Is it because of the mild, moist climate? Is it that the high banks provide special conditions of microclimate and soil that favour wild flowers? Or is it a matter of time? If the hedges of the West Country survive from a much earlier age than those of other parts it would mean they have had more time to develop that diversity which comes with age. Maybe it's all of these reasons combined.

The further west you go the bigger the banks tend to be and the less importance is attached to the hedge on top. In Cornwall the banks are massive and usually stone-faced, the shrubs on top may be nothing more than a bit of gorse or even heather, and the bank itself goes by the name of hedge. There are similar banks in many parts of Wales, especially the south and west. In fact Pembrokeshire and Cornwall have a very similar feel to them, with high, rocky sea-cliffs surrounding a country of small, banked fields, dotted with whitewashed, black-slated farmhouses. Hedgebanks are found in other parts of the country though they are usually smaller. On the whole, the older a hedge is the more likely it is to stand on a bank. Whether it also has a ditch is more a matter of whether the soil needs draining.

Another clue to the age of a hedge is the course it traces. Ancient hedges may be straight or crooked but recent ones are almost always straight. The contrast between the small, irregular fields of ancient countryside and the large, rectangular ones of the planned countryside is usually quite clear. The c- and s-shaped curves of former open-field strips and the dog-legs of former furlongs indicate enclosure by agreement, probably during early modern times. (See pages 21-22.) But a curving hedge doesn't always have this origin. It may follow

A Devon hedgebank in all its glory.

the course of a stream, sometimes a stream that no longer flows because the land has been artificially drained. Or it may follow the break of a slope, so as to put steep and flat land into separate fields.

Recent

Those pure hawthorn hedges don't stay pure forever. Like any other ecosystem they become more diverse with time. The first woody colonists are usually elder, ash, blackthorn, rose and bramble. Hazel, dogwood and maple are slower to arrive and their presence in a hedge suggests that it's ancient, though they will come in more quickly if the hedge joins onto an ancient wood.

This extract from my notebook features two hedges that appear to have been colonised after planting, one ancient and one recent.

High Stoy, Dorset

There's a drove with hedges on both sides. One is shown on a map of 1616, the other isn't.

Old Hedge, pre 1616	*New Hedge, post 1616*
Shrubs:	*Shrubs:*
Mostly hazel with some sycamore, blackthorn and pussy willow.	*Mostly hawthorn and blackthorn with some elder, sycamore and hazel.*
Herbs:	*Herbs:*
Lots of bluebells, also red campion, lords and ladies, lesser celandine and bracken.	*Mostly red campion with some lesser celandine, a little dog's mercury and very little bluebell and ramsons.*

187

Red Campion.

The drove is situated right on the edge of the planned countryside, on the northern rim of the Dorset chalk downs, which stretch southwards from here all the way to the sea. One end of the drove abuts onto the upper edge of an ancient woodland which occupies the steep slope that marks the end of the chalk hills. From that high point you could throw a stone into the ancient countryside of the Blackmore Vale that lies below. The recent hedge appears to have been originally planted as a mix of hawthorn and blackthorn while the ancient hedge shows every sign of having been planted as pure hazel. Both have subsequently been colonised by three species of shrub or tree, which gives the younger hedge a higher species count.

This is unusual, as older hedges are usually more diverse. Even the list of shrub species from both hedges is fairly similar. What distinguishes them is the proportions of the different species in each hedge, one being mainly hazel, the other mainly thorn. The same applies to the herb layer. The species list is much the same either side of the drove but the proportions are different. Bluebells, which dominate the ancient hedge, are true woodland wildflowers while red campion, which is dominant in the recent one, is more of a hedgerow species.

This was just a quick list I jotted down in passing. If I'd had the time it would have been interesting to compare the ends of the hedges nearest the wood with those furthest from it to see what effect distance from the wood has had on the distribution of shrubs and herbs.

The mixture of hawthorn and blackthorn was occasionally used in enclosure-act hedges instead of pure hawthorn. Blackthorn is a useful hedging plant as its suckering habit helps to keep the hedge thick at the bottom. Another variation on pure hawthorn was to include some standard ash trees. It's usually pretty easy to distinguish between a hedge planted with ash standards and one that has been colonised by ash after planting. The planted ash trees are now at the end of their mortal span. They are either over-mature or they have already been felled and have regrown in a multi-stemmed form like a coppice stool. They will also be fairly evenly spaced along the length of the hedge. Self-seeded ash trees are likely to be younger and more randomly spread.

Self-Sown

Some recent hedges are entirely self-sown, the hedgerow equivalent of recent semi-natural woodland. They grow up along field walls and fences, which make convenient perches for birds which excrete the seeds of hawthorn, bramble and other berry-bearing bushes. Ash and sycamore seeds, light enough to be carried by the wind but big enough to be able to get going in a grass sward, are also common. The level of diversity in the hedge is usually low at first and increases over time as new species colonise.

Whether or not a hedge self-seeds along a particular wall or fence depends on the frequency of grazing. A few years of continuous arable crops or silage-making can give the shrubs the break they need. There's always a narrow strip at the edge of the field where the plough and the mower don't reach. On a roadside a hedge is most likely to form on the side of the fence nearest the road, where it's protected from grazing. You can sometimes see self-sown hedges in the process of getting established. On the chalk downs of Wiltshire you may see hawthorn bushes scattered at random along the line of a roadside fence, neatly trimmed to a uniform height and shape as though they were a continuous hedge.

Hooper's Rule

Taking all hedges together, ancient and recent, planted and self-sown, there's a tendency for older ones to be more diverse. This is partly because of the historical change from planting mixed hedges to pure hawthorn ones and partly because the longer the hedge is there the more opportunity there is for new species to colonise. In fact it has been suggested that you can actually date a hedge by counting the number of tree and shrub species in it. This idea was the brainchild of Max Hooper and his colleagues, who were investigating hedges at Monks Wood Experimental Station in Huntingdonshire during the 1970s. By studying old maps and other historical documents they were able to date some of the local hedges. They compared these dates with the number of tree and shrub species in the hedges and found there was a direct relationship between the two: one woody species per hundred years of age.

It wasn't an exact match, but close enough to deserve further investigation. They recorded hedges in different parts of the country and most of the results they gathered supported the hypothesis. However there was one area in Shropshire where the hedges were known to be late but were nonetheless very diverse. Evidently there had been no hawthorn nursery in the locality at the time the land was enclosed and the hedges were planted with mixed shrubs in the old style. When Max Hooper and his colleagues published their findings they emphasised that the idea should be "treated with caution and not used as an immutable universal law".* Nevertheless, it caught the imagination of professionals and amateurs alike and soon came to be known as Hooper's rule. Many people gave it, and some still give it, much more authority than its originators ever claimed.

The method is simple. Choose three random thirty-yard (30m) sections of the hedge, or just one or two if it's too short. They shouldn't include the ends of the hedge and should be well scattered along its length. Try to resist the temptation to choose especially diverse sections that will give you a high count! Include all woody species except scramblers like brambles and wild rose and climbers such as ivy and old man's beard. Then take the average of your samples.

It can become quite addictive. Regardless of whether it can really give you an accurate date, it's a good way to get to know a hedge – and to brush up your

* *Hedges*, E Pollard, MD Hooper & NW Moore, Collins, 1974.

tree and shrub identification skills. I always feel a sense of delight when I come upon a particularly diverse hedge. I also feel a sense of wonder. A hedge like this is as much a link with the past as an old parish church or the gravestones in its churchyard. It's a living thread that connects my world with the world of the people who planted it. It gets me wondering about them. Who where they? Why did they plant it? What tools did they use? What clothes did they wear?

Natural Influences

Over the years it's become clear that Hooper's rule really can't be used with any confidence. More pockets of country have emerged where people went on planting mixed hedges into the age of parliamentary enclosures. Such places are mainly outlying areas of enclosure in predominantly ancient countryside, places where there perhaps wasn't enough demand to make a nursery business worthwhile and there was plenty of woodland to provide wild seedlings. Likewise, early hedges were sometimes planted with one species of shrub rather than a mixture, as the drove at High Stoy illustrates.

There are also several natural influences on diversity that aren't related to the age of the hedge. The acidity of the soil is one of them. Here in Europe, alkaline soils support a wider range of plants than acid ones, and shrubs like spindle, wayfaring tree and dogwood will never be found in a hedge on an acid soil, however old it is. The climate is another. The natural diversity of trees and shrubs is greater in the south of Britain than in the north, and at low altitudes compared to the hills. The nearness of seed parents also has an effect. If the hedge joins onto an older hedge or ancient woodland it will usually have a higher count. Although the end of the hedge will be colonised first, in the end all of it will be affected. Finally, some plants are so competitive that they can take over a diverse hedge and reduce it to a pure stand, which can give an old hedge a very low count.

I've known elder do this. It's one of those plants that inhibit the growth of its neighbours by putting out chemicals that are poisonous to them. It's also a competitive plant that responds very vigorously to a nutrient-rich soil, and the combination of chemicals and competition can suppress and kill other trees and shrubs. The most extreme example I've seen was a windbreak of alternate elder and damson trees, planted around a vegetable plot with the aim of combining shelter with an edible yield from both species. Although damson is the toughest of fruit trees and often used in windbreaks, after only ten years it had all been killed, leaving a pure stand of elder. I would suspect any pure elder hedge of once having been more diverse.

Elm Hedges

More common is the pure hedge of suckering elm. There are two kinds of elm in Britain. One is the wych elm, which is a single species, and the other is a group of several species which all have a suckering habit. The wych elm is more common in woodland than hedgerows, reproduces by seed and never suckers. The suckering elms have lost the ability to reproduce by seed and are more characteristic of hedgerows than of woods.

The tall elm trees which used to be such a feature of the landscape have largely disappeared from British hedges since the outbreak of Dutch elm disease in the 1970s, but elms are still there as virtual shrubs. It's their suckering habit that has saved them. The fungus that causes the disease is spread by bark beetles that feed on medium- to large-sized elms. It inevitably infects a young suckering elm when its trunk diameter reaches about twenty centimetres. But plants smaller than this are safe and can produce more suckers without ever growing to mature size.

It's this same suckering habit that has made elms such strong competitors in hedges. Reproduction by seed is not easy in a hedge, as the competition for light and water from the established shrubs is intense. But a new sucker has the support of all the established plants in the clone and this gives it the edge over a seedling. Other shrubs can co-exist with elm but they can't compete when it comes to reproduction. So, as all plants must die in the end, elm eventually replaces the others. Its size and vigour also play a part. Blackthorn and dogwood are two hedgerow shrubs that also sucker but they don't take over the way elm does.

Elm leaf.
Note the
asymmetric
base, which is
typical of all
British elms.

The bare poles of dead elms in untrimmed hedges have become a familiar part of the landscape, often giving an uncared-for and scruffy look to parts of the clay country. But in the east of England you can still see living elms of tree size in the hedges. The so-called English elm, the commonest suckering species over central England, is totally susceptible and always dies, while the East Anglian species has some resistance. The non-suckering wych elm, by contrast, is quite resistant and seems to survive more often than it succumbs.

The difference is in the genes. Sexual reproduction, which in plants means reproduction by seed, allows a species to change its genetic makeup through time. Different plants have resistance to different strains of disease and sexual reproduction can throw up individuals which have resistance to new strains. There have been repeated epidemics of elm disease from Neolithic times to the 1930s. The present one is unusually severe but not unique. Through these long ages the wych elm has had the opportunity to develop new resistance while the suckering elms, restricted as they are to vegetative reproduction, are stuck with the genes their ancestors had thousands of years ago.

As for the difference between the English and East Anglian elms, it has recently been discovered that the English elms are all just one clone. Every single tree in the country is genetically the same individual, descended by vegetative reproduction from one seedling tree that grew at some time in the dim past. That individual happens to have no resistance at all to the current strain of the disease. The East Anglian elms have a bit more genetic variation.

Like grey squirrels, rhododendron and oak mildew, all of which have had significant effects on the landscape, the present epidemic of elm disease is a product of globalisation. It came to Britain on infected timber imported from North America. How it will end is hard to predict. The fungus that causes the disease is capable of genetic change and may become less virulent in time. It also has its own parasite, a virus, and this in its turn may become more virulent and act as a control on the disease. One way or another this epidemic is likely to pass just as all the previous ones have.

HEDGE SHAPES

Like any other semi-natural ecosystem, hedges develop under a blend of both natural and human influences. We manage hedges with the aim of keeping them compact and dense while they continually try to grow upwards and outwards. A hedge needs to be high enough and dense enough to keep animals in the field, but no bigger than necessary because the more it grows the more it competes with the grass or other crops in the fields. As hedges grow there's a constant tendency for the upper branches to grow vigorously and shade the lower part, which makes it thin and gappy. So controlling the size of the hedge helps to keep it dense at the same time. Browsing by farm animals can also thin out the lower part of a hedge, so there's often a wire fence on one or both sides to protect it. Sheep browse harder than cattle and being smaller animals they do it at just the height where the hedge is weakened by shading. Sheep also make more use of any resulting holes than cattle do, as they can fit through smaller gaps and take more interest in escape.

Grown-out Hedges

Maintaining a hedge costs time and money and in these days of expensive labour and financial squeeze some hedges are left to their own devices. A common pattern of change is for the trees, including both standard trees and ones that were previously kept trimmed to shrub size, to become dominant over the shrubs. The combination of shade and root competition from the trees weakens the shrubs. They are usually finished off by browsing and by the animals barging their way from one field to another through the resulting holes. The hedge gradually turns into a line of trees with a distinct browse line on them.

A grown-out hedge. Note the browse line.

From a distance, a landscape full of grown-out hedges of this kind can look more attractive than one ruled by tight little hedges of trimmed shrubs. But these big hedges are dying. Like an overgrazed wood, they won't survive longer than the lifespan of the trees. These days more hedges are lost by neglect than by deliberate grubbing out. It's a constant process that goes on unobtrusively without the noise and fuss of bulldozers or the ugly gash of bare soil that proclaims that a hedge has been removed.

Even while they survive these lines of trees have already lost most of the useful functions of a hedge. They are no longer a barrier to farm animals. The nesting habitat for hedgerow birds is gone and the hedgebank habitat severely degraded by trampling. As for shelter, a line of trees like this doesn't slow the wind but speeds it up. When the wind blows against the dense crowns of the trees some of it is deflected up and over them and some of it is deflected downwards, where it joins with the ground level wind to blow through the line of bare trunks with redoubled force.

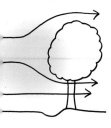

192

The Blackthorn Sandwich

A neglected hedge with blackthorn in it can develop in quite a different way. Blackthorn is a suckering shrub armed with formidable thorns that enable it to spread out from the hedge into the pasture on either side, even in the face of browsing. Only mowing, topping or arable cultivation will stop it. It tends not to out-compete the established shrubs in the hedge in the way that elm does, so eventually the hedge becomes a sandwich, with blackthorn as the bread and the original hedge as the filling. The mass of blackthorn suckers keeps the hedge dense at the bottom. It becomes an excellent nesting habitat for song birds and a hedge like this which is both tall and dense provides just the shelter that bats and butterflies need in order to travel around the landscape from one piece of habitat to another. But the hedgebank habitat is degraded by shade. If the blackthorn is continuous along the hedge it can make an effective barrier to farm animals but it's a net loss to the farmer because it takes up so much land.

Sometimes a gap develops between the fringe of blackthorn and the original hedge, especially where the main shrub in the hedge is hazel. When other trees and shrubs are neglected they grow mainly upwards but once hazel has reached a modest height it grows outwards, over the top of the shorter blackthorn. It shades the blackthorn nearest to the hedge and weakens it, while the outer edge of blackthorn continues to spread into the field. Sooner or later cattle find their way behind the outer belt of thorn and trample down the weakened plants behind. As they spend more and more summer days in the cool shade of the hazel they barge out a green tunnel between the original hedge and the belt of thorn.

A blackthorn sandwich.

A bramble fringe.

A hazel hedge that is fringed with bramble rather than blackthorn can also develop this structure. It can happen without the help of animals, as shade alone is enough to kill the brambles nearest the hedge. What started out as a hazel hedge with an understorey of bramble ends up as a hedge with a line of bramble parallel to it.

Coppicing

There are basically three ways of managing a hedge: coppicing, laying and trimming.

Coppicing means cutting the entire hedge down to the ground and removing all the cut material. You don't see it done very often but it can be the best remedy for a seriously overgrown hedge. It's difficult to either lay or trim a hedge composed of large-diameter stems, and coppicing also gives the best opportunity to plant new shrubs where there are gaps, because for one season at least there's no competing shade. Of course the hedge has to be fenced while the shrubs regrow but a laid hedge generally needs fencing at first too.

A variation on coppicing that you sometimes see is what might be called high coppicing, cutting the overgrown shrubs at around a metre above the ground. I think people do this because they shy away from full coppicing, which looks too much like destroying the hedge. But on the whole it's not a very good idea. After years of competition and self-shading the remaining stems are rather far apart and largely twigless. The regrowth comes from the top of the cut stems rather than the base and this leaves the bottom of the hedge gappy. It's hard to remedy this by planting because any new plants will suffer the shade of taller neighbours. This gives a hedge that is thin at the base and thick above, which is exactly the wrong way round: it's no barrier to animals, especially sheep; rather than give shelter it will intensify the wind at ground level; and it makes a poor habitat for wildlife.

Laying

A laid hedge looks very different to a coppiced one but in fact the two methods have much in common. In both cases all the stems are cut at ground level so that new growth will spring from the base. The difference is that in laying not all of them are cut right through and removed. The over-large, crooked or awkward ones are cut out but a selection of medium-sized, straight stems are cut three-quarters of the way through and bent over to form the new hedge. This doesn't kill the stems: all the vital tissues are located just underneath the bark and enough of them remain in situ for the stems to survive and put on new growth.

Hedge-laying at my field.

There's no job I enjoy more than laying a hedge. It's always done in winter, when the trees and shrubs are dormant. The winter has a quality of quietness. It has a shy, easily-missed beauty, with a thousand shades of brown and grey. The brown-backed fieldfare and the russet redwing provide the accent, rather than the bright wildflowers of spring and summer. When you lay a hedge you're working with plants to create a living structure that is always a blend of your own intentions and nature's. The size, shape and species of the shrubs in the hedge will influence the form of the finished product in equal measure to your own style of hedge-laying.

There are, of course, regional styles of hedge-laying. I was brought up with the Somerset style, which produces a big, thick hedge laid between two rows of stakes. Midland style is much neater and more regular, with a single line of stakes down the centre and the living stems woven between them, like a wattle hurdle. But this neat regularity is much easier to achieve with the recent, single-species hedges of the planned countryside than with the anarchic ancient hedges of Somerset. I still use the Somerset style, not just for tradition's sake but because it seems to me the best way to work with the hedges round here. Travelling the other way from my home, into the West Country and Dorset, you come upon a different style again. Here the freshly-laid hedge doesn't need to be a barrier to sheep and cattle as it grows on top of a bank that does that job quite adequately. So the hedges are laid very low, almost flat to the bank.

The Lancashire and Westmorland styles are similar to Somerset, with two rows of stakes, while the Cumberland style is similar to West Country. But over most of England the single-stake Midland style, or variations on it, is the norm. Most of the Welsh styles are broadly similar to the English Midland style, with a single line of stakes. But in South Wales, from Monmouthshire to Pembrokeshire, the hedgebanks are higher and the traditional hedge is much the same as in the English West Country.

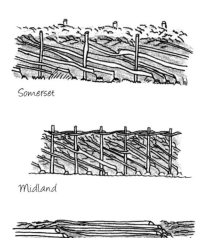

Somerset

Midland

West Country

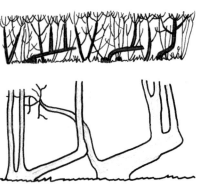

Clipped hedge, grown-out hedge & isolated tree all with signs of former laying.

This hedge has regrown both from the laid stems and from the rootstock, left of centre.

Sometimes these days you can see a style of hedgelaying that can only be described as nominal. Everything is cut and removed except for a line of single stems, laid flat to the ground so that the tip of one just reaches the butt of the next. Really this is coppicing rather than laying. It's much quicker and cheaper than real laying but presumably still gets the grant payment for laying and perhaps that's why it's done.

In the first summer after laying, a laid hedge starts to regrow. The shoots that spring from the base of the cut stems will eventually renew the hedge, just as in coppicing. But shoots also spring from the laid stems themselves and grow up vertically, giving the hedge a wispy upper storey over its dense lower layer. From this point on the hedge is normally kept in shape by regular trimming. Bit by bit the laid stems are superseded by new growth from below but they can persist for a long time, either alive or dead. In a regularly trimmed hedge they stay much the same size they were when they were laid and are hard to see among the dense twiggy growth except in winter time. But if the hedge is neglected and becomes gappy some laid stems will grow bigger and bigger, still lying at the tell-tale angle which shows that they were once cut and laid. Occasionally you may even see an isolated tree which bears the signs of once having been laid, clearly the sole survivor of a hedge which has since been lost.

Trimming

Traditionally a hedge would be trimmed for a number of years and then, before it started to get thin and gappy at the bottom, left to grow tall so it could be laid again. These days that rarely happens. Laying is labour-intensive while trimming is done by machine, so constant trimming has become the norm. It's done with tractor-mounted flail cutters, which cut the twigs and chop them up into little chips that can be left to decompose on the ground. This saves the labour of removing the trimmings. It must also gradually increase the level of nutrients in the hedgebank soil and thus reduce the diversity of herbaceous plants growing there, though this is a slow process and it's hard to point to a place where it has definitely happened.

Most hedges are trimmed every year, at least here in the west of England, where they are a functional part of the farm. In some parts of the east, where hedges are more of an amenity than a tool of the farmer's trade, things can be different.

Huntingfield, Suffolk

In this part of Suffolk there are some huge fields with all their hedges removed, but they alternate with areas where there are still plenty of hedges. The hedged areas have a really good feel to them. As hedges have no economic use here they survive through the goodness of heart of individual farmers. The custom seems to be in most cases to trim the sides but not the tops, so they are very tall. The hedges are ancient and mixed, full of singing birds now, in May. You get a feel of what Suffolk must once have been, though it does feel eerie without any farm animals.

Back to Somerset, two days later

After the snowy scenery of Suffolk with the hawthorn in full bloom, Somerset is drab. Here the hedges are cut every year and it makes such a difference. As we drove out of the station I suddenly noticed it and it came as a shock.

Sometimes you have to go away in order to really understand your home landscape. I'd never realised before how little we allow the hawthorn to flower round here. Hawthorn only flowers on twigs in their second year of growth, so trimming every year means it never flowers. Come to that I didn't appreciate how much it was flowering in Suffolk till I got home and saw the contrast. The note I made in Suffolk makes no mention of the blossom.

What I saw in Suffolk is not universal in arable areas. The Vale of York, for example, is very much planned countryside, with big rectangular fields and pure hawthorn hedges. Few hedges seem to have been removed but they are kept very small by trimming. Regional variations can be as much a matter of local custom as of geography.

Small, neat hedges often suffer from over-trimming. The smaller the hedge the cheaper it is to maintain because you don't have to make so many passes with the trimmer. Once along the top and one pass for each side is very economical but it makes a hedge that's too small to be viable in the long term. All the new growth is concentrated near the cut ends at the top of the stems and eventually the hedge becomes little more than a row of sticks with tufts of twigs at the top. Then the shrubs start to die, leaving gaps, and eventually it becomes nothing more than an irregular row of isolated shrubs. Sometimes it can be hard to tell whether you're looking at an old hedge in the process of dying or a new one in the process of self-seeding along a fence line. Uncontrolled sheep browsing can also turn the bottom of a hedge into a row of sticks. If the hedge is being assaulted from above by excessive trimming and from below by sheep it can deteriorate quickly, as in this example. The wispy

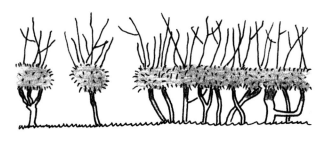

twigs above are the current year's growth and will be removed next time the hedge is trimmed.

Nevertheless a trimmed hedge can stay in good condition for many years if it's well treated. In central Somerset where I live there are plenty of thick, dense hedges that show no signs of deteriorating after several decades of trimming. They keep cattle in without the aid of a fence or at most with a single strand of wire. They stay dense, partly because they are mixed hedges and include shrubs that either sucker or branch lower down than hawthorn, and partly because of their size. Many of them reach up to head height and are broad in proportion, which gives the shrubs enough space to develop and maintain a healthy shape. Big, thick hedges like these are good for nesting birds. They give good security from predators and accommodate those species that like to nest a bit higher from the ground. They also give good shelter to farm animals.

Lynchetts

I introduced the term 'strip lynchett' in the historical chapter to describe medieval cultivation terraces. (See page 20.) But a different kind of lynchett can form along a hedge line that runs across the slope, as a result of soil erosion.

A hedge acts as a dam to soil as it moves down the slope and the accumulated soil on its uphill side can build up to the point where it makes a distinct terrace. Meanwhile soil is eroded from the field immediately below, increasing the height difference between the uphill field and the downhill one.

A lynchett

Soil erosion hardly happens in permanent grassland yet lynchetts are quite common in hilly parts of the country where there's little sign of the plough. But there's hardly a field anywhere in Britain that hasn't been ploughed at some time in the past. The amount of erosion that happened, and thus the height of the lynchett, is a product of three things: the steepness of the slope, how erodible the soil is – in general clay resists erosion better than sand – and how often it was ploughed. When a hedge is removed the lynchett usually remains as a grassy bank running across the slope.

TREES

Hedgerow Trees

In the past hedgerow trees were grown either as pollards or for timber. A bit of firewood, some tool handles and the occasional piece of timber to repair a house were useful products in the rural economy. Whenever a hedge was laid the hedger would leave a few young saplings to grow on, just as a woodsman would leave a few standards when he cut the coppice. As mechanical trimming has taken over, fewer and fewer trees have been left. Machines are designed to work fast, without interruption. It takes time to locate a suitable sapling, stop the trimmer just before you get to it, start again just after it, then go back and trim the shrubs round it by hand. It's so much simpler just to keep driving. And why would anyone bother? The small yield of timber or poles that were useful in the past are irrelevant in the modern mass-production economy.

Photographs of hedged landscapes from the 1950s or before have a distinctly antique look these days. It's not just that they are in black and white, you also feel you're looking at a subtly different country, softer and at the same time more solid. The difference is in the abundance of hedgerow trees. If you're able to take the photo back to the place where it was taken you'll probably see a stark contrast between the old view and the new. Some people say it was the Dutch elm epidemic of the early 1970s that transformed the landscape. Indeed, in areas where elm was the dominant hedgerow tree there was a sudden change at that point. But the same process went on just as surely though more slowly in other places. It's not the death of trees that's changed the landscape but the fact that they are no longer being replaced. A sudden change like Dutch elm disease is obvious but a gradual change slips by unnoticed.

The trees in the old photos aren't just more abundant, they are also more varied in age. Today almost all hedgerow trees are mature or old. A hedge where saplings have been left to grow into trees is a rare and pleasant surprise in the landscape. Trees are important wildlife in themselves and, by increasing the structural diversity of a hedge, they increase the number of niches available to other creatures. For example, song birds will only nest in a hedge where there's a song perch for the male, however suitable it may be in other respects.

Growing trees in hedges has always been a bit of a compromise between the growth of the tree and the growth of the hedge. A tree weakens the hedge beneath it both by shading and by root competition. You'll often see a gap in the hedge underneath a broad-boughed tree. So the interests of the hedge had to be balanced against the value of the tree. In the past shade was kept somewhat in check as pollards were regularly cut and timber trees were pruned. But these days both pollarding and pruning are very rarely done.

Hedgerow trees also reduce the yield of crops in the fields, mainly by shading. A tree in a north-south hedge doesn't have as much effect as one in an east-west hedge because its midday shade falls on the hedge itself rather than on the fields. Looking around I see no evidence that farmers in former times took this into account when choosing which trees to promote, but it's one of the many tools which can be used now to design a landscape which is both biodiverse and productive.

Despite the negative effect on the hedge most farmers keep their mature hedgerow trees. A neighbour of mine said he'd never cut down the hedgerow trees on his farm like his cousin had done because, "It doesn't look like Somerset any more over there." Most of us feel it's worth paying a modest price to maintain that recognisable quality which makes a place not just any place but our home. Even when the hedge itself is grubbed out the trees are often spared, although they compete with the crops and make tractor work more difficult. In some fields you can trace the course of a former hedge by a line of old trees dotted along it.

Shelterbelts and Windbreaks

A shelterbelt is made up of several lines of trees and a windbreak only one.

Shelterbelts aren't common in the British landscape. They take up a fair bit of land, which farmers and landowners may be reluctant to 'lose' in the sense of planting trees on it. Nor is there much return in terms of timber. The outer rows of trees aren't drawn up, so they become too branchy for timber unless they are pruned. But pruning wouldn't be worthwhile economically and would make the belt pretty useless for shelter. (See the drawing on page 192.) As with hedges, the negative effect on the crops is concentrated near the shelterbelt and is often quite visible, while the positive effect is spread out over the field and doesn't show up. The gain in yield outweighs the loss but it doesn't look like that.

Single-line windbreaks are also uncommon. They need a little more care and attention than a multi-row shelterbelt because the loss of even a single tree would create a gap and a gap forms a wind tunnel that intensifies the wind rather than slowing it down. On the other hand they take up less land. For both these reasons they are more suited to high-value crops, where management is more intensive and land more valuable. In this country they are almost exclusively used for orchards, which are particularly vulnerable to wind, both at blossom time and when the fruit hangs heavy on the bough. If you see a windbreak in the landscape you can be almost sure that there's an orchard at its foot or, if there isn't, that one was grubbed out recently.

The trees used most often in windbreaks are poplars and alders. Both grow fast and straight and there are varieties available which keep their lower branches well, to avoid a thin, gappy bottom. Conifers are less often used because a permeable barrier has a more calming effect on the wind than a solid one, which causes gusts and eddies. Where conifers are used they are usually wide-spaced so as to allow some of the wind to pass between them.

FIELD WALLS

In many hilly areas hedges give way to dry-stone walls. One reason for this is the climate. It can be difficult to establish a good strong hedge in the cold, windy and wet conditions of the hills. Stone wall country may also be a sign that the ground was originally so stony that people couldn't start farming till they'd got rid of the stones. Not every place had such a surplus of stone and sometimes you'll see small field quarries that were used once the surface stone had run out. But occasionally there was so much stone that even the field walls weren't enough to use it all up: it was the unusual pattern of field boundaries on the map that made me feel St Braivels Common, on the edge of the Forest of Dean, was worth a visit.

St Braivels Common, Gloucestershire, February

This place has always looked fascinating on the map. It's a landscape of tiny fields with scattered farms and cottages, which contrasts with the larger fields and compact village of St Braivels itself. It has no unenclosed land at all, despite being called a common. What could be its history?

In a word, it's stones. The Common lies on a great dome of hard sandstone and has a sandy soil. Originally there must have been a lot of loose stones on the soil surface because all the fields are walled and their small size indicates there was a lot of stone to get rid of. In fact there was so much that in some places the walls weren't enough to use it up and there are neat piles of stones the size of a small house, made simply to get the excess stones out of the way. Compared to the loamy, stone-free soil near the village it must have been an unattractive place to cultivate and was left as common land for long enough to acquire its name. Then at some point population pressure must have risen so high that the task of clearing the stones from the land became a necessity. Most of the walls now have hedges growing up beside them and the landscape has a mellow, mossy feel to it.

June

Coming here in summer is very different. You can hardly see the stone walls now the hedges beside them are in leaf. What a beautiful little world it is! There are a remarkable number of flower-rich meadows, dominated at the moment by ox-eye daisies. Along the narrow green lanes there are foxgloves and lovely crooked-limbed oaks, both old and young. (See picture on page 42) We came here to photograph the stone piles but with the trees in leaf and the herbaceous plants grown tall we couldn't get a good shot.

"This is now the preserve of the rich," said Cathy. Too true! Each of the cottages is probably on the site of a shelter thrown up by a family of land-hungry squatters but today these cottages are within commuting distance of three major cities.

Different ranges of hills have their distinctive styles of wall and these are partly determined by the nature of the local stone. The sleek, smooth walls of the Cotswolds are the product of the thin, even-shaped stones that the Cotswold limestone yields. Mendip walls are much more chunky; you couldn't make a neat Cotswold wall with the irregular lumps of Mendip limestone. No doubt there are also cultural reasons, including the date they were built. The parliamentary enclosures brought the values of the new industrial age to the countryside. Just as the hedges of the time were pure hawthorn and the field layout rectangular, the walls tend to be uniform and regular. Stone-walled fields which were enclosed by agreement in an earlier age not only follow the characteristic curves and dog-legs of the former furlongs, they also tend to be built in a more informal style, with more variation in height, width and shape.

Although walls don't need regular cutting like hedges, they do need maintenance. Stones fall off from time to time and sometimes whole sections can fall down. Repairing them is a slow and skilled job and once they have been let go it can be a huge job to get them back in good condition. I know a small farm of about a hundred acres on the Mendips where the new owners were quoted a price of thirty thousand pounds to put all the walls in order. There's no way that present-day farming can support that kind of cost. A strand of barbed wire alongside the wall is a cheaper solution and may also save the wall from further damage by discouraging cattle from rubbing themselves on it. In some parts of the country the walls are fenced even where they haven't broken down. This is mostly where the local walling style is tall and narrow, which makes a wall more vulnerable to the odd push from an itchy cow.

Just like hedges, walls can disappear from the landscape if they are neglected, but it's a slower process. Bit by bit they tumble down till there's nothing there but a long, low pile of stones. Over the years any inert object lying on the soil surface will eventually be buried by the earthworms. They constantly bring soil up from below and deposit it as worm casts on the surface and this gradually raises the soil level relative to any solid object like a stone. Where the soil is deep whole buildings can be buried a metre or more below ground level. This is one reason why archaeologists spend so much time digging. But on the thin hill soils where most field walls are found there's often not enough depth to bury even a low heap of stones and even after hundreds of years a slight grassy bank may remain. On hills made of rocks like granite, where the soil is too acid for earthworms, the ruins of walls may stay on the surface more or less forever.

On the whole walls haven't been lost so much through deliberate destruction. Even with modern machinery it's much more expensive to shift the thousands of tonnes of stone which go to make up a wall than to grub up and burn a hedge. In any case stone walls aren't often found on the high-value arable land where most of the hedge-grubbing has happened.

Wildlife of Walls

Walls are challenging environments for wildlife, with little or no soil, wide fluctuations in temperature and summer drought. But some plants and animals can adapt to these conditions and even take advantage of them.

Lichens can live on the surface of the stones. A lichen is a combined organism, half fungus and half alga. The alga provides food by photosynthesis while the fungus protects it from the extreme conditions of microclimate that prevail on rocks and the bark of trees. Without any soil, they are dependent on the air for both moisture and mineral nutrients. This makes them sensitive to air pollution and the presence of lichens is an indicator of unpolluted air. It varies according to species: on the whole the ones which form a flat crust are more tolerant than the ones which branch like miniature bushes. Lichen experts can read the prevailing level of air pollution quite accurately by noting which species are present and which are not. As they depend on wind-blown dust for nutrients and raindrops for water, and only part of the combined organism is able to photosynthesise, it's no wonder that their growth rate is infinitesimally slow. They couldn't compete with other plants and are mostly found on surfaces where nothing else can grow.

Mosses are only a bit more competitive than lichens and also benefit from the absence of vigorous plants but they need more moisture. They are more common in the constantly damp climate of the west or where a wall is shaded by trees.

Some of the plants that survive the extreme dryness of summer walls are ones whose true home is far to the south. Pennywort or navelwort is a Mediterranean plant but its native range includes the south and west of Britain. It lives happily on the walls and stone-faced hedgebanks of the West Country. Both its common names come from the shape of its leaves, which are circular with a soft dimple in the middle. They are thick and fleshy so as to store water into the drier days of summer. Stonecrops are common plants on walls and have even fleshier leaves, each one like a little water tank.

Basking reptiles find the dry heat of a wall an asset. Being cold blooded, reptiles have to get heat from the sun to warm their bodies up to get active and go hunting. The hard, pale surface of the stone reflects the energy of sunlight onto any body resting on it, rather than absorbing it as vegetation does. Lizards climb better and can hide more easily in the holes between the stones than snakes, which are more often seen at the foot of a wall, where they benefit from the shelter as well as the reflected heat.

Both bush-like and crust-forming lichens grow on these twigs, indicating a low level of pollution.

14

Roads and Paths

THERE'S NOTHING more enticing than a path through the woods that curves away from you into the unknown. A road which bends between tall hedges over the brow of a hill is hardly less inviting. The intrigue of not knowing what lies beyond has been the subject of many a poem. It may seem prosaic by comparison to pore over those same roads and tracks on a map but this is one aspect of landscape reading where maps and direct observation complement each other especially well.

In many parts of the countryside you can see where an older road has been superseded by a newer one. The earlier road often takes a more hilly route than the newer. Steep slopes weren't so much of a problem in the days when walking, riding and pack horses were the main means of transport, and the most economical route was usually the straightest rather than the flattest. In fact valley bottoms, with their wet clay soils, were often impassable in the days of unsurfaced roads. But as wheeled transport became more common the most

I always want to know what's just around the curve.

economical route was more often one that avoided the steepest slopes even if that meant a slight detour.

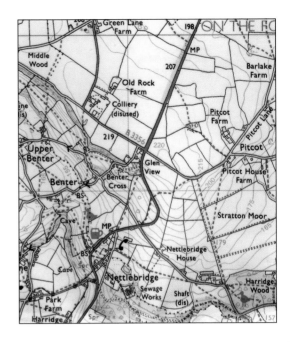

The older, straighter roads may show both their age and importance by the way the field pattern is formed around them. Roads that cut across the field pattern must be younger than the fields. Old country lanes of lesser importance usually conform to the field layout rather than govern it, sometimes following the boundaries of the fields in a series of right-angled bends. Some of these old lanes are still in use and tarmacked, some are now green lanes or footpaths and others have disappeared altogether. Where a straighter, more important road has gone out of use you can sometimes see a continuous hedge line that ghosts its former course along the edge of several fields. It may continue the line of a surviving road towards some destination that has since disappeared, such as a disused ford on a river or a deserted village. Or in hilly country it may be replaced by a section of new road that takes an easier route up the hill, curving in and out of the contours to find the gentlest way up.

Nettlebridge,
Somerset.

These patterns can often be seen more easily on a map than on the ground. This map shows Nettlebridge in Somerset, where the Roman Fosse Way cuts straight across a steep valley. The present main road follows the Roman route on the flat plateau to the north but in the valley it loops around it, first on one side then on the other. The old route remains partly as a narrow lane and partly as a hedgeline with a footpath alongside it, shown on the map by a dashed green line.

Turnpikes and Drove Roads

Many of the improved roads were turnpikes. Built mainly during the eighteenth century, they were financed by tolls. Though the toll gates have long gone you can still see the distinctive toll houses beside many country roads. The three-sided facade, with one side facing the road and the others at forty-five degrees

The toll house at
Westhay, Somerset.

to it, enabled the toll-keeper to see what was coming in either direction. They are usually sited at a road junction, where they could catch more than one stream of traffic.

Turnpikes were specifically designed for wheeled traffic, which wanted a hard surface and was prepared to pay for it. Travellers who didn't need it and didn't want to pay avoided them if they could. So the improvement of the main roads may have helped to define the drove roads, a network of green lanes dedicated to the long-distance transport of meat on the hoof. Welsh and Scottish drovers walked hundreds of miles behind their cattle on the way to the markets in England.

Within Wales, farms that offered hospitality to the drovers and their herds would plant a clump of Scots pines by the roadside as a sign. Some of these clumps are still there, often on droves that have now become part of the motor road network. Most of the present trees look too young to have been there in the days of droving and must have been replanted. Even today you can occasionally see a new group of young pines planted beside a mature clump.

I've also heard it said that the best blackberries in Wales are to be found along the drove roads. The bramble is an unusually variable plant, with some three hundred sub-species recognised in Britain alone. There's a great difference between the best fruiting ones and the worst. The drovers would pass by many different types on their travels and could afford to be choosy. So as they went on their way, excreting the seeds of what they had eaten, they spread the very best blackberries along the sides of the drove roads. At least that's the story I heard.

Enclosure-Act Roads

In the planned countryside the network of village lanes was swept away along with the open fields and replaced by new straight roads. They are sometimes so straight that people take them for Roman roads. They usually have very wide verges, which might seem strangely wasteful for an age that was so keen on productivity. Roads and their verges were part of the common land of the parish, so they could be used as common grazing. Verges were the poor person's pasture and many a cottager would keep a goat or even raise a couple of bullocks on 'the long acre'. But the spirit of the times was against common land and this was just the kind of self-reliance the enclosers were keen to stamp out. They wanted the poor as dependent labourers. The reason why the verges are so wide is that they were not planned to be hard surfaced; that came much later. In wet weather a narrow unsurfaced road would soon become impassable, while the traffic on a wide road would be spread over a wider area and the road would remain usable. Wide roads were a mark of efficiency rather than a waste of land.

When you're travelling by car, the first clue that you're in planned countryside can sometimes be the roads rather than the layout of the fields, especially if your view is confined by tall hedges.

Blackdown Hills, Devon

Driving along a straight road with wide verges and hedges of almost pure beech, I'm clearly in enclosure-act country. Then suddenly the road curves and becomes

slightly sunken. The hedges are now mixed and they come in to the sides of the road, leaving no verge. In a moment I'm in a village.

On the hills of the eastern part of the West Country – the Blackdowns, Exmoor and the Quantocks – beech was used instead of hawthorn when the commons were enclosed. The straightness of the road and its wide verges were also diagnostic. By contrast, the stretch of curving, slightly sunken road with no verge and mixed hedges was quite clearly ancient. It survives in the middle of the planned countryside because it's the village street and in England the villages themselves were left alone by the process of enclosure. Emerging from the other side of the village I was in planned countryside again till the road suddenly took a dip, heading down off the Blackdown plateau. Immediately I was back in the ancient countryside of winding lanes and mixed hedges.

Holloways

One thing about that village street which is characteristic of old roads is that it's sunken. Roads wear away through time. Look carefully at almost any village street and you'll see that the level of the houses and gardens is higher than that of the street itself, if only slightly. In fact sunken roadways are usually the most visible sign of a deserted medieval village in what is now a grassy field, though other earthworks may be present too. But it's not only in villages that roads are sunken. Broadly speaking, the older the road the more likely it is to have been worn away below the level of the surrounding fields, so sunken roads are characteristic of ancient countryside. In some places a road can be so sunken as to form an obvious gully and this is known as a holloway.

The steepness of the slope affects the formation of holloways. The impact of feet and wheels compacts the soil in the roadway and wears away the vegetation. When rain falls it can't penetrate the compacted soil so it runs along the surface and takes the soil with it. The steeper the slope the faster the water flows and the more soil it carries away. Look at any holloway and you'll see how closely its depth matches the steepness of the slope. As the slope increases so does the depth of the holloway and as it levels out again the holloway peters out.

Sandy soils are more erodible than clays, so the sandier the soil the less slope is needed to form a holloway. Holloways are typical of sandstone hills, which have both the slope and the soil type that favour them. In fact there are some sandstones that are almost as erodible as the soil itself and the holloway cuts down through the bedrock just as it did through the soil. On the Yeovil sands of south Somerset you can see deep, vertical-sided gullies on land that only slopes very gently. The famous diarist Gilbert White described the same thing on the greensand at Selbourne in Hampshire. On less erodible rocks holloways usually erode down to a solid base and then stop. On chalk this may be a layer of flints, consolidated by the traffic of the ages. On limestone it may be the top surface of the bedrock. In the old green lane at Ragmans Farm there's an exposed slab of limestone bedrock, and running through it is a neat, narrow groove cut by generations of iron-tyred cart wheels, or maybe the sledge runners of an earlier age.

ROADSIDE VEGETATION

Holloways

Hart's tongue fern.

The hedges are left unmanaged more often on a holloway than on other roadsides, because the steepness of the terrain makes them less accessible. Even on quite large roads the branches from either side often meet over the top and little lanes can become shady green tunnels. The characteristic plants of these dark places are ivy and the hart's tongue fern, with its shiny, undivided fronds that do look like huge tongues. Mossy tree roots are often exposed on the steep sides. Beech roots in particular can grow into fantastic shapes, giving a Tolkeinesque feel to these places that always have an air of being just a little removed from the rest of the landscape.

West Country Lanes

True holloways shouldn't be confused with West Country lanes which, having a tall hedgebank on either side, feel as though they are sunken even if they are level with the surrounding fields. These West Country banks are famously rich in wildflowers. The mix of herbaceous plants is often different from one bank to the other; especially where the road runs east to west so one side is south-facing and sunny while the other is north-facing and shady. This extract from my notebook gives an example.

South Devon

An east-west lane near the sea with very low hedges. The vegetation is similar on both sides – cow parsley, nettles, alexanders, red campion, bluebell, herb Robert etc. – but alexanders is dominant on the south-facing bank and nettles on the north-facing. In a similar lane nearby with high hedges, nettles are dominant on both sides.

The distribution of nettles in these hedges may not be related to the abundance of plant nutrients in the soil, as it so often is. As well as responding to high levels of nutrients they are also quite shade-tolerant plants. Alexanders is a naturalised plant from the Mediterranean, originally introduced as a pot herb. It belongs to the cow parsley family but instead of the familiar flat plates of white flowers it has pom-poms of greenish-yellow flowers. It mostly grows near the sea. As you get within a mile or two of the south Devon coast you start to see it in the hedgerows along with cow parsley. Perhaps it needs the milder winters of the coast to survive.

Verges

Most roadside verges are much less colourful than the West Country banks and the plants that grow there tend to be those competitive ones that readily respond to high levels of nutrients. Roadsides receive extra nitrogen from the exhaust gasses of passing vehicles and plant nutrients accumulate there over the years because they are not removed by grazing or mowing. If a verge is mown the mowings are left there and they enrich the soil as they decompose. The typical mix of plants is tall, coarse grass with nettles, hogweed, cow parsley, goosegrass and bindweed. The occasional splash of colour is added by meadow cranesbill, common mallow, rosebay or great hairy willowherb. Sometimes you'll see a verge overgrown with bracken and that's usually a sign that you're on a sandy soil.

There are a few verges here and there where a more delicate and diverse grassland has survived. Some local authorities have recognised them as mini nature reserves and put up discreet signs to that effect. I've only seen these on minor roads where there's little traffic.

Roadside soils can be affected by the salt that's applied when snow falls. On major roads it can build up to the point where coastal plants colonise the verge, even far inland. You may have noticed a swathe of small white flowers along the central reservations of dual carriageways and motorways in early spring. This is Danish scurvy grass, a native plant despite its name, which isn't a grass but a small member of the cabbage family. There are several species of scurvy grass, which all live by the sea, are edible and have the strong, sour taste that goes with a high level of vitamin C, the cure for the sailors' chronic illness.

Another roadside curiosity are the occasional apple trees that, like scurvy grass, suddenly spring into focus at blossom time. They have grown from the cores tossed out of the windows of passing cars. Domestic apples don't come true from seed so it's unlikely that the fruit of these trees will be good to eat. But they add a little colour to the scene and a little distinctiveness to the roadside landscape. You can see them by railway lines too.

Roadsides can also act as a refuge for plants that have lost their niche in the wider countryside. The common poppy, for example, is an annual that needs disturbed soil in order to germinate. It used to grow in cornfields because the annual disturbance of ploughing gives just the conditions it needs. Wheat fields red with poppies were a favourite theme of the impressionist painters towards the end of the nineteenth century. Not long afterwards the cornfields of northern France were torn apart with high explosive in the First World War and this brought up the biggest flowering of poppies ever seen. Its seed stays viable in the soil for a long time and the massive disturbance of the war brought up many years' poppies at once. As a symbol of peace and hope amid the hell of war the poppy is still with us, but it's largely gone from the cornfields because it's easily killed with herbicides. Every now and then some roadside works on the site of a former cornfield brings up a batch of buried seed and the blood-red blooms splash their colour along the verge as they used to over barley and battlefields alike.

Verges aren't completely independent of the fields around them and sometimes you can see how the neighbouring land has affected the vegetation of a verge. I have an example in my notebook from a walk I took on the Cotswolds.

River Windrush, Oxfordshire

The narrow flood plain and steep southern bluffs are grassland, grazed by a few beef cattle and horses or shut up for hay. Everywhere else as far as the eye can see is continuous arable. In a farmyard I saw the remains of a milking parlour, just the pit where the cowman used to stand with all the above-ground parts removed – a relic of the days of mixed farming. The adjacent milk room is now an artist's studio. I didn't see a single working farmyard, only modernised farmhouses and cottages.

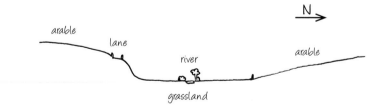

I walked upstream by the river and came back along the lane that connects Burford and Little Barrington. The disordered vegetation of its verges is a relief

> from the arable on one side and dull grassland on the other. The northern verge is
> full of meadow cranesbill, knapweeds and other wildflowers. The southern verge,
> which lies just downhill from the arable land, has some meadow cranesbill but
> is dominated by nettles, cow parsley and goosegrass. Presumably this contrast is
> due to the runoff of nutrients from the arable land.

Cow parsley and goosegrass, like nettles, are plants that indicate a high level of nutrients.

Where a road crosses unenclosed land the verge may seem to merge seamlessly with the surrounding grassland, heath or moor. But if you look carefully you may see a strip of vegetation that's influenced by the road, often due to the use of limestone chippings, which reduce the acidity of the roadside soil. This can happen in two ways: lime can be leached from the surface chippings by rainwater and deposited beside the road; or, if the surface is limestone gravel rather than tarmac, limey dust raised by traffic will settle out nearby. The effect is most often seen in the composition of the plants. On a heath there may be a definite concentration of gorse beside the road and the little yellow tormentil may be replaced by the lime-lover, creeping cinquefoil.

Paths

On unsurfaced tracks and paths the plants need to be resistant to trampling and soil compaction. The centre of a well-used path is usually bare. A little further out, or on a less well-used path, you find much the same suite of plants as in gateways. (See page 149.) Both greater plantain and pineapple weed are common. Further out again there's a zone dominated by plants that are moderately tolerant of compaction and trampling. They include white clover, dandelion and silverweed, whose yellow flowers could be mistaken for buttercups at first sight, though the silvery sheen on its feathery leaves is quite unmistakable. All these plants survive trampling because they are low growing and have tough, elastic tissues that resist physical impact. They are also good at reproduction by seed because they often get killed during a spell of heavy traffic and need to recolonise when it gets lighter again.

Woodland paths are usually bare, as few plants tolerate both trampling and shade. One exception is the lesser celandine, with its little rounded leaves and flowers like yellow stars. It's a tough, ground-hugging plant that readily regenerates from its pea-like tubers that, as many gardeners know, are almost indestructible. In an ancient wood it may be mixed in with the other flowers over much of the woodland floor but will make a pure stand in wet areas or in compacted soil, such as on a path.

Lesser celandine.

SHADOWS OF THE COUNTRYSIDE

Lanes, paths and hedgerows are one element of the countryside that can be carried over into the urban landscape. Woods and even meadows sometimes get built around and survive amid a sea of bricks and mortar but they aren't so much part of the town as bits of encapsulated countryside, whereas country lanes and roads can sometimes determine the layout of the town itself.

You can see this in the neighbourhood where I live now, an area of mostly council housing that was built on the edge of Glastonbury in the 1960s and early '70s, known as Windmill Hill. If you compare the historical map from the early 20th century with the current Ordnance Survey map you can see that the old network of lanes and footpaths is still there and has been added to rather than superseded. The neighbourhood is a flat hilltop and there used to be one lane that zigzagged across it. (See map on left.) It was typical of those crooked lanes that originally wound their way between the furlongs of the open fields and were preserved when the fields were enclosed by agreement. (See pages 21-22.) It's marked on the old map as Windmill Field Lane. The first three sections of it are now called Windmill Hill Road and are streets of houses. There's also a curved street, towards the upper right of the 2008 map, which appears to follow the line of a C-shaped strip in the former open fields. (See map on right.)

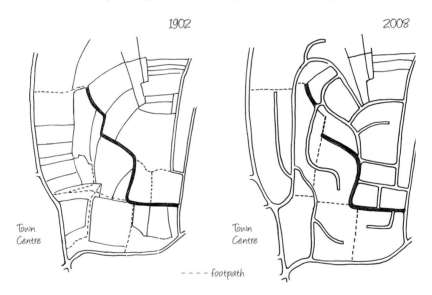

1902   2008

Town Centre   Town Centre

- - - - footpath

The fourth section of Windmill Field Lane has been demoted to a footpath. On one side it still has the old mixed hedge that was there when it was a country lane and on the other a garden hedge of lonicera. (See photo opposite.) There are other footpaths on the hill, some of them with a rural hedge on one side, others completely urbanised. Most of them are on the slopes, connecting the flat hilltop with the old town at the bottom. Comparing the two maps, you can see that

The fourth, narrow section of Windmill Field Lane, now a footpath.

they are mostly still where they were a hundred years ago. The old map shows several 'nurseries' on the hilltop, probably meaning market gardens. Gardening is labour-intensive and the paths must have been used by people from the town walking to work and back, as hardly anyone lived on the hill in those days. Today they are mainly used by schoolchildren who live on the hilltop and go to the school at the bottom.

In the past footpaths probably came and went according to need. I suspect that most of the paths on Windmill Hill only came into use when the nursery business developed, with the coming of the railway, and workers needed to come up from the town. When the nursery land was built on, the original purpose of the paths was swept away, but not the paths themselves because by then they had become legal rights of way. The Rights of Way Act of 1949 fossilised the path network as it was in that year, just at the dawn of mass car culture. Or rather it fossilised those parts of the network that landowners admitted to.

The last section of what was once Windmill Field Lane is marked only by a garden hedge, now mostly exotic shrubs but with two old oaks and a pollard ash, remnants of the laneside hedge, standing up above them. On the line of another hedge nearby there was till recently an old native maple, but it started dying back and was removed as a safety hazard. That hedge had survived more or less intact till a couple of years previously. It gave this corner of the housing estate a pleasant, slightly rural feeling and a connection with the countryside that surrounds it. It gave us elderflowers in summer and blackberries in autumn. Then one day a gang of workers arrived and ripped it out. Only after the event I found out that some of the neighbours had asked the council to remove it because they thought

213

it was unsightly. Now those neighbours have a view of a row of concrete garages, enlivened with a little graffiti.

The urbanising of the vegetation acts like a ratchet. The relics of the rural landscape die one by one and are never replaced. New trees may be planted but they are urban trees, often of exotic species. Meanwhile the trees that were planted when the houses were built grow bigger and impart more of their character to the landscape. On Windmill Hill a patch of ash, sycamore and conker trees, planted just after our house was built, is now a tall woodland, where children have carved dens into the steep bank and woodpeckers feed in the treetops. The urban landscape has an interest and often a charm of its own but it is distinctively urban and develops vegetation that has little connection with what went before. Its layout, on the other hand, often has much more of the countryside in it than we ever imagine.

TIME AND SPACE

This look at an urban landscape may be a fitting way to end the book, since most of us live in towns and what we see in our daily lives can be just as interesting as what's far away. You don't need to make an expedition to a famous nature reserve to get started. In fact you may begin to read the landscape from the car or bus on your way there: here a coppice wood, there a plantation, further on a steep slope that's succeeding to scrub.

I often spend a train journey with a book lying unopened in my lap because I can't take my eyes off the fields, woods and rivers as they fly by. This is not a superficial way of reading the landscape, because what you lose in detail you gain in breadth. In the space of an hour or two you can, if you're lucky, see several distinct landscapes come into sharp focus. This page from my notebook records a journey when I had just such luck.

Waterloo to Templecombe, Somerset

Sandy country – oak, birch and bracken. Pine and heather in the very sandy bits.

Chalk – railway verges thick with hawthorn, some ash, occasional yew and the white pom-poms of wayfaring tree. Wide open fields. You can often see the chalk itself, both where rabbits have made scars in the railway cuttings and in the arable fields.

Nadder Valley – vegetation very mixed; no clear message. Lovely intimate country, with alders and willows beside the little rivers.

Blackmore Vale – big, thick hedges with the spikes of dead elms sticking up through them.

Although the country I passed through was fairly flat – at least I couldn't see much in the way of hills from the railway line – the distinct bands of vegetation we passed through were very clear.

Oak, birch and bracken are a classic community of plants, telling more than any one would have done on its own. None of them are confined to sandy soils, especially not oak, but seeing all three together and not much else was a clear sign of sandy country. On the other hand pine and heather are strong indicators. They only grow spontaneously on soils which are really acid and poor in plant nutrients. What I was looking at here was heathland which had succeeded to pinewood, keeping the heather as an understorey.

There was no obvious change in the relief which told me that we'd passed from sand to chalk but the plants did so immediately. Although hawthorn and ash will grow anywhere, wayfaring tree is a strong indicator of alkaline soil, and yew of dry soil. Seeing the white rock itself just confirmed the message of the plants.

The Nadder Valley is more typical of the countryside at large than the extremes of sand and chalk but that didn't make it any less interesting. I enjoyed tracing the courses of the streams by looking out for water-loving trees as we flashed past.

The Blackmore Vale, at the point where the railway line crosses it, is a wide, flat sweep of land with few farms, no villages and massive thick hedges. It has the feel of heavy clay and this was confirmed by the dead remains of suckering elms in every hedge.

Of course you see more detail as soon as you swap wheels for feet. My notebook is full of insights I've had on a first visit to a place. If you work as a permaculture consultant a single visit is often all you get. This is usually enough for the purpose of giving some basic advice on how to work harmoniously with the land. But no-one would pretend you can prepare a full permaculture design based on one day's observation. For that you really need to live with the land for a year or more, getting to know it as it changes through the seasons. The same applies if you're just reading the landscape for pleasure: the more intimately you know a place the more it reveals its secrets.

Even a second visit can be valuable. I find I often notice as many things the second time round as the first. The mind can only take in so much at once and sometimes a change will have occurred which reveals something new. This can even happen when you've known the place for years.

An example comes from Ragmans Farm, a place I know well because my teaching work takes me there several times each year. At the top of a small rise there are two maple trees standing by a gateway. Although they look to be the same age, one is more than twice the size of the other. The smaller one is visibly shrinking as branches die back while the other grows bigger every year. I'd never even wondered why until one year the land was let out to a neighbour who rotated his cattle round the farm on a different system from the one that had been used before. The new regime meant that the cattle passed back and forth through this gateway more frequently and two prominent tracks of bare soil appeared where they walked.

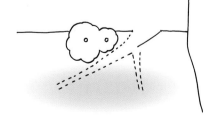

At once it was obvious that the smaller tree was suffering from soil compaction in the root zone. The most heavily used track went much closer to it than the large one. In previous years, when the impact of the cattle wasn't enough to make a clear bare-soil path, it was still enough to harm the tree, though not enough for me to realise what was going on.

However well you know a place there's always more to learn, not just because the landscape itself is always changing but also because our perception of it changes and grows. This, above all, is what makes landscape reading so fascinating.

Further Reading

GENERAL

The Hidden Landscape: a journey into the geological past, by Richard Fortey, Jonathan Cape, 1993. A readable account of the rocks of Britain.

The History of the Countryside, by Oliver Rackham, Dent, 1986. The best book on the history of the landscape.

The Ecology of Urban Habitats, by Oliver Gilbert, Chapman & Hall, 1991. A fascinating account of how the urban landscape works.

FIELD GUIDES

These are books that help you identify wild plants and animals. The most useful for landscape reading are ones that cover wildflowers and trees. When choosing a guide the main points to bear in mind are:

The key

- This is the first step to identification. It usually takes the form of a series of questions with multiple answers that progressively narrow the possibilities down to a single species. Some are easier to use than others.
- Trees are usually keyed by leaf shape but a useful feature is a second key for use in wintertime based on twig shapes and buds.
- Wildflowers are usually keyed by the blooms but in general they are more difficult to key than trees and some wildflower books lack an overall key.
- The best way to assess the effectiveness of a key is to use it, so an opportunity to borrow a guide from a friend to try it out can be useful.

Illustrations

- In general, hand-painted illustrations are better than photographs. The illustrator can paint a typical example, avoiding both the idiosyncrasy of individual plants and confusing backgrounds.
- Tree guides often have really awful illustrations, hardly more than a series

of lollipops with 'oak', 'beech' and 'walnut' under them. The overall shape of a tree is usually more affected by its environment and history than its species. The most useful illustrations are detailed ones showing leaves, twigs, buds and flowers.

Size and range covered

- A smaller book is easier to carry around with you but if it's too small there may not be enough information on each plant for a secure identification. The wider the range of plants covered by the guide the less space there will be for each entry, or the book will be inconveniently large and heavy.
- Many guides cover parts of the continent as well as Britain, which results in a lot of unnecessary entries if you're only going to use it here.
- Some tree guides include a lot of species that are only found in parks or arboretums and have no relevance to landscape reading. A useful range of trees is: all the native and naturalised species; the most commonly planted forestry trees, both conifer and broadleaved; fruit trees; and a few very common ornamentals. This would cover over 99% of the trees in Britain but less than half the species count. The native shrubs should be included too. Many of them are useful indicators and they are an important part of the landscape in their own right.

Distribution maps

- These show the geographic range of each plant. If they are included in a guide they can save a lot of time because a quick glance at the maps can often rule out several species from the range of possibilities. They are much more useful for herbaceous plants than for trees because trees have been so widely planted.

My favourite guides are:

Wild Flowers by Colour, by Marjorie Blamey, A&C Black, 2005. The ideal book for beginners, designed with easy identification as the top priority.

Wild Flowers of Britain and Ireland by Marjorie Blamey, Richard Fitter and Alastair Fitter, A&C Black, 2003. A more advanced book, suitable for people with some previous knowledge of wild plants. As well as wildflowers it covers trees, grasses and ferns, so you only have to carry one book, but the entries for these latter groups are very brief compared to those in a specialist guide.

Trees and Bushes in Wood and Hedgerow, by Helge Vedel and Johan Lange, Methuen, 1960. Still the best tree guide, though sadly out of print. Second hand copies are available on the internet.

How to Find and Identify Mammals, by Gillie Sargent and Pat Morris, The Mammal Society, 2003. Not really a field guide because it's A4 size and wouldn't slip into your pocket, but good for identifying the tracks and signs of wild animals.

ADVANCED

Plantatt, by MO Hill, CD Preston & DB Roy, Centre for Ecology and Hydrology, 2004. A table of all the native and naturalised plants of Britain giving ecological information for each, including their soil preferences, based on the work of Heinz Ellenberg in central Europe.

It has its limitations. Firstly, plants don't necessarily behave in the same way in Britain as they do in central Europe. Secondly, it's not possible to express all the nuances of plant behaviour in a table. For example, some plants may tolerate a wide range of soil moisture and others may be restricted to a narrow range but both kinds have their soil moisture preferences expressed by a single number on a scale of one to twelve. Nonetheless, the 'Ellenberg numbers' are a valuable resource for reading indicator plants.

Glossary

Aftermath – grass that regrows after a hay crop has been taken

Alga – singular of algae

Alkaline – the opposite to acid

Alluvium – soft mineral sediment deposited by rivers

Annual – plant that completes its life cycle in one year. See *biennial* and *perennial*

Arable – land used for crops such as cereals, rather than grass

Aspect (of a slope) – the direction it faces relative to north, south, east and west

Biennial – plant that completes its life cycle in two years. See *annual* and *perennial*

Biomass – the overall weight of plant and animal material, living and dead, in an ecosystem

Biotic – caused by a living thing, plant or animal

Browse line – line on trees or shrubs below which the leaves and twigs have been eaten by grazing animals

Burn (Scots) – stream

Climax – the supposed final, stable stage of natural succession

Clone – group of plants that results from vegetative reproduction from one parent and are thus genetically identical

Combe (pronounced 'coom') – small, narrow valley

Deciduous – tree that loses its leaves in winter

Emergent – erect plant that has its lower part in water and its upper part in the air

Exotic plant – one that is not native to the country where it grows

Fallow – arable land that is temporarily resting, usually for one year, with no crop grown

Herbaceous – plant with no woody parts, including herbs, grasses etc.

Invertebrate – animal without a backbone, e.g. insect, worm, mollusc

Leat – artificial water channel

Loam – soil containing a mixture of sand and clay

Lynchett – terrace formed on a hedge line by soil erosion on the downhill side and deposition on the uphill. See also *strip lynchett*

Maiden – tree that has been neither coppiced nor pollarded

Mast year – year in which a tree produces abundant seed

Monoculture – crop in which all the plants are of one species

Omnivorous – animal that eats both plants and animals

Osier – willow grown on short rotation for basket making

Perennial – plant that lives for more than two years. See *annual* and *biennial*

Phytoplankton – microscopic plants living in water

Poaching – baring and compaction of the soil by trampling during wet weather

Primary wood – land that has been wooded continuously since the end of the last Ice Age. See *secondary wood*

Pure stand – group of plants, either wild or cultivated, all of the same species

Rhizome – root-like structure of herbaceous plants, usually running horizontally through the soil

Secondary wood – land that is now wooded but has been cleared at some point in the past and then recolonised by trees. See *primary wood*

Semi-natural ecosystem – one in which all the plants are self-sown but the structure has been determined by human activity such as grazing, mowing or coppicing

Spar, thatching – long wooden staple used by thatchers to fix the thatch to the roof

Species – a distinct group of plants or animals which can interbreed with each other successfully, e.g. apple, cow. See *variety*

Strip lynchett – medieval cultivation terraces.

Suckering – formation of new shoots from the root of a parent plant

Tuber – large, fleshy *rhizome*, e.g. the edible part of the potato plant

Vale – valley

Variety – a distinct subdivision of a species, e.g. Cox's orange pippin, Bramley. See *species*

Vegetative reproduction – plant reproduction by means other than seeds, e.g. *suckering*

Water table – level in the soil or porous rock below which it is waterlogged

Windthrow – uprooting of trees by the wind

Woody plants – trees and shrubs

Index

Books to empower your head, heart and hands

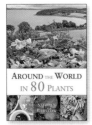

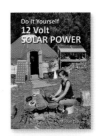
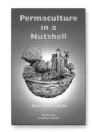

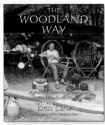

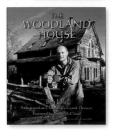

Subscribe to

permaculture
practical solutions for self-reliance

Permaculture magazine offers tried and tested ways
of creating flexible, low cost approaches
to sustainable living

Print subscribers have FREE digital and app access
to over 20 years of back issues

To subscribe, check our daily updates
and to sign up to our eNewsletter see:

www.permaculture.co.uk